DIVINE ACTION
AND PROVIDENCE

PROCEEDINGS OF THE LOS ANGELES THEOLOGY CONFERENCE

This is the seventh volume in a series published by Zondervan Academic. It is the proceedings of the Los Angeles Theology Conference held under the auspices of the Torrey Honors Institute, Biola University, in January 2019. The conference is an attempt to do several things. First, it provides a regional forum in which scholars, students, and clergy can come together to discuss and reflect upon central doctrinal claims of the Christian faith. It is also an ecumenical endeavor. Bringing together theologians from a number of different schools and confessions, the LATC seeks to foster serious engagement with Scripture and tradition in a spirit of collegial dialogue (and disagreement), looking to retrieve the best of the Christian past in order to forge theology for the future. Finally, each volume in the series focuses on a central topic in dogmatic theology. It is hoped that this endeavor will continue to fructify contemporary systematic theology and foster a greater understanding of the historic Christian faith amongst the members of its different communions.

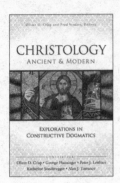

CHRISTOLOGY,
ANCIENT AND MODERN:
Explorations in Constructive
Dogmatics, *2013*

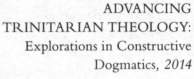

ADVANCING
TRINITARIAN THEOLOGY:
Explorations in Constructive
Dogmatics, *2014*

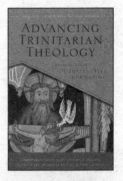

LOCATING ATONEMENT:
Explorations in Constructive
Dogmatics, *2015*

*THE VOICE OF GOD IN
THE TEXT OF SCRIPTURE:*
Explorations in Constructive
Dogmatics, *2016*

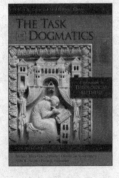

THE TASK OF DOGMATICS:
Explorations in Theological
Method, 2017

*THE CHRISTIAN
DOCTRINE OF HUMANITY:*
Explorations in Constructive
Dogmatics, *2018*

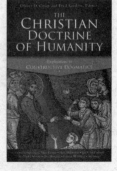

Oliver D. Crisp *and* Fred Sanders, Editors

DIVINE ACTION
AND PROVIDENCE

Explorations in
CONSTRUCTIVE DOGMATICS

———————— CONTRIBUTORS ————————

William J. Abraham, Oliver D. Crisp, Christine Helmer,
Brenda Deen Schildgen, Philip G. Ziegler

ZONDERVAN ACADEMIC

Divine Action and Providence
Copyright © 2019 by Oliver D. Crisp and Fred Sanders

ISBN 978-0-310-10688-3 (softcover)

ISBN 978-0-310-10689-0 (ebook)

Requests for information should be addressed to:
Zondervan, *3900 Sparks Dr. SE, Grand Rapids, Michigan 49546*

Image on page from William Perkins, *The Workes of that Famous and Worthie Minister of Christ, in the Universitie of Cambridge, M. W. Perkins.* 3 vols. Printed by John Legate, Printer to the Universitie of Cambridge, 1608. Courtesy of the H. Henry Meeter Center for Calvin Studies, Calvin University.

Cover design: StoryLookDesign
Cover photo: Everett – Art / Shutterstock

Printed in the United States of America

19 20 21 22 23 24 25 26 27 28 /LSC/ 15 14 13 12 11 10 9 8 7 6 5 4 3 2 1

*We dedicate this volume to our friends and colleagues in
the Torrey Honors Institute at Biola University and
the School of Theology in Fuller Theological Seminary
for seven years of hospitality. We couldn't have run
these conferences without your good graces.*

Thank you.

CONTENTS

ACKNOWLEDGMENTS

THE EDITORS WOULD LIKE TO THANK Professor Clinton E. Arnold as Dean of Talbot School of Theology, and the faculty and administration of Biola University for their support for the Seventh Los Angeles Theology Conference (LATC) in January of 2019, out of which these published proceedings grew. We are especially grateful for the invaluable assistance of Jessamy Delling, who oversaw the practical running of the event through the Torrey Honors Institute and made the event run as smoothly as it did. Thanks too to Fuller Theological Seminary for its ongoing support of LATC, and to Allison Wiltshire in particular for her administrative assistance. This is now the seventh time that we are able to record grateful thanks to our editor and colleague, Katya Covrett, for her collaboration and insight before, during, and after the fun and frolics of conference proceedings. She remains an editor extraordinaire.

CONTRIBUTORS

William J. Abraham—is Albert Cook Outler Professor of Wesley Studies and Altshuler Distinguished Teaching Professor at Perkins School of Theology, Southern Methodist University. He earned his BA from the Queen's University, Belfast, his MDiv from Asbury Theological Seminary, and his DPhil from Oxford University. He also holds an honorary DD from Asbury Theological Seminary.

Oliver D. Crisp—is Professor of Analytic Theology, Institute for Analytic and Exegetical Theology, School of Divinity, University of St. Andrews, Scotland. He received the BD and MTh degrees from the University of Aberdeen, a PhD degree from King's College, University of London, and a DLitt from the University of Aberdeen.

David Efird—is senior lecturer, University of York, UK. He holds an AB degree from Duke University, an MDiv from Princeton Theological Seminary, an MSc from Edinburgh University, and a DPhil from Oxford University. He is an ordained priest in the Church of England.

Julián E. Gutiérrez—is an independent scholar. He holds a BScEng degree from Agrarian University of Colombia, a BMS from Jorge Tadeo Lozano University, an MA in theology from Talbot School of Theology, Biola University, an MTh in systematic theology from the University of Aberdeen, and a PhD in divinity from the University of St. Andrews.

W. Ross Hastings—is Sangwoo Youtong Chee Professor of Theology, Regent College, Vancouver, Canada. He holds a PhD in chemistry from Queen's University in Kingston, Ontario, Canada, an MCS from Regent College, Vancouver, and a PhD in divinity from the University of St. Andrews, Scotland.

Christine Helmer—is professor of German and religious studies, Department of German and Department of Religious Studies, Northwestern

University. She holds a PhD from Yale University and an honorary DTh from the University of Helsinki.

Jonathan Hill—is senior lecturer in philosophy of religion, University of Exeter, UK. He holds the BA and MPhil degrees from the University of Oxford and a PhD in philosophy from the National University of Singapore.

R. David Nelson— is senior acquisitions editor for Baker Academic and Brazos Press, and editor of *Lutheran Forum*. He received his BA in history and English literature from the University of Alabama at Birmingham, an MDiv from Beeson Divinity School, Samford University, and a PhD in Divinity from King's College, University of Aberdeen.

Brenda Deen Schildgen—is distinguished professor emerita of comparative literature, University of California, Davis. She earned a BA in English and French at the University of Wisconsin, an MA in religious studies at the University of San Francisco, and an MA and PhD in comparative literature at Indiana University, Bloomington.

Nathaniel Gray Sutanto—is associate minister at Covenant City Church, Jakarta, Indonesia, and is ordained by the International Presbyterian Church. He is also adjunct lecturer in systematic theology at Westminster Theological Seminary. He received a BA in philosophy and another BA in biblical and theological studies from Biola University. He went on to earn an MA in religion at Westminster Theological Seminary before receiving his PhD in systematic theology from the University of Edinburgh.

David Worsley—is an associate lecturer in philosophy at the University of York, UK. He holds a BA in politics, philosophy, and economics, an MA in political philosophy, an MA in philosophy, theology, and ethics, and a PhD in philosophy from the University of York.

Philip G. Ziegler—is professor of Christian dogmatics in the Divinity Department of the University of Aberdeen, Scotland. He holds a BA from the University of Toronto, an MA in theology from the University of St. Michael's College, an STL from Regis College, and an MDiv and ThD from Victoria University and University of Toronto.

INTRODUCTION

A distinction between creation and "preservation" or between the initial and "continuing" creation has been rightly used to warrant that there was a first existence of creatures at a zero point of time. But such distinctions can have no other metaphysical or religious significance. The world is no less dependent on God's creating word at any moment of its existence than it was at the beginning. God's creating word no more waits upon its auditor now than at the beginning.

—ROBERT W. JENSON[1]

THE CLAIM THAT GOD ACTS IS at the heart of the Christian message of salvation. The Christian God is, after all, a God who creates, sustains, and redeems his creatures (as Jenson goes on to point out in the remainder of his two volume *Systematic Theology*). The very first words of the biblical text begin with a claim about God's action: the beginning, when God created the heavens and the earth. It records act after act, interaction after interaction, episode upon episode where God intervenes—culminating in the incarnation, life, death, resurrection, and ascension of Christ, who (it is claimed) is God incarnate. The actions don't stop there either: the records of the early church in the later New Testament documents tell of how God works by means of his Holy Spirit in the lives of the early Christians, sustaining and enabling them to withstand great hardship, proclaim the message of salvation, and witness signs and wonders performed by key leaders of the emerging Christian movement.

Yet this biblical effusion of divine acts in the created world stands in stark contrast to the marked aversion to such language in contemporary

---

1. *Systematic Theology*, vol. 1, *The Triune God* (New York: Oxford University Press, 1999), 9.

discussion of divine providence. Often in recent accounts of providence, theologians preface their views with a jeremiad about how the doctrine has fallen on hard times and how it has been reconceived in modernity.[2] It is a problematic doctrine, so it is often said, one that has been made difficult since the scientific revolution and the concomitant reconception of the natural world as something entirely independent and causally closed.[3] This can be seen in Pierre Simon Laplace's oft-repeated response to Napoleon upon being asked where the deity fitted into his scientific worldview: "I have no need of that hypothesis."

But why must doctrines of providence be on the conceptual back foot? Rather than explore the issues the doctrine raises for the intersection between science and theology (something that has been done numerous times elsewhere),[4] this volume considers providence in its dogmatic register, as John Webster used to say. However, not all of the chapters attempt to restate a version of the doctrine for today. There are also essays that question its place amongst the traditional theological loci and worry about its history and reception (e.g., the contributions by Christine Helmer and Brenda Schildgen, and, to some extent, by Philip Ziegler). The contributors are aware of the problems the doctrine raises. And they deal with important ways in which it has been rethought in modern theology, either in terms of particular thinkers (Schleiermacher, Bavinck, Barth), or particular schools of thought (e.g., apocalyptic readings of Paul, postliberalism, analytic theology). Nevertheless, there is a decided emphasis upon giving constructive accounts of the doctrine or aspects of it even when the constructive component is bound up with a project that involves theological retrieval. As with previous volumes in this series, there is a breadth of views represented, as well as a breadth of theological commitment. Lutherans, Reformed, Anglican, Methodist, evangelical, Free Church—all these traditions can be found represented in the essays that follow. This has been part of the

---

2. See, e.g., Charles M. Wood, *The Question of Providence* (Louisville: Westminster John Knox, 2008); and John Webster, "Providence," in *Christian Dogmatics: Reformed Theology for the Church Catholic*, ed. Michael Allen and Scott R. Swain (Grand Rapids: Baker Academic, 2016), 148–64.

3. Although, see Alvin Plantinga, "What Is 'Intervention'?" in *Theology and Science* 6, no. 4 (2008): 369–401 for an argument that rejects the view that there is a special problem of divine "intervention" that modern theologians must address.

4. See, e.g., important studies by Nicholas Saunders, *Divine Action and Modern Science* (Cambridge: Cambridge University Press, 2002); Arthur Peacocke, *Theology for a Scientific Age: Being and Becoming—Natural, Divine, and Human* (Minneapolis: Fortress, 1993); Alvin Plantinga, *Where the Conflict Really Lies: Science, Religion, and Naturalism* (Oxford: Oxford University Press, 2011); John C. Polkinghorne, *Science and Providence: God's Interaction with the World* (London: SPCK, 1989); and the essays in *The Oxford Handbook of Religion and Science*, ed. Philip Clayton (Oxford: Oxford University Press, 2006). The field is large and diffuse. This is just an indicative sample of the literature.

DNA of the Los Angeles Theological Conference series since its inception, and we are delighted to continue in that vein of ecumenical, constructive dogmatics here. With this in mind, we turn now to provide an overview of the chapters that follow.

Oliver Crisp kicks off the volume with an essay that seeks to open up discussion of meticulous accounts of divine providence. Meticulous providence is the view that presumes, as Crisp puts it, that the scope of divine preservation, concurrence, and governance in divine providence encompasses *all that comes to pass.* Crisp argues that this doctrinal claim is compatible with rather different and incommensurate metaphysical pictures, giving rise to a range of possible views of providence that would count as "meticulous." He explores two such pictures that give the lie to the common misapprehension that meticulous accounts of divine providence must be deterministic in some sense. On Crisp's account, this is not necessarily so. He outlines a secondary cause account that is consistent with theological soft determinism and a concursus account that is consistent with a stronger account of libertarian free will. The upshot of his discussion is that meticulous providence is a broader, more "roomy" doctrine than is sometimes thought.

Next up is William Abraham, a Methodist philosophical theologian who is in the midst of an extensive four-volume work on divine action and agency in Christian theology. In his wide-ranging chapter, he focuses on nonmeticulous versions of divine providence. He rejects attempts to cast divine providence in the language of "double agency," where there is the human agent and some mysterious divine agency that together bring about a given action. Framing his discussion with two concrete examples of providence, Abraham argues that the right way to think about these matters is in terms of a specific notion of divine agency. This should focus on instances of personal agency that we can apprehend, using these as test cases of divine action "from below," so to speak, as opposed to accounts that begin "from above," that is, via some theory about divine action abstracted from particular instances of such putative action.

In the third chapter, Julián Gutiérrez focuses on the identity of the God of providence with particular reference to the theology of the English Puritan theologian Stephen Charnock (1628–80). Gutiérrez presents Charnock as an exemplar of the Reformed scholastic tradition, and the goal of the chapter is to offer a constructive retrieval of a classic model of providence. The chief benefit of this model, and its promise for contemporary theology, is the careful attention it gives to identifying the agent of providence. Such an approach stands in notable contrast to much modern discussion of providence, which presupposes a rather featureless divine agent behind events in the world. The result of such inattention to the character of God is not just an underdeveloped account of God but also a flattened and unenlightening view of providence itself. A retrieval of Charnock's exposition of providence could help to make up for these defects.

In the fourth chapter, Christine Helmer contributes this volume's most negative take on providence, which she calls a "deflationary account." Helmer begins by noting that the doctrine has had no fixed place in the long history of theology but has made its home sometimes in the doctrine of God, sometimes in the doctrine of faith, sometimes in eschatology, and so on. She then focuses on the cultural production and theological reception of providence in the early modern period, where it became largely associated with anxieties about assurance of salvation. Helmer turns to Martin Luther's theology of divine hiddenness as an example of Christian faith that was unhindered by the widespread, dysfunctional preoccupation with providence and straightforwardly calls for contemporary theology to jettison the theology of providence.

In chapter 5, Nathaniel Gray Sutanto considers providence from a neo-Calvinist point of view, with special attention to the usefulness of the doctrine within the culture of the modern university and its thought forms. Sutanto's chapter retrieves Herman Bavinck's (1854–1921) organic model of divine providence, drawing from his untranslated *Christelijke wetenschap and Christelijke wereldbeschouwing*. What is unique about Bavinck's approach is that it is less an apologetic argument for providence and more of a performative account showing the fruits of affirming a meticulous model of divine providence. Likewise, Sutanto commends this approach and indicates how the doctrine of providence can support Christian intellectual life today.

In chapter 6, W. Ross Hastings engages the theology of Karl Barth in order to construct an account of asymmetric concursus between divine and created agents. Divine agency and creaturely agency, he argues, must be compatible in a way that preserves the fecundity of creational realities yet recognizes the primacy of divine freedom. This chapter explores their concurrence in two areas: in Christology, where the divine nature is asymmetrically related to the human, and in Barth's anthropology, which features a similar asymmetric compatibilism.

In chapter 7, Brenda Deen Schildgen considers providence using the tools of a historian of ideas. She explores the way providence has formed the Christian theology of history, or rather the variety of Christian theologies of history that have been developed in different eras. Beginning with the Bible and early Christianity, she examines the theologies of well-known figures such as Eusebius (263–339 CE) and Augustine (354–430 CE) but also figures such as Lactantius (240–320 CE) and Orosius (c. 375–c. 418 CE), whose influence is often overlooked. After some attention to Thomas Aquinas, Schildgen focuses on the way modern political regimes (from South African apartheid to American manifest destiny) have functioned with a secularized notion of providence and concludes with some counsel about how to keep in place the necessary distinction between sacred and secular.

In chapter 8, R. David Nelson considers divine agency in light of the recent apocalyptic turn in Pauline studies. Contemporary apocalyptic theology portrays God's action in the world as always "new," creatively and redemptively disrupting the "old," which is governed by sin, death, and the devil. While appreciating the apocalyptic turn, Nelson points out that the fundamental task of Christian theology requires the confession of continuity in God's ways. To that end, Nelson draws on Thomas, Calvin, and Barth to show how to conceptualize the connections between the old and new actions of God.

In chapter 9, Philip Ziegler undertakes to clarify providence by attending to its antithesis, the devil's work. Introducing this theme means expanding from reflecting on two agents (the divine and the human) to considering a "three-agent drama." Ziegler's account of the grammar and function of the doctrine of providence is markedly dramatic and pragmatic as a result of reckoning theologically with the work of the devil in relation to God's sustaining and governing sovereignty. Largely by way of an extended dialogue with Gustaf Aulén, Ziegler recommends a concentration of the doctrine of providence within the soteriological sphere.

In chapter 10, Jonathan Hill considers rival accounts of divine action, with a special interest in examining whether Christians should adopt some kind of occasionalism. In strong occasionalism, God causes all mental and physical events; in weak occasionalism, God only causes physical events. Alvin Plantinga has recently defended the latter. Critiquing that account, Hill argues that strong occasionalism is preferable to weak occasionalism. Yet in doing so, Hill also claims that whether one should be an occasionalist at all comes down to which theory of diachronic identity one favors.

In chapter 11, David Efird and David Worsley consider how divine action and divine providence relate to eschatology, and in particular the beatific vision. Their motivating question is why God does not actualize our ultimate good right now. The chapter considers divine providence to be compatible with human freedom and divine action to be compatible with a law-governed creation. Together these help create a unified theory of God's love for us and his desire that we love him too. Further, Efird and Worsely argue that divine hiddenness is a feature of God's love.

May these essays extend discussion of the doctrine of Scripture and our hearing of its various voices today, *ad maiorem dei gloriam.*

Oliver D. Crisp and Fred Sanders, April 2019

CHAPTER 1

METICULOUS PROVIDENCE

Oliver D. Crisp

Q. What do you understand by the providence of God?
A. God's providence is his Almighty and ever present power, whereby,
as with his hand, he still upholds heaven and earth and all creatures,
and so governs them that leaf and blade, rain and drought, fruitful and
barren years, food and drink, health and sickness, riches and poverty,
indeed, all things, come to us not by chance but by his fatherly hand.
—*Heidelberg Catechism, Q. 27*

THUS THE *HEIDELBERG CATECHISM*, and it is difficult to think of
a better, more evocative characterization of meticulous providence than
that. Put in more prosaic language, we might say that if providence is the
general theological term we give to divine preservation, concurrence,
and governance with respect to the created order, meticulous providence
is (very roughly) that species of doctrine which stipulates that the scope
of divine preservation, concurrence, and governance encompasses *all that
comes to pass*.[1] There are many biblical passages that suggest such a view.

---

1. In a previous treatment of providence, I wrote that meticulous providence is the view that
"God orders all things that come to pass, such that no event occurs without his concurrently
bringing it about in conjunction with mundane creaturely causes" ("John Calvin on Creation and
Providence," in *Retrieving Doctrine: Essays in Reformed Theology* [Downers Grove, IL: IVP Academic,
2010], 3–25; 13). That is approximately right, but the way of stating the matter here is, I think, more
accurate. David Fergusson puts it like this: "Everything that happens is willed by God and serves
some end—nothing lies outside the scope of divine volition and intentionality." *The Providence of
God: A Polyphonic Approach* (Cambridge: Cambridge University Press, 2018), 1.

For instance, Proverbs 15:3 tells us that the eyes of the LORD are in every place, beholding the wicked and the good. Proverbs 16:33 states that "the lot is cast into the lap, but its every decision is from the LORD." Matthew 10:29 has Jesus saying, "Are not two sparrows sold for a penny? Yet not one of them will fall to the ground outside your Father's care." And in the opening chapter of Ephesians, we read that we are "predestined according to his purpose who works all things after the counsel of his will" (Eph 1:11). Paul, in addressing the Areopagus in Acts 17, is reported as saying that God gives "to mankind life, breath, and everything." And quoting the pagan poet Epimenides with approval, he goes on to say that "in him [i.e., God] we live and move and have our being." The writer to the Hebrews observes that God upholds "all things by the word of his power" (Heb 1:3). This is just a small sample of the many biblical passages that suggest God's providence is meticulous in nature.[2] Nevertheless, there are a number of ways in which this could be construed—different metaphysical pictures with which these biblical passages are consistent.

For instance, does meticulous providence mean God directly and immediately causes all things distinct from himself—along the lines envisaged in occasionalism, the doctrine according to which we are merely the occasions of God's action in creation, not actually causing anything ourselves? (This view can be found in the work of Jonathan Edwards and Nicholas Malebranche, amongst others.)[3] Or is it, as *The Westminster Confession* 5.2 claims, that God "orders" all that comes to pass "to fall out, according to the nature of *second causes*, either necessarily, freely, or contingently" (emphasis added)? (This, or something very like it, is the sort of view one can find in the theology of John Calvin and many of his successors.) Perhaps the fundamental theological claim of meticulous providence should be construed to mean God *concurs* with every creaturely action so as to ensure a particular outcome obtains in every circumstance. On this view, effects are produced by both God and creatures immediately and simultaneously. (This doctrine, which can be found in many versions of Thomism, is also a position adopted by some in the Reformed tradition.)[4] Finally, it may be that God ensures

2. It is often said that providence is a *term* imported into Christian theology from ancient pagan philosophy. Even if that is right, the *concept* of meticulous providence (as I understand it here) is clearly present in a number of biblical texts.

3. For discussion, see Steven Nadler, *Occasionalism: Causation among the Cartesians* (Oxford: Oxford University Press, 2011); and Oliver D. Crisp, *Jonathan Edwards on God and Creation* (New York: Oxford University Press, 2012).

4. For discussion of this in the Roman Catholic tradition, see Alfred J. Freddoso, "God's General Concurrence with Secondary Causes: Why Conservation Is Not Enough," in *Philosophical*

that the world he creates includes exactly the history it does, down to the smallest detail, by bringing about that world in which human creatures make the particular set of free choices he desires them to make. (This view is consistent with Molinism, or the doctrine of middle knowledge, which is one of the most popular accounts of providence amongst contemporary analytic theologians, though it is historically a Jesuit position.)[5]

There are other views besides these, of course. I mention these four because they are important fixtures in the history of theological discussion of providence and because they illustrate the fact that one can agree that the scope of God's providence is indeed meticulous and yet construe that in very different ways—including ways that do not presume some version of theological determinism. God's meticulous oversight of all that comes to pass could mean he is the sole immediate cause of all that comes to pass; or the immediate cause of some but not all things (because he utilizes secondary or creaturely causes); or a concurring "cause" bringing about things immediately and in conjunction with the immediate causal activity of creaturely agents; or by means of some other act of divine ensurance[6] that makes certain that human free actions unfold precisely as he intends. Yet clearly these are very different views about the nature of divine oversight of creation, each of which can plausibly be said to be versions of meticulous providence.

Rather than offer an overview of all of these various options, which can be found elsewhere in the literature,[7] I will focus on two rather different ways of construing meticulous providence with a view to showing that the doctrine is more expansive than might be thought at first glance. It is "roomy" enough to include within its bounds accounts of providence that are determinist as well as accounts that are libertarian. This somewhat

---

Perspectives, vol. 5, *Philosophy of Religion*, ed. James Tomberlin (Aterscadero, CA: Ridgeview, 1991), 553–85; Freddoso, "God's General Concurrence with Secondary Causes: Pitfalls and Prospects," *American Catholic Philosophical Quarterly* 68, no. 2 (1994): 131–56. For discussion of this matter in the Reformed tradition, see Richard A. Muller, *Divine Will and Human Choice: Freedom, Contingency, and Necessity in Early Modern Reformed Thought* (Grand Rapids: Baker Academic, 2017), chap. 8.

5. There are also those within the Reformed tradition who claim that a version of Molinism is consistent with Calvinism. See, e.g., Terence Tiessen, *Providence and Prayer* (Downers Grove, IL: InterVarsity, 2000).

6. Here I am using the term ensure rather like Paul Helm's repurposing of the archaic English word *ensurance*, that is to connote the action or means of *ensuring* or *making certain*. See Helm, "Discrimination: Aspects of God's Causal Activity," in *Calvinism and the Problem of Evil*, ed. David E. Alexander and Daniel M. Johnson (Eugene, OR: Wipf and Stock, 2016), 145–67; 156.

7. A useful primer can be found in Dennis W. Jowers, ed., *Four Views on Divine Providence* (Grand Rapids: Zondervan, 2011). A rather different approach can be found in the essays collected together in Francesca Aran Murphy and Philip G. Ziegler, eds., *The Providence of God* (London: T&T Clark, 2009).

unexpected thesis has theological implications for how we frame our discussions of meticulous providence, as I shall indicate at the end of the chapter.[8]

To this end, the argument proceeds as follows. In the first section, I shall set out a number of preliminary conceptual distinctions. Then, in a second section, I shall outline two distinct accounts of meticulous providence. The first of these I shall call *the secondary cause account*. It follows in broad outline the sort of view that is defended by Calvin and some of his intellectual heirs in Reformed theology, though it is not identical to the views of Calvin, strictly speaking. On this view, God determines the history of the world bringing about all that comes to pass, usually mediately, by means of secondary causes such as creaturely agents. The second view I shall outline I will call *the concurrence account*. As already intimated, it follows the general outline of an approach to meticulous providence that can be found in Thomist thought.[9] Nevertheless, the version I shall outline does not utilize Thomist metaphysics. It is inspired by a Thomist approach rather than being Thomist strictly speaking. The substance of this account of meticulous providence is that God's act of concurrence with creaturely causes does not infringe the libertarian freedom of creatures but somehow preserves it whilst also ensuring all that comes to pass. Having given an outline of these two versions of meticulous providence, I turn in a third section to assess these two ways of thinking about divine action in creation, closing with some reflections on the theological upshot of this comparison.

PRELIMINARY CONCEPTUAL DISTINCTIONS

To begin with, we need to expand upon the notion of meticulous providence. Thus far I have said this is the view according to which the scope of divine preservation, concurrence, and governance encompasses all that comes to pass. Preservation, concurrence, and governance are the three traditional dogmatic heads under which providence is usually discussed. They are not necessarily distinct divine actions but more like different modes of the one divine act, or different aspects of the one action of divine

---

8. The presumption that meticulous providence is inherently deterministic is commonplace. One recent example is David Fergusson, who says, "the classical doctrine emerged in the west with its typical stress on divine sovereignty, double agency, a distinction between primary and secondary causes, and a compatibilism that affirmed both human freedom and divine determinism." *Providence of God*, 59; see also 75.

9. I have been helped in preparing this chapter by some essays by W. Matthews Grant and Hugh McCann, two contemporary Christian philosophers indebted to the Thomist tradition, even if they don't always follow Thomist metaphysics to the absolute letter.

providence. God is said to preserve the world he has created in existence by the immediate exercise of his power. For defenders of meticulous providence, without such an act of divine preservation, the creation would immediately cease to exist. God also acts in concurrence or "agreement" with creaturely actions, without which no creaturely action would take place. So God's providence is necessary in order for creatures to act as well as continue to exist. And God governs his creatures by means of his constant oversight of the creation, ordering all things to the goal or consummation for which he has ordained the created order in the first place. Thus there is nothing that obtains in creation without God's preservation of, concurrence with, and government respecting that thing. Absent God's preservation of, concurrence with, and government respecting that thing at each moment of its existence, it would not exist. In this way, according to the doctrine of meticulous providence, all that exists in creation is in some important sense *radically* dependent on God's preservation, concurrence, and government. The idea is similar to the way in which a person's thoughts are radically dependent upon their continuing to think those things in order for the thoughts in question to continue to exist.

Now, meticulous providence so understood is often thought to be equivalent to determinism. I take it that determinism is, in the words of Peter van Inwagen, "the thesis that the past *determines* a unique future."[10] That is, the past determines *exactly one* future physical state of affairs. Put a bit more expansively, suppose that the past up to midday yesterday is summarized in the proposition p. To this, add a complete account of the laws of nature, summarized in the proposition l. Determinism is the view according to which the conjunction of p plus l entails a unique future state of affairs. In other words, $p + l$ entails that you are reading this sentence right now rather than, say, basking in the sunshine on Manhattan Beach, skiing at Big Bear, or whatever.[11]

Of course, there are different sorts of determinism. Usually, when analytic philosophers talk about determinism, they are interested in *physical* or *causal* determinism. (I shall use these two terms interchangeably since I presume that causation is a relation that obtains between physical things.) Philosophers are interested in the way in which one thing may causally affect another in the physical universe in which we live. So causal determinism

---

10. Peter van Inwagen, *An Essay on Free Will* (Oxford: Oxford University Press, 1983), 2. Emphasis original.
11. For discussion of this point, see Kevin Timpe, *Free Will: Sourcehood and Its Alternatives*, 2nd ed. (London: Bloomsbury Academic, 2013), 13–14.

is the thesis that a particular event, y, is causally necessitated by x, if x is some acting thing or some event, such that, given x, the unique event y *must* happen because x *makes* it happen.[12]

By contrast, theologians like to talk about *theological* determinism. This is not the same thesis as causal determinism because the idea is that God, an immaterial agent, determines a unique future for the created order. This includes the physical creation but does not comprise it. For presumably there are many things that are not physical in the created order, such as angels and demons. Yet on the theological determinist view, God is said to determine their actions as well. What is more, some theological determinists seem to think that God's meticulous oversight of the creation, which involves his ordaining all that comes to pass, does not involve him physically or causally bringing things about in the world. His action is logically prior to physical causation and is sometimes said to be what informs or gives rise to such physical causation.[13]

Be that as it may, one clear difference between theological determinism and causal determinism is that according to theological determinism, it is *God* that determines what comes to pass, whereas on causal determinism, physical events in the past plus the laws of nature determine a unique future physical state of affairs. Perhaps God utilizes physical events to bring about unique future physical state of affairs. If that is right, then at least some versions of theological determinism imply some version of physical or causal determinism. Nevertheless, the two theses are conceptually distinct.

With this in mind, let us turn next to compatibilism and incompatibilism and how they bear upon meticulous providence. In this context, compatibilism is the thesis that determinism is compatible with human free will and moral responsibility. Notice that I use the term *determinism* without qualification in the previous sentence. This is because whatever sort of determinism is in view, the issue is whether that form of determinism

---

12. Adapted from Katherin A. Rogers, *Freedom and Self-Creation: Anselmian Libertarianism* (Oxford: Oxford University Press, 2015), 10–11.

13. One historic example of this sort of idea can be found in the idea of physical premotion. This term of art was made famous in the *de auxiliis* controversy between Báñezians and Molinists in the sixteenth century Iberian peninsula. It states that nothing in creation acts without the predetermination of God. There is what we might call a divine "motion" or action that obtains prior to any physical action in creation—hence a physical premotion. For discussion of this, see the introduction to Jowers, ed., *Four Views on Divine Providence*, 17; Thomas P. Flint, *Divine Providence: The Molinist Account* (Ithaca, NY: Cornell University Press, 1998); the editorial introduction to Louis De Molina, *On Divine Foreknowledge: Part IV of the Concordia*, ed. and trans. Alfred J. Freddoso (Ithaca, NY: Cornell University Press, 1988); and especially R. J. Matava, *Divine Causality and Human Free Choice: Domingo Báñez, Physical Premotion and the Controversy De Auxiliis Revisited* (Leiden: Brill, 2016).

(whether causal, theological, or whatever) is consistent with human free will and moral responsibility. We might also worry about the free will and moral responsibility of other nonhuman creatures such as angels or primates. But we need not trouble ourselves with such complications here. It is sufficient for our purposes to focus on the free will and moral responsibility of human creatures irrespective of whether there are other rational creatures that also have free will and moral responsibility.

If compatibilism is the thesis that determinism is compatible with human free will and moral responsibility, incompatibilism is the thesis that determinism is incompatible with human free will and moral responsibility. Either determinism is true, or human free will and moral responsibility is true, but not both. There is no possible state of affairs in which both determinism and human free will and moral responsibility is compossible, on this way of thinking.

Next, let me say something about libertarianism, since this will be important for the concurrence account. There are various ways of construing libertarianism. I will put it like this. Libertarianism is the view according to which incompatibilism is true, and determinism is false. That is, libertarianism states that determinism and the combination of human free will plus moral responsibility are not compossible and, in addition, that determinism is false. Some people think that libertarianism also requires commitment to some form of the principle of alternative possibilities, according to which a person has free will only if she or he could have done otherwise.[14] But it is not clear to me that this is a *requirement* for libertarianism, though it is a common feature of much contemporary libertarianism. It seems to me that the following claims could all be true:

1. Incompatibilism
2. The denial of determinism
3. Agents are the source of actions that are free
4. Those actions that are free actions are actions for which humans are morally responsible

In this respect, I am understanding free will as a kind of *control condition*, that is, some control upon action in virtue of which human agents are held

---

14. In its modern guise, this principle derives from the work of the Princeton philosopher Harry Frankfurt. See Frankfurt, *The Importance of What We Care About: Philosophical Essays* (Cambridge: Cambridge University Press, 1998), chap. 1. For a helpful recent discussion of the issues, see Timpe, *Free Will: Sourcehood*, chap. 5.

morally responsible.[15] It could be argued that although these four claims are consistent, each being a necessary condition for libertarianism, they are not sufficient. For, so it might be thought, one must add to this the principle of alternative possibilities in order to have a set of necessary and sufficient conditions for libertarianism. But perhaps not.

Consider, for example, the case of Anselm of Canterbury.[16] His view seems to be that human free will requires something like the four conditions stated above. But he also thinks that the truly free person is one who measures up to the standard set by God—to that rightness or rectitude of will (*rectitudio*) that involves acting in accordance with God's will. The truly free person, on Anselm's view, seems to be one who acts rightly according to the rectitude of will *for its own sake,* not as a means to some other end, so that the truly free agent rightly desires what she ought to desire.[17] Such a person is the source of her or his action, not God. Nevertheless, it is not obvious that such a position requires a principle of alternative possibilities, or some similar idea of metaphysical wiggle room or *leeway,* in order for the action in question to be free and one for which the creature is morally responsible.[18] The alternative to such rectitude, for the Anselmian, is the dereliction of one's moral duty to follow divine commands. Far from being an alternative that is enjoyed by the truly free individual, that is only a "choice" in the Pickwickian sense of being the privation of some good state that ought to obtain. The truly free person, for the Anselmian, is the source of his or her choice and has rectitude of will for its own sake. Indeed, from an Anselmian point of view, it is possible to be in a state in which such rectitude is the only live option, as presumably is the case for those who are glorified as well as elect angels and God himself. This, for the Anselmian, is a more morally exalted state than one in which there is the real prospect of some wiggle room or leeway to choose some alternative.

---

15. See Kevin Timpe, *Free Will in Philosophical Theology* (London: Bloomsbury Academic, 2014), 7.

16. See especially Anselm's three dialogues *On Truth* (*De veritate*), *On Freedom of Choice* (*De libertate arbitrii*), and *On the Fall of the Devil* (*De casu diaboli*), as well as his much more substantial piece, *On the Harmony of God's Foreknowledge, Predestination, and Grace with Free Choice* (*De Concordia*), all of which can be found in translation in *Anselm: Basic Writings,* trans. Thomas Williams (Indianapolis: Hackett, 2007). Useful discussion of Anselm's view can be found in Sandra Visser and Thomas Williams, *Anselm* (Oxford: Oxford University Press, 2008), chap. 11, an interpretation I find persuasive. For a rather different approach to Anselm, one that claims he does hold to a principle of alternative possibilities for free will *tout court,* see Katherin Rogers, *Anselm on Freedom* (Oxford: Oxford University Press, 2008); and *Freedom and Self-Creation: Anselmian Libertarianism* (Oxford: Oxford University Press, 2015).

17. See Anselm, *On Freedom of Choice* 3, in *Anselm: Basic Writings,* 151.

18. At least not on all occasions. See discussion of this point in Visser and Williams, *Anselm,* chap. 11.

Of course, this analysis of libertarianism might be disputed. I raise the point about Anselm in order to show that there are theological cases where something like libertarianism seems to be in view, and where a principle of alternative possibilities or some other, similar sense of metaphysical leeway does not appear to be a requirement of the analysis of such free will—instead, sourcehood is the fundamental issue. We can distinguish these two sorts of libertarianism by referring to them as *leeway libertarianism* and *sourcehood libertarianism*, respectively.[19]

The leeway libertarian thinks that in addition to the four components to libertarianism I have outlined thus far—namely, incompatibilism; the denial of determinism; the claim that agents are the source of actions that are free; and the claim that those actions that are free actions are actions for which humans are morally responsible—what is needed is some sort of principle of alternative possibilities in order for a creaturely action to count as one that is truly free and for which the person concerned is morally responsible.

By contrast, the sourcehood libertarian is like the Anselmian: she thinks that what is required for libertarian freedom is our four components: incompatibilism; the denial of determinism; the claim that agents are the source of actions that are free; and the claim that those actions that are free actions are actions for which humans are morally responsible. Add to this the claim about the possession of rectitude of will for its own sake, which is a kind of teleological claim about the right ordering of the will, and we have the major aspects of what the Anselmian thinks is needed in order for a creaturely action to count as one that is truly free and for which the person concerned is morally responsible. Unlike the leeway libertarian, what is most important here is that the creaturely agent is the source of her action.

We are now in possession of a rough and ready concept of meticulous providence. We also have in our possession several further distinctions relevant to our discussion. These are physical or causal determinism and theological determinism; compatibilism and incompatibilism; and leeway and sourcehood versions of libertarianism. As I have already indicated, normally meticulous providence is thought to imply some sort of soft theological determinism or compatibilism. It is thought to be contrary to incompatibilism because the incompatibilist denies that meticulous providence and human free will are compossible, which is the very thing the defender of meticulous providence affirms. And meticulous providence is commonly thought to be contrary to libertarianism because God's meticulous oversight

---

19. There are also leeway and sourcehood versions of compatibilism, but we won't treat them here.

of all things is often thought to be antithetical to libertarian accounts of human agency.

With these distinctions in mind, we may now turn to sketch out two versions of meticulous providence. The first is a version of theological compatibilism that is consistent with a broadly Calvinian view of the matter. The second, which is the concurrence account, appears to be consistent with libertarianism.

TWO VERSIONS OF METICULOUS PROVIDENCE
THE SECONDARY CAUSE ACCOUNT

Let us begin by recapping our rough-and-ready version of the meticulous providence doctrine. This was that meticulous providence is (very roughly) that species of doctrine which stipulates that the scope of divine preservation, concurrence, and governance encompasses *all that comes to pass*. The defender of a secondary cause account of meticulous providence construes this general claim in terms of a version of theological compatibilism. Now, we have seen that compatibilism is the thesis that determinism is compatible with human free will and moral responsibility. So theological compatibilism is the thesis that God, being the agent that determines all things, is compatible with human free will and responsibility. But compatible how? One way to answer this is to suggest that human free will is the power an agent possesses to act in accordance with her desires—a rather "thin" account of human free will, to be sure, but one that is consistent with determinism. It is also consistent with moral responsibility. According to some compatibilists, *where* the desires in question originate is not salient for ascription of moral responsibility. *That* the desires are had by the agent in question and inform her choice is salient, however. Thus, for example, the Princeton philosopher Harry Frankfurt thinks that the origination of the conditions that give rise to my choosing to choose an action, and my choosing it in an ordered hierarchy of desires and choice, is not relevant to either my freedom or my moral responsibility for the action in question. If I choose a particular thing and choose to choose it, then whether my first- and second-order desires were ultimately due to some other agent like God or not, I am the one choosing as I do, and I am the one morally responsible for my action. As Frankfurt puts it,

> The only thing that really counts is what condition I am in. How I
> got into that condition is another matter. If I'm in the condition where

I'm doing what I want to do and I really want to do it, i.e., I decisively identify with my action, then I think I'm responsible for it. It makes no difference how it came about that that is the case. If it *is* the case then it follows that I am fully responsible.[20]

The defender of the secondary cause account of meticulous providence can claim something similar. I am morally responsible for choosing according to what I desire, and desire to desire, and this is true even if I am not the *ultimate source* of my first- and second-order desires.

An example will make the point clearer. Suppose I intentionally slap Jones. I desired to slap Jones, and I desired to desire to slap Jones. That is, my first- and second-order desires were in agreement so that—to borrow another term from Harry Frankfurt—I chose to slap Jones *wholeheartedly*. In other words, there were no conflicting first-order or second-order desires complicating my motivation for acting as I did in slapping Jones. Not only that, but in acting as I did, on the basis of such motivation, I am responsible for slapping Jones rather than (say) shaking his hand. For I acted upon what I desired, and desired to desire; I was in my right mind at the time, and I was not coerced or forced into action by others. In short, my desires were ordered toward this particular action. But clearly this is consistent with me being determined to act as I did by God.

From this example we can see that, plausibly, provided my choice is *wholehearted* in the Frankfurtian sense of the term, I am responsible for the choice I made in slapping Jones irrespective of whether I could not have chosen otherwise, and irrespective of whether the conditions for that choice originate outside me in the action of God.

We can now apply this view of theological compatibilism to the issue of divine action in secondary causation. It is important not to mistake the scope of the claim being made about secondary causation here. The view is not that God sets up the world so that secondary causes do all the work after the first moment of creation as a kind of absentee landlord along the lines of deism. Rather the claim is that God determines all that takes place but that this includes the use of creaturely causes, such as creaturely free choices, as the means to his ends. We creatures are proximate or secondary causes of particular actions for which we may be morally responsible, even where God is the primary or ultimate cause of what takes place.[21]

---

20. Harry Frankfurt, "Discussion with Harry Frankfurt," *Ethical Perspectives* 5 (1992): 32. Emphasis original.

21. Calvin makes similar claims in his work. For instance, "I distinguish everywhere between

Take, for instance, the example of Pharaoh often cited in connection with discussions on meticulous providence. God hardens Pharaoh's heart as the Scripture says (Exod 9:12). Yet it is Pharaoh who desires to reject the overtures of Moses as God's viceroy, and Pharaoh who sought to resist the liberation of the Hebrews. He desired to desire this course of action (second-order desire), and he desired it (first order desire) and freely chose it. He acted upon it, though the ultimate source for this course of action lies outside Pharaoh in the secret counsels of God (Deut 29:29). Read alongside Proverbs 21:1, it is clear that the heart of the king in the hand of the LORD is like a water course that God directs wherever he will—though we know not how God does this. Pharaoh's action is directed by God, but it is the desire of *his*—that is, *Pharaoh's*—heart. He chooses it *wholeheartedly*, as Frankfurt would say. And for these reasons, he is responsible for the choice he makes and the action that follows from that choice.

Put in more concrete theological terms, Pharaoh is the proximate cause of his action in rejecting Moses's overtures for release. But the ultimate source of his choice is God's ordination and plan of salvation (cf. Gen 50:20). God determines that Pharaoh will harden his heart and ensures this comes about by means of the circumstances in which he places Pharaoh as well as by direct action upon him as he makes the choice he does to reject Moses's overtures. But the choice itself is Pharaoh's choice, not God's choice.

An obvious line of criticism of this view is what is sometimes called *the controller objection*,[22] which is an objection to the claim that agents can be morally responsible for choices where they are not the ultimate source of those choices. We can put it like this: If God controls our actions like the actions of Pharaoh in the biblical story of the exodus, then it is difficult to see how anyone—Pharaoh or anyone else—is truly blameworthy. For God determines all that comes to pass; he is the primary cause of Pharaoh's hardness of heart, not Pharaoh. But to return to Frankfurt's earlier point, why think that is *salient* for the ascription of blame? If Pharaoh chose as he did wholeheartedly, then the fact that his choice was determined by God does not exonerate him. To think that it exonerates him is to conflate the issue of the ultimate source of his choice with the question of culpability for the choice. The ultimate source of the choice may not be Pharaoh;

---

primary and secondary causes and between mediate and proximate causes." John Calvin, *The Secret Providence of God*, ed. Paul Helm, trans. Keith Goad (Wheaton: Crossway, 2010), 101.

22. For a recent iteration of this, see Katherin Rogers, "The Divine Controller Argument for Incompatibilism," *Faith and Philosophy* 29 (2012): 275–94, and a response by John Ross Churchill, "Determinism and Divine Blame," *Faith and Philosophy* 34 (2017): 425–48. Rogers also discusses this in the first chapter of *Freedom and Self-Creation*.

it may be God, if theological determinism is true. But, so the defender of the secondary cause account of meticulous providence thinks, this issue is conceptually distinct from the matter of culpability. Source must be distinguished from blame. Those who follow Frankfurt's lead in this matter will say that moral responsibility depends on the wholehearted choice of the agent. It is Pharaoh's choice; Pharaoh who desires to desire as he chooses; and Pharaoh who desires as he chooses and makes the choice he does. He is the proximate source of his choice though not necessarily the ultimate source. But this fact alone—the fact that Pharaoh is only the proximate source of his choice—does no work in shifting moral responsibility from Pharaoh for making the choice he does. For it is *his* choice, not God's choice, and (presumably) he made it wholeheartedly.

THE CONCURRENCE ACCOUNT

Let us turn to the concurrence account as a second, and rather different, way of construing meticulous divine providence. There are different versions of concurrence in the history of theology. Sometimes this sort of view is set up as a doctrine that includes a claim about divine universal causation. An important constituent of the view is that God is the cause of all that comes to pass.[23] But, as I have already intimated, God cannot be a *physical* cause because he is not a physical object, any more than a soul can be the physical cause of the neural changes in the brain of a human person for those who think humans are body-soul composites. (How could it be? Immaterial beings like souls are literally *nowhere*, *pace* St. Thomas. They have no mass and no location, and they are not extended in space—or so it seems to me.) Although he would balk at that last assertion, Aquinas is willing to admit that "the very act of free will [in creatures] is traced to God *as to* a cause."[24] So perhaps in keeping with Aquinas we may say that God is not a physical cause, strictly speaking, though we might speak of his action in meticulous providence using causal language as a kind of placeholder for the divine immediate bringing about of creaturely action. Let us do so, speaking with the vulgar whilst thinking with the learned, and refer to such divine action as *causal-like action*.[25]

---

23. Thus W. Matthews Grant in "Divine Universal Causality and Libertarian Freedom," in *Free Will and Theism: Connections, Contingencies, and Concerns*, ed. Kevin Timpe and Daniel Speak (Oxford: Oxford University Press, 2017), 214–33.

24. *Summa theologiae* 1.22.2 ad 4. Emphasis added.

25. Compare Matava: "While God's creative causality is *analogous to* efficient causation, divine causality is not any sort of causality we know from created causes. God's causality is sui generis. Divine transcendence must be seen all the way through." *Divine Causality*, 320. Emphasis original.

Now, there are many accounts of the notion of "cause," and I do not propose to go into them in detail here. Suffice it to say that many modern philosophers regard the notion of cause as a kind of brute or primitive unanalyzable concept with which we are saddled. Humean regularity theory is one such view that has been very popular amongst modern philosophers. A rough version of the view goes like this. We see one billiard ball strike another billiard ball, and we infer from this that the one ball in striking the other causes the motion of the second ball. The regularity with which we encounter such circumstances leads us to think that there is a constant conjunction between the striking of one ball against another, the motion this gives to the second ball, and so on. Nevertheless, we don't really know what it is for the first billiard ball to *cause* the other to move, such that its motion is the effect of being struck by the first ball. Rather, we observe a certain regularity obtaining between the motion of one ball and its motion upon being struck by the other ball. Through a certain regularity of such conjunctions, the one thing following the other, we come to infer that there is a cause and effect.[26]

Apply this to the case of God bringing about the actions of creatures, including the action of free creaturely agents like humans. What would it be for God to act in a causal-like manner? I have no idea any more than I have an idea of what it would be like for a soul to act in a causal-like way upon a body. But if the notion of causation used in more mundane circumstances to refer to physical causal relations is primitive or basic or unanalyzable, then the fact that God's causal-like action is at least as mysterious as notions of physical causation should not be particularly troubling. Or at least it should be no more troubling than the case of physical causation (for those who think of physical causation as something brute or unanalyzable).[27] Nevertheless, I can say something about the circumstances or state of affairs that give rise to such divine action. Recall our three modes of providence: preservation, concurrence, and government. On the concurrence view, God is said to preserve creatures in existence for all moments after the first moment of their existence. Concurrence is that particular manner of preservation that has to do with God concurring with the actions of

---

26. This is famously the view of David Hume, and his regularity theory is still with us today. See Hume, *Enquiry Concerning Human Understanding*, ed. P. H. Nidditch, 3rd ed. (Oxford: Oxford University Press, 1975 [1777]), 7.1.50.

27. A point made with some force by William Hasker in *The Emergent Self* (Ithaca, NY: Cornell University Press, 1999), 150–52. A similar claim about apophaticism with respect to the "how" of divine ensurance can be found in Helm, "Discrimination," 156–60.

free creatures so as to ensure that they occur. Without this particular sort of active preservation on God's part, the action in question could not so much as be intended, let alone executed by the creature in question. God governs the world in such a way that it proceeds in an orderly manner according to the physical laws that he has put in place in the act of creation (whatever analysis we give of such laws) toward the end or goal that he has ordained for it.

Now, we might describe God's concurrence as his immediate or basic act of will that ensures that the volition of the creaturely agent obtains. His act is logically, but not necessarily temporally, prior to the creature's action in volition. And it is a necessary condition of that action—indeed, a hypothetically necessary condition. In a recent paper on the subject, W. Matthews Grant has proposed that God has reasons for concurring with the volitions of creaturely agents but that strictly speaking, there is nothing in virtue of which God brings about the effect of the creaturely volition.[28] "God's willing, choosing, or intending E [the creaturely volition] is not an act distinct from God's causing E," he says.[29] For there is nothing intrinsic to God in virtue of which God brings about the volitional effect in the creaturely agent. "Rather," he remarks, "God's causal act consists entirely in items extrinsic to God, that is, in E [the creaturely volition] plus the causal relation between God and E."[30]

Put in a more dogmatic register, if God is an absolute sovereign over all he has created and is metaphysically and psychologically independent of his creation (existing *a se* or from himself), then his concurrence with creaturely action cannot affect or change his being. And if God is metaphysically simple, there can be no act of concurring with particular creaturely volitions "in" God, so to speak. For that would imply the very notion of metaphysical complexity in God that many traditional defenders of concurrence want to deny. Instead, according to Grant's way of construing matters, there is God, God's reason for concurring with the creaturely volition, and the relation that obtains between God and the creaturely volition—though this cannot be a "real" relation, that is, one that actually presumes some sort of real or intrinsic change in God.

How would such an account of divine, universal, causal-like action in concurrence make sense alongside something like a libertarian account of

---

28. See Grant, "Divine Universal Causality and Libertarian Freedom," esp. 220–22.
29. Grant, "Divine Universal Causality and Libertarian Freedom," 220.
30. Grant, "Divine Universal Causality and Libertarian Freedom," 221.

human freedom? Here we must return to our earlier distinction between sourcehood and leeway accounts of free will. Previously I intimated that some philosophers distinguish between accounts of the metaphysics of human free will that maintain the basic issue is the source of the action (hence "sourcehood" accounts) and those that think the basic issue is some kind of leeway, or alternative possibility, at the moment of choice (hence "leeway" accounts).[31]

Recall our earlier characterization of libertarianism as the conjunction of the following four claims:

1. Incompatibilism
2. The denial of determinism
3. Agents are the source of actions that are free
4. Those actions that are free actions are actions for which humans are morally responsible

I said that some libertarians think that these four conditions are insufficient and that to them must be added some sort of principle of alternative possibilities, which acts as a kind of leeway condition. By that I mean it adds the claim that a truly free action is one according to which a person has free will only if she or he could have done otherwise—that is, if there is some leeway at the moment of choice.

But what if we adopted a basically Anselmian account of free will and applied that to our concurrence version of meticulous providence? Would that help us make more sense of the concurrence account? Perhaps it would. Here is how such a view might go. First, we have already seen that according to meticulous providence, the scope of divine preservation, concurrence, and governance encompasses *all that comes to pass.* Next we have seen that the concurrence view adds to this general theological claim the following ideas: that concurrence is an immediate or basic act of will that ensures the volition of the creaturely agent obtains; that it is an act that is logically, but not necessarily temporally, prior to the creature's action in volition; and that it is a necessary condition of that action—indeed, a hypothetically necessary condition, that is, one that must obtain once God has freely ordained it.

Now, the difficult thing in concurrence accounts is specifying how it is that God's concurring action may be a necessary condition for human agency without the view collapsing into theological determinism. For the

---

31. This is made particularly clear by Timpe in *Free Will: Sourcehood.*

concurrence theorist wants to preserve an account of creaturely freedom that is stronger than that of the secondary-cause view. The concurrence theorist wants (at the very least) some sort of source libertarianism. For in keeping with other libertarians, the concurrence theorist agrees that if an agent is truly free in her choice and resulting action, she must be the source of that action.

But this is just where the Anselmian account may be of assistance. For the Anselmian agrees that the free agent must be the source of her choice and resulting action, and she denies determinism is true with respect to free creaturely actions. So one possible way to be a concurrence theorist is to say something like this.

> God's meticulous providence encompasses all that comes to pass. From the *Godward* side of things, this involves an act of concurrence with every free creaturely action. Such an act of divine concurrence is an immediate or basic act of will that ensures that the volition of the creaturely agent obtains. It is an act that is logically, but not necessarily temporally, prior to the creature's action in volition; and it is a hypothetically necessary condition, that is, one that must obtain once God has freely ordained it. Nevertheless, it is a libertarian free choice of the creature. One fundamental aspect of this from the *creaturely* side of things is that this means the choice and resulting action in question must originate with the free choice of the creature. The creature must be the source of that choice, not God. That is, the action, though divinely ordained, cannot be determined. But this does not require, in addition to this sourcehood condition, a leeway condition as well. For the fundamental issue (from an Anselmian point of view) is acting freely according to rectitude of rightness of will for its own sake. Thus, truly free choices and the actions that issue from them are rightly oriented to the goal that God has ordained. Creaturely choices that do not have this feature fail to measure up to God's goal for them; they are deficient in important respects.

Of course, this raises yet further issues having to do with divine sovereignty and aseity. If this picture is right, then what is the source of God's knowledge of these free creaturely choices? And here there may well be a cost (for those who want to pursue this Anselmian version of a concurrence account). For it looks like it cannot be Godself that is the source of this knowledge, as is the case in traditional Thomist versions of concurrence. For then the source of the creaturely choices in question would ultimately lie outside the creature in God's eternal act of self-reflection. Instead, the Anselmain could say that the source of these choices, being the creature herself, is what gives rise to the divine knowledge that the creature in question will do one thing rather than another. So God's ordination of all that comes to pass is, on this view, contingent in some important respects upon the actual choices creatures will make in the circumstances in which God places them.[32]

EVALUATION

What have we learned? To begin with, we have seen that meticulous providence is a doctrine that has a number of different species. We have focused on two of the most prominent in the history of theology, namely, the secondary cause and concurrence views, though in each case I have given my own version of the doctrine in question. The secondary cause view as I have construed it is a picture of providence consistent with theological determinism of a compatibilist variety. That is, it presumes that God's providence ensures all that comes to pass either directly, through God's immediate agency, or (more commonly) indirectly by means of secondary causes. But whether directly or indirectly, God is in some fundamental sense the one who is the ultimate source of these actions, even when the scope of his providential action includes the agency of human creatures as proximate sources. It might be worried that the defender of the secondary-cause view has to work harder to show that her position does not reduce human agency to a kind of instrument by means of which God brings about his plans. (This is one way to construe the controller objection raised earlier.) I do not think that this is a necessary consequence of the view, but it is easy to see why it would occur to critics. To this end, I offered Frankfurt's notion of wholeheartedness in choosing as one way of ameliorating this sort of worry that the defender of a secondary-cause view might take up.

By contrast, the concurrence view as I have outlined it tries to have its theological cake and eat it too, so to speak. On this way of thinking, God is, in some sense, "causing" what obtains to obtain. Yet creatures are freely choosing to act in accordance with God's will not merely in an instrumental sense but in a sense that includes a full-blown idea of their own sourcehood as moral and causal agents. There are costs with this view as well. These are principally in giving a clear account of how God's meticulous ordination

---

32. Something like this view is set out by Katherin A. Rogers in *Perfect Being Theology* (Edinburgh: Edinburgh University Press, 2000).

of free creaturely acts does not violate the conditions of their sourcehood, and in giving some account of divine knowledge of these free creaturely choices that does not jeopardize divine sovereignty and aseity. In neither case have I sought to defend the view in question against all objections. Instead I have tried to give a charitable account of each view in order to show by way of example that there are (at least) several different ways to be a defender of meticulous providence.

Of course, these are not the only live options when it comes to meticulous providence, as I have tried to indicate at the beginning of this essay. But our task was not to give an overview of all the live options, let alone all the logically possible ones. Rather our task was to give an account of two rather different options that demonstrate that meticulous providence is consistent with different—indeed incommensurate—metaphysical pictures of God's action in the world.[33] Many of my Reformed colleagues will worry that I have cast the net too broadly: can a view such as the concurrence one set forth here truly represent a version of meticulous providence if it is able, in the final analysis, to embrace a libertarian account of freedom? Yet one of the lessons that I think recent work on the history and metaphysics of free will has to teach the theologian is that these matters are becoming ever more complex as more work is done in this area. Too often when tackling issues of free will and divine sovereignty as they bear upon the doctrine of providence, theologians seem content to trot out tired old clichés: Calvinists versus Arminians (if you are a Protestant), or Báñezians versus Molinists (if you are Roman Catholic). But the literature on the metaphysics of free will, as well as some of the historical work being done in this area, should give us pause for thought. Matters are not quite so cut and dry. For my part, one important lesson here—whichever view of providence one opts for—is this: this is a complex and fraught area of theological inquiry, and we would do well to pause, and take a moment to listen to those with whom we disagree on these matters before marching in to reassert the superiority of whichever particular view we currently hold. For, as Karl Barth has shown us in a rather different context, reading providence from history is a dangerous business—as dangerous, perhaps, as thinking that my particular view of this matter is the last word. Providence—whether we think it is meticulous or not—has a way of upending all our neat devices in the end.

---

33. Some readers may detect here an echo of previous attempts by the present author to say similar things in a different context about the breadth of Calvinism as a theological tradition (e.g., Crisp, *Deviant Calvinism: Broadening Reformed Theology* [Minneapolis: Fortress, 2014]). That is intentional.

CHAPTER 2

PARTICULAR PROVIDENCE AND THE DETAILS OF DIVINE ACTION

William J. Abraham

AS A PIETIST OF THE LOWER ORDER, let me begin with two stories from a common source that pinpoint the challenge I want to take up in this chapter. For security reasons the identity of the human agents involved will remain anonymous; however, I can vouch for the veracity of the material I am about to share. The testimony is for me unimpeachable. So here is story one.

My friend Magnus was recently invited to speak at a public meeting in Hamburg to an immigrant audience on why Muslims should come to Christ. As he was fully launched in his presentation, a man in the audience began to heckle. Puffing arrogantly on a cigarette, he proceeded initially to deploy a series of old chestnuts familiar to many who are hostile to the Christian faith: "Where did Adam find wives for his sons?" "Do you really believe that the sun stood still?" (drawing on Josh 10:12). "Did Jesus turn water into wine?" Given that Magnus asserted that he did indeed do this, the man added mischievously, "He could have started a profitable tavern." Then events took a turn for the worse.

> At this point, the heckler [he] placed his hand on his groin—an exceedingly offensive gesture in my culture. It was clear to me that the man's intention was not illumination but disruption. He was there to subvert and sabotage the objectives of that gathering. I was there to foster faith and he was there to spread doubt. Who he was and how he had come into the congregation,

I was not certain. Neither did I know how to stop him hijacking the meeting. He was working hard to provoke an angry response from me. So, when he made that offensive gesture, I was grieved and felt embarrassed. I bowed my head, and in my heart I prayed, "Father, the spirit of your adversary has come into this meeting to dishonor your holy name. It is not me who is being mocked. He is mocking you. I am only your servant trying to sow the seed of belief; he is sowing the seed of unbelief. Please help me." As I lifted my eyes from my Bible and sternly looked at him, smugly puffing on his cigarette, he once again placed his hand on his groin as a gesture of defiance and insult. However, this time, no sooner had he done that when suddenly a long burst of fire jetted out from between his legs. It was as though a rocket engine had been fired off from between his legs, shooting out flames. People around him leapt out of the way to avoid catching fire amidst gasps of shock. He himself flew off his chair, and as he stood up hopping, fire was jetting out from his front and forming a pig tail–like flame from his behind. In seconds, his entire midsection was engulfed in flames. Several of the men huddled around him and covered him with their jackets to quench the flames. He was taken to a hospital. Later we learned that apparently, the cigarette lighter in his trousers' pocket had begun to leak. And when he put his hand on his groin, the cigarette between his fingers had ignited the lighter fluid and caused the burst of flame shooting from underneath of his legs from the opening of the cigarette lighter. It was extraordinary that his injuries were minimal.[1]

Let's for the moment take this example as a case of particular and special providence. We can contrast this with general and ordinary providence and with extra-special providence represented by miraculous intervention made visible by a violation of a law of nature. I do so because it depicts a situation where prima facie God answers prayer in order to meet a very specific need of one of his servants, yet there is no miraculous intervention, even as the divine action involved is not best captured by speaking of God merely sustaining the laws of nature and preserving human agents in being. The action of God is particular and special rather than simply generic and ordinary, yet it is not miraculous in the proper sense of that term.

Moreover, by providence in this instance I am assuming the following three conditions. First, there is the active power of God at work in the world, so God is intimately involved in nature and history. Second, there

---

1. Personal communication, December 2018.

is the foreknowledge of God, so God acts taking into account what will happen up ahead. Third, God acts in order to further the good purposes of God either in judgment or in salvation, so God acts prudently to provide for future circumstances and eventualities.

For the record, I think that this was how it was interpreted by my friend Magnus even though he might not be interested in the second-order analysis I have just supplied. Thus, he rounds off his testimony in this fashion.

> Once we reassembled together, numerous jokes followed. Many in the audience believed that the Lord had kindled a fire under him to shut his mouth. But some dismissed what had happened as coincidence. For me there was no question who had set the pants of that discourteous, insolent scoffer on fire. I learned early on in my faith that it is a perilous and terrifying thing to ridicule the Lord or his servants since one runs the risk of becoming an object lesson of God's sense of humor or his wrath. The Lord immediately blessed the meeting organized by my friends in Hamburg, and after the meeting, several people in that audience committed their lives to Christ.[2]

The first option represents the action involved as a miracle; the second as a mere coincidence, that is, nothing above and beyond the ordinary working of the laws of nature and human agency; the third as the very specific action of "The Lord setting pants on fire," that is, as an act of special provision in a situation of great need that results in part in the blessing of the meeting and the conversion of unbelievers.

Aside from the delightful humor buried in this testimony, ordinary Christians are a tad reluctant to accept this theological reading of the whole episode. It is rare to hear examples of what our ancestors used to call the "awful providence of God." Our ancestors, however, readily saw the providential hand of God in judgment and not just in God bringing about positive good out of evil or good out of good. Furthermore, our ancestors had the theological courage to tackle the host of questions that these commitments evoked. They wrestled with the relevant issues of foreordination, predestination, divine determinism, freedom, contingency, human agency, responsibility, theodicy, causality, divine sovereignty, and divine glory that naturally came from following through on the first-order language of theology and piety. It is a mark of the richness and fecundity of contemporary theology that these issues are now back on the table.[3]

---

2. Personal communication, December 2018.
3. Two recent collections of essays are worthy of note: Francesca Aran Murphy and Philip G.

My aim is to zero in on one and only one dimension of the ensuing discussion, namely, whether we can tackle the challenge of specifying the more precise actions of God involved in cases of particular and special providence. In order to make the issue as vivid as I can, I turn now to my second story. This time my friend Magnus was in northern Europe, planning to spend a day teaching Bible in a refugee housing center. He writes,

A friend of mine had offered to drive me there since it was a few hours away. Usually, before I go to these camps, I buy some fruit, pastries, meat, and bread to ensure that we will have a meal together and make the occasion more enjoyable for the refugees. In the morning, he came. As we were driving to the store, the engine light in my friend's car came on. He said, "I don't think it will be safe to drive this car. I have to take it to a mechanic's shop. I will not be able to go with you. Can we postpone going today?" I explained that I didn't have many days left. I had promised these folks to be with them, and to cancel would deeply disappoint them. Therefore, I told him to take me to the grocery store and then attend to his car. I would take the train afterward. He dropped me off in front of the store and left. Once I had finished shopping, I went to the cashier to pay. As I reached in my coat pocket, I realized I did not have my wallet. I had left it next to my bed in my room. That meant I could not buy my train ticket or bus ticket to the train station, or pay for the food I had just selected. I would have to put the food back on the shelves, walk for thirty or forty minutes to the apartment to get my wallet, and take the bus to the shop and then to the train station. That meant a significant delay. I was aggravated with myself. I apologized to the cashier and told her that I had forgotten my wallet. I offered to put the things back on the shelves. As I turned around with my cart, a tall man with white hair and striking, big, blue eyes was standing right behind me. He asked, "Will you allow me to pay?" I profusely thanked him and said, "I have forgotten my wallet. I need to go to my apartment to get it since I also need money for other things this morning." He said, "I know!" I was puzzled as to what he meant, but my mind was irritated

---

Ziegler, eds., *The Providence of God* (London: T&T Clark, 2009); and Paul Kjoss Helseth, William Lane Craig, Ron Highfield, and Gregory Boyd, *Four Views on Divine Providence* (Grand Rapids: Zondervan, 2011). Useful earlier discussions are available in Maurice Wiles, ed., *Providence* (London: SPCK, 1969); and in Jacob Viner, *The Role of Divine Providence in the Social Order* (Princeton: Princeton University Press, 1972). Charles M. Wood, *The Question of Providence* (Louisville: Westminster John Knox, 2008) and Michael J. Langford, *Providence* (London: SCM, 1981) provide useful clarification of the issues involved. Genevieve Lloyd, *Providence Lost* (Cambridge, MA: Harvard University Press, 2008) provides a fascinating cultural history related to the doctrine of providence.

and distracted by my absent-mindedness. He repeated, "Please let me pay, and I will take you to where you need to go." I thanked him and agreed that on one condition I would let him pay: that he would let me pay him back as soon as we were at my apartment. He nodded. He paid for the food items and walked me to his car in the garage. I gave him the address where I was staying. He looked at it and said, "Okay." But then, rather than driving in the direction of the apartment, he drove to the train station. He stopped in front of the station and said, "I won't be long." A few minutes later, he came back and handed me two tickets—one for going exactly where I needed to go and one for coming back. With the tickets, he also gave me fifty euros and said, with great emotion and emphasis, "Christ is with you! God bless you, dear friend!" Before I could say anything, he handed me my two grocery bags, waved goodbye, and drove off. As he drove away, I was certain I had I had just encountered something out of the ordinary. How did he know that I was planning to take the train that morning? How did he know where I was going? He had not asked, and I had not told him. He did not know who I was and what I was doing. In a secular nation, why would he say, "Christ is with you! Bless you, dear friend!"? I went to the platform to catch my train, but I was in a daze with regard to the encounter. There were too many inexplicable details![4]

We now have before us two stories which instantiate cases of particular and special divine providence over against ordinary, general providence and over against extra-special, miraculous providence. My question is this: Can we be more precise here? Can we legitimately speculate about the specific divine actions that may be involved in cases of providence like these?[5] The motivation behind this deeper move is twofold. First, I think that specification is at the heart of really robust doctrines of divine action. This follows from the conceptual point that "action" is a very general concept, like "happening" or "event." Much work on divine action ignores this crucial feature of the grammar of action discourse, eagerly hoping that, say, spelling out the grammar of general action discourse will provide

---

4. Personal communication, December 2018.
5. Note that I am looking for more than a set of criteria for demarcating cases of particular and special providence in contrast both to generic, ordinary providence and to extraordinary miraculous intervention. In very general terms these special acts of God exhibit a distinctive purposiveness visible to the outsider as coincidences and interpreted by the believer as acts of God. My question takes us deeper by asking if we can further specify the more precise divine actions that might be in play and then suggesting that this resolves the challenge of the compatibility between particular providence and human freedom.

the foundation for all talk about special acts of God.[6] Second, by reversing this way of thinking and beginning from below with the specific action predicates given to us in Scripture, tradition, and piety, we can test our proposed accounts of particular, special providence.[7] Such providence characteristically involves cases where God works in, with, and through human actions, that is, human actions which are good and human actions which are evil. Traditionally, one of the deep worries is how we can preserve a vision of intimate divine action and genuine human freedom. Attending to the details of divine action, I suggest, permits us to resolve this dilemma.

A widely canvassed theory of double agency does not really help us. I mean by this a theory (whatever its conceptual and metaphysical ingredients) where every human act is interpreted both as a genuinely human action and as a genuinely divine action. Specification is crucial at this point. The human agent in story one set about mocking God, disrupting the meeting, fully intending to do so. It is simply incoherent to turn around and describe this set of actions as divine actions where God mocks God, disrupts the meeting, fully intending to do so. We are misled at this point by deploying the surface grammar of action discourse, whether applied to human agents or God. We fail to see the glaring contradiction because we fail to specify what precisely the relevant action is in the pertinent context under review. Given the radical openness of the concept of action, we somehow think we are being conceptually and theologically profound by insisting that we can see the same event from two different angles, or by claiming that we have two different orders of causality, or by claiming that there is no competition between divine and human action. All these dodges evaporate once we specify what the human agent is doing. We cannot with a straight face say that God mocks God, disrupts a meeting where the gospel is being preached, and does all this and more deliberately. To be sure, once we become aware of the obvious conceptual and moral difficulties involved, we naturally reach for theories of privation, have resort to unnecessary paradox, or run to take refuge in divine mystery. However, these simply introduce a whole new set of dodges that hide the obvious mistake of thinking of God mocking God, of God disrupting the meeting, and so on.

Nor will it do to suggest, as David Bentley Hart has recently done, that a doctrine of creation *ex nihilo* interpreted in terms of a theory of

---

6. I deal with this issue at length in *Divine Agency and Divine Action*, vol. 1, *Exploring and Evaluating the Debate* (Oxford: Oxford University Press, 2017).

7. I assume here that if our vision of providence does not deal with instances of particular, special providence, then our account is radically incomplete.

transcendental causality will somehow take care of business.[8] Hart is at pains to deliver us from thinking of causality in terms of mechanical causality. The divine order of causality as exhibited in creation *ex nihilo* somehow involves a radically different order of causality; creation *ex nihilo* somehow takes us into a world of transcendence and is constituted by agency and action which is beyond the realm of the determined and determining. Truth to tell, to speak of creation *ex nihilo* is an *aporia* which remains forever imponderable once we try to translate it into causal terms. We are not to think of God as an Agent who can stand in the same order of human agents. God knows the good and evil acts of his creatures and reacts to neither. If we were to think in these terms, then we reduce God to a being among lesser beings, a force among lesser forces. We must place divine causality altogether beyond the finite economy of created causes.

To be sure, Hart does not entirely give up the language of causality. Thus, he keeps intact a distinction between primary and secondary causality; he resolutely insists on the possibility of divine permission over against the language of absolute divine determination; and he deploys some kind of doctrine of analogical predication. However, we should not be misled by these concessions, for they are carefully housed within an obscurantist vision of the divine "who is transcendently present in all beings, the ever more inward act within each finite act."[9] If we take the latter head-on, then we face a disjunction: either this is simply one more instance where the theologian is trading on the open concept of action and has not really said anything of consequence, or it leads us straight back into a doctrine where the primary and critical primary act in each finite act is brought about by God. So God, after all, is the crucial agent in the evil acts of the mocker in story one. Frankly, we have gone off into causal la-la-land in an effort to avoid the standard problems in deterministic doctrines derived from Aquinas and Calvin.[10]

Hart in fact is working with false alternatives. He thinks our only

8. David Bentley Hart, "Providence and Causality: On Divine Innocence," in *The Providence of God*, ed. Francesca Aran Murphy and Philip G. Ziegler (London: Bloomsbury, 2009).

9. Hart, "Providence and Causality," 35.

10. Hart is scathing in his rejection of the standard theories on offer at this point. He holds that any strict doctrine of omnicausality is false because it cannot deliver on the authenticity of genuine freedom. It will not do to say that if God had supplied the relevant efficient grace, then evil human acts would not have occurred and that this is sufficient for genuine human freedom. If God could have halted the exercise of the capacity to do evil either by an act of physical promotion or by an act of infallible, efficient concurrence, then God is clearly implicated in evil in a way that is morally unacceptable. I share Hart's judgments at this point, even as I find his dismissal of Molina unpersuasive.

options are some kind of mechanical causation (what is often called efficient causality) or some kind of transcendental causality that cannot be accommodated within our thinking about finite, creaturely causes. It is little wonder that if these are our only alternatives, then we will be driven to think of divine causality in terms of some kind of mechanism which enables God to interact with nature and history. Finding none, Hart opts for the transcendentalist alternative. What is missing here is the obvious possibility of causality understood as personal agency; it is precisely this notion that is in play when we think of analogical predication as applied to divine action. Just as human agents take prudent action by anticipating the future to the best of their knowledge and provide for various contingencies, so God acts prudently on the basis of his foreknowledge to provide for various contingencies. There is no need to get into a logical lather about such discourse; it is clearly analogical, and we know instinctively how to make the analogical adjustments.

Here the language of causality is much too crude to help; indeed, with a host of thinkers, I am convinced that our standard notions of causality are ultimately derived from our own experience and conception of human personal action where we perform a host of varied actions as creatures made in the image of God. To be sure, the logic of personal agency and causation remains contested, but we know enough about its contours to make headway in the challenge presented by that range of providential acts where God acts intimately in human affairs without infringing on the genuine freedom of human agents. Before I turn to this, let me clear the decks with respect to Hart's muddled commentary on creation *ex nihilo*. The crucial move to make here is that this particular, specific act of God is a basic act.[11] It is done straight off, akin to the way in which human agents do things straight off without performing other acts. Once this is in place, we can then proceed to explore if we can get a handle on why God created the universe. Perhaps God did it as an act of sheer generosity, like an artist creates a magnificent work of art; or perhaps God creates it to provide a place for the incarnation of his Son; or perhaps God creates it in order to create a space for the whole panoply of creaturely reality that we discover every day before our eyes. Exploring the logic of creation, rather than taking us off into an obscurantist metaphysics of transcendental causality, takes us right into the logic of everyday accounts of human agents

---

11. The seminal essay on this topic is Arthur C. Danto, "Basic Actions," *American Philosophical Quarterly* 2 (1965): 141–48.

and actions. Hart's unhappy disjunction eliminates this way of thinking by intellectual bluster and sheer fiat.[12]

John Webster is much more on track when, in typical fashion, he admonishes us to keep the kind of proposal canvassed by Hart at arm's length. Given that both Webster and I take theology to be constituted in a deep way by reflection on divine agency and divine action, I find his work on providence profoundly illuminating initially but ultimately unsatisfactory.[13] We are both pulling the same rope, a rope that goes back at least as far as the work of Karl Barth. The deft illumination, aside from his cautionary methodological suggestions, is that he insists that our doctrine of providence take as its subject matter reflection on what he terms the primary material of all theology, namely, the doctrine of God as triune. We might call this Webster's platitude.[14] One way to think of this is to see this move as a reminder: The agent involved in providence is not the god of the philosophers or the god of the various versions of liberal Protestantism but the triune God—Father, Son, and Holy Spirit. So, treatments of providence must be rooted and grounded in the doctrine of the Trinity. "God's immanent triune perfection is the first and last object of Christian perfection and governs all else. And that perfection is abundant, giving life and sustaining what is not God, and which is the object of economic reflection."[15] Put in an apt way in respect to providence, he then notes that the necessary conceptualities we deploy can only bear some of the weight needed to do our work.

In the doctrine of providence, the language of causality and agency is a matter in point, because refinement of such language is sometimes

---

12. To be fair to Hart, he brilliantly notes that the omnipotence of God is depicted in the amazing act of creating genuinely free creatures. Thus, speaking of human autonomy, he writes, "It is in his power to create such autonomy that God's omnipotence is most abundantly revealed; for everything therein comes from him: the real being of agent, act and potency, the primordial movement of the soul towards the good, the natural law inscribed in the creature's intellect and will; the sustained permission of finite autonomy; even the indetermination of the creature's freedom is an utterly dependent and unmerited participation in the mystery of God's infinite freedom; and, in his eternal presence to all time, God never ceases to exercise his providential care or to make all free acts the occasions of the greater good he intends in creating." See "Providence and Causality," 45.

13. I am grateful to Felipe do Vale for bringing this to my attention. I have never been persuaded by Webster's sterling account of Scripture nor by his wonderfully nuanced recovery of the Reformed tradition, but I share his passion to develop a genuinely theological theology that takes divine agency and divine action as its central concern.

14. Formally we might capture this as a rule for interpreting divine actions: For every action y performed by x, then the triune God and only the triune God counts as x.

15. John Webster, "On the Theology of Providence," in Murphy and Ziegler, eds., *Providence of God*, 159. Compare: "God's external acts are in accordance with his inner nature; his providence expresses his omnipotent holiness and goodness and wisdom, his infinite resourcefulness in being for us" (168).

thought to be essential to successful exposition. The doctrine cannot, of course, manage without such language—all theology has is borrowed from elsewhere. But good dogmatics will be keen to retain a sense of that the borrowing is *ad hoc*, not principled, and to let the real work best be conducted as an exercise in biblical reasoning, a conceptual, schematic representation of what theology is as told by the prophets and apostles.[16]

Materially then, the doctrine of providence must above all else satisfy this condition: Its subject matter will be God's immanent triune perfection. "God's (his) works *ad extra*, though indivisible, manifest the properties of the persons to whom they may especially be appropriated. The Father determines the course of created time; the Spirit causes creaturely causes; and the Son intervenes to draw back creation from ruin so that it may attain its end."[17]

So, our analytic powers must be subservient to our deployment of and governance by the Christian doctrine of God and its economic entailments. "Only in this way can the identities and agents of the history of providence, their modes and ends, be protected from formalization."[18]

Webster provides here a salutary warning. In any treatment of the host of divine actions that crop up in theology proper, the identity of God is crucial. All the actions of God are actions of the triune God; this is the right way to identify the agent involved. The case of providential acts of God is no different from other actions like creation *ex nihilo*, the election of Israel, the atonement in Christ, baptism in the Spirit, and so on. However, precisely because it is a theological platitude that is crucial to the exposition of *all* divine action, it cannot but remain utterly general. It is something we need to repeat to ourselves when we are tempted to lapse into making the relevant subject the God of generic theism, or the household god of Being borrowed from ancient metaphysical speculation, or the first cause of degenerate natural theology, or the Rambo god of much liberation theology. However, Webster's platitude will not help us in coming to terms with the kind of cases of providence that is our quarry in this chapter. Nor will it help to be sent off to do more dramatic-historical description of

---

16. Webster, "On the Theology of Providence," 161.

17. Webster, "On the Theology of Providence," 167. Webster's proposal requires extensive work on the doctrine of appropriations but I am skeptical that will take us very far in providing careful description of the particular divine actions at the heartbeat of theology proper.

18. Webster, "On the Theology of Providence," 162. And its initial method will be that essentially of fresh exposition of Scripture or more specifically of dramatic-historical description. Its first task is "an analytic-expository task, in which it attempts orderly conceptual representation of the content of the Christian gospel as it is laid out in the scriptural witness." Webster, "On the Theology of Providence," 161.

biblical texts because the stories that mirror the contemporary examples I cited provide us with next to no guidance on how to proceed.[19] They pose exactly the same kind of theological puzzlement that my examples do. Thus, it will come as no surprise that when it comes to the actual details of his doctrine of providence, Webster retells those standard Thomistic and Reformation themes that have been around for centuries.[20]

It is time to shift our perspective and lean fully into the language of personal agency, even if in the end we should keep such discourse at arm's length in order to stay close to the rough ground of Scripture, creedal confession, and personal piety. So, here is my speculative proposal regarding my two stories.

Take story two first. In this instance God provides my friend Magnus with the crucial financial resources needed to take a trip to spend a day with Christian converts in a refugee housing estate. Think of the divine action this way. In very general terms God sends along a total stranger who provides the necessary funding. However, this is much too generic. After all, the funding could have come from an anonymous donor responding to a fundraising letter. What is striking is that the stranger shows up at exactly the right time, offers graciously to help, knows the exact place to which Magnus is travelling, buys the tickets needed, throws in an extra fifty euros for good measure, and identifies Magnus from the outset as a Christian. We can agree with Webster that the divine action is that of the all-sufficient Trinity who acts freely and abundantly out of his endless resources. But this does not begin to tell us how to interpret this instance of providential care. So, think of it this way. The stranger is a man of devout faith, someone who lives in intimate fellowship with his Lord and Savior, and who daily offers his life to God. He shows up in the grocery store and encounters my friend enmeshed in a small-scale but highly significant crisis as far as his ministry is concerned. Surely the relevant details with respect to divine action are that God tells the stranger by means of person-relative revelation who Magnus is, the city to which he is headed, and the amount of money he will need.[21] Given the submission of the stranger to the divine

---

19. The classical case is that of Joseph and his brothers as developed in Exodus. For my treatment of this example that follows the logic developed here, see *Divine Agency and Divine Action*, vol. 3, *Systematic Theology* (Oxford: Oxford University Press), 153–55.

20. See his treatment of secondary causality, "On the Theology of Providence," 169–71. It is interesting that the more recent work on providence takes us straight back into the divisions that have been central on providence across the ages.

21. Efforts to eliminate this element of divine speaking are doomed to failure at this point. See for example the interesting work of Vincent Brümmer, "Farrer, Wiles, and the Causal Joint," *Modern Theology* 8 (1992): 11–12. Brümmer is skeptical about being able to identify the relevant speech acts of God and holds that immersion in the tradition of the church is sufficient to enable us to read

will, it is a small thing for God to motivate and prompt him to supply the need involved.[22] However, in order for this to happen, we have an act of special and particular providence: God is actively involved in our lives, God foreknows the future contingencies, and God, acting on that foreknowledge, provides for the relevant need. So, God is actively involved in the lives of both Magnus and the stranger; God foresees the breakdown of the car and foreknows that my friend will forget his wallet; and God prompts the stranger to show up, informs him of what is going on, and motivates him to take care of the need.

Take this one step further. Is the stranger free with respect to his actions in this instance? Think of it this way: Suppose that the stranger wakes up and, noticing that he needs groceries, decides to go to the store and buy groceries. He freely forms the intention to buy groceries. However, there are many ways to execute this intention. He can go to various stores, decide on the best time to go, get in line at a certain moment, and so on. There is no one way to achieve his intentions and perform the action of buying groceries. We might formally say that the execution of the action is radically underdetermined. It is precisely this open space in the expression of his intentions and execution of his actions where God can intervene by prompting, providing relevant information by revelation and apt motivating inspiration. So, this can truly be an action where there is synergism and cooperation between God and the free human agent. The human agent gets to buy his groceries and help a fellow believer in crisis, and God brings it about that my friend's acute problem is solved. We can even speak of genuine double agency that preserves freedom. The provision of need is both an act of the stranger and an act of God.

What about my first story? Think of it this way. The heckler hears about the meeting where my friend is speaking and decides to attend. While there he acts deliberately to disrupt, to make life difficult for the speaker, and ultimately to mock God. He also decides to puff arrogantly on his cigarette. All this he does freely and deliberately. He could have done something else that evening, but this is what he chose to do of his own free will. The effect on my friend is predictable: after answering the fake questions as

---

events in terms of divine action. Formation in the tradition is indeed important, and in many cases, tradition provides sufficient paradigms and parallels to serve as the relevant resource. However, the tradition itself depends on being able to identify the speech acts of God, and his skepticism is unpersuasive.

22. In the case of truly deep believers we can think of them possessing through the work of the Spirit the very mind of Christ (Rom 12:1–3) so that they naturally and automatically read the world and perform their actions without needing any kind of fresh input from the divine.

best he can, he bows his head in prayer when the visitor proceeds to mock God by grabbing his groin. The rest is now familiar; the visitor's cigarette lighter begins to leak, the gas is lighted by the cigarette, and fire shoots out from between his legs. The tables are turned. God mocks the mocker by setting him literally on fire. We have an act of awful providence, an act of divine judgment carried out in public. This is how my friend describes it, drawing on his formation in the faith and on the vast experience of his relationship with God through a whole series of ordinary and sometimes hair-raising events. So how might we explore this further?

Apply the same logic as I have just done in the case of story two. The visitor hears about the meeting, decides to show up, and freely decides to mock the servant of God. He forms the intention to mock God. However, this intention and action can be carried out in a host of ways. He could have persisted in asking awkward questions; he could have started a public row with the folk in his row of seats; he could have started singing in a loud voice; he could have told lewd jokes to his neighbors. As he thinks through the options, he considers various ways—thinking informally rather than according to some formal calculus, as we do all the time in performing purposive actions. In the range of options open to him, he can go this way or that way in executing his intentions and doing what he voluntarily decides. However, God is also present in the meeting, and God has his particular plans for the meeting. Anticipating what is going to happen, some of the executions of the visitor's intention fit better with God's intentions than others. Suppose we think of God intending to bless the address, persuade folk to come to faith in Christ, protect my friend from humiliation, and the like. It is clear that some of these intentions can be carried out when the visitor acts this way rather than that way to achieve his particular intentions. Thus, God prompts the visitor to carry out his intentions by placing his cigarette next to a leaking lighter with the predictable result that fire will shoot from between his legs. Here again we have a case where the mocker gets what he intends, and God gets what he intends. Put in terms of providence, God is not absent from the lives of his rebellious creatures as they are wont to think; he foreknows what their intentions and plans are, and he acts in a hidden manner without miraculous intervention to see to it that the execution of those intentions and plans fit with God's intentions and plans to ensure that all things work together for good for those who love God.

What I have done here is simply draw on aspects on the logic of personal, purposive agency to throw light on one dimension of any robust doctrine of particular providence, that is, those cases where God acts to bring good out of good and to bring good out of evil. I have not sought to deal with other kinds of providential acts represented by the preservation of creation, or by direct miraculous intervention, or by God sending rain on the just and unjust, or by God causally connecting disobedience with disaster.[23] My aim is strictly limited. But the class of providential acts I have in mind is not marginal; clear examples show up in Scripture and personal experience, and they have long been identified as cases of particular and specific providence. At one level my analysis is deflationary. We do not need to get lost in theories of primary and secondary causality, or theories of "caused causes," or proposals about God somehow creating the free actions of creatures, or grand theories of necessity and contingency, or apophatic accounts of transcendental causality where we lose our semantic bearings, or on meaningless notions like impossible possibilities. Yet the analysis has real substance and provides a clear way to provide a vision of those providential acts where God works to achieve his ends without undermining the free actions of human agents.

Let me conclude by dealing briefly with two objections to my proposal, one theological and one philosophical. First, does my proposal not commit me to a vision of God as a cosmic snooper and manipulator and thus undermine any robustly Christian vision of God as holy, loving, and righteous? The answer to this is quite simple. As Webster has rightly emphasized, the agent in all divine action discourse is the triune God of the gospel. The objection simply ignores this platitude and smuggles totally unworthy conceptions of God as the relevant agent into our deliberations. On the contrary, what my proposal secures is an account of God who is resolutely ingenious in acting in our lives and in human history. God does not sit on the sidelines; rather God finds ways to use even rebellious sinful actions to further his good purposes as revealed in Christ. Perhaps the issue here is that we balk at predicating judgment of divine providential action, for few would want to say that the action of God in story two can be described as a cosmic snooper and manipulator. If this is the case, then my response is that a God who does not truly judge us fails to maintain any distinction between good and evil and leaves us in a sorry predicament as far as human evil is concerned. What strikes me in the divine response to evil is the extraordinary restraint and mercy depicted in Scripture. I have

---

23. This is a standard theme of the Deuteronomistic histories of the Old Testament challenged with noble ferocity by the book of Job.

a long list of folk whom it would be pleasure to see bumped off by God, say, by sleep apnea, or a heart attack in the middle of the night. Happily, divine judgment is in God's hands, not ours; we can safely leave it there.[24]

Second, some may be uneasy about the place of person-relative revelation I have introduced in story two. My proposal commits me to a very robust vision of possible divine speaking and thus opens up a raft of epistemological questions about how we might provide warrants for such a claim. The answer to this is also relatively simple. First, this chapter is not a contribution to the epistemology of theology; it is an exercise in theology proper understood broadly as a deflationary account of divine agency and divine action. Within this, I am focusing on the constructive as opposed to the apologetic task of systematic theology. Second, conceptually I have long been convinced that without robust forms of divine speaking, we are doomed to agnosticism in our claims about divine agency and divine action. It is not enough, as some have suggested, to reduce divine speaking either to the intensity of our response to wondrous events or to projections of our desires on to the mind of God. The fatal flaw here is that these options cannot account for the specific propositional content of the relevant revelation in story two; we need genuine divine impartation of specific information without which the story becomes incoherent. To be sure, it would be useful to talk to the stranger and hear his side of the story on what God did, but that is not essential, even though it opens up a path for further phenomenological investigation of the life of faith. To repeat, without authentic divine speaking, the stranger could never have done what he did to further the purposes of God for my friend Magnus. Most believers are content to read what happened as a wonderful act of special divine providence; we do not need to know exactly how God worked behind the scenes. However, if we fail to do the philosophical and theological work that is our happy vocation, we will fall prey to a raft of abstractions about causality and a host of other topics, as is common in discussions of providence, ancient and modern. We may even be tempted to shift from being Pietists of a lower order and become Pietists of a higher order who give away the store.

---

24. For me this introduces a radically different problem in theodicy from the standard problems covered in the literature.

CHAPTER 3

WHO IS THIS KING OF GLORY?

Recovering the Identity of the God of Providence

JULIÁN E. GUTIÉRREZ

INTRODUCTION

Tracing the doctrinal development of divine providence in history can be an elusive task for multiple reasons. On the one hand, there were no major studies on the doctrine of providence written during the earliest centuries of Christianity; it appears that providence was not a chief object of theological inquiry during the patristic era. On the other hand, those who were interested in providence treated it fragmentally as a motif subsidiary to the doctrine of creation.[1] Additionally, most discussions about divine providence during this time took place in consideration of polemical (apologetics), pastoral, and exegetical concerns, which did not necessarily seek a methodical formulation of the doctrine.[2]

---

1. In *Creation* (Grand Rapids: Eerdmans, 2014), 52, David Fergusson notes that the church fathers thought of divine providence as a notion integrated with every doctrine, including the coming of Christ and the expansion of the church. This fact might partially explain why providence was not treated as an independent subject during the patristic period.

2. See Fergusson, *Creation*, 51–52; David Fergusson, *The Providence of God: A Polyphonic Approach* (Cambridge: Cambridge University Press, 2018), 9–10. For an extensive study on the history of the doctrine of providence from the experiential point of view, consult Mark W. Elliott, *Providence Perceived: Divine Action from a Human Point of View* (Berlin: De Gruyter, 2015).

Even though the doctrine of providence is barely developed in Scripture, it is noteworthy, nonetheless, that most theologians, from the earliest times until the advent of modernity, have acknowledged it as an integral part of the Christian faith. The earliest church fathers did not intend to offer a meticulous explanation of the doctrine of providence, yet they concurred in their polemics against Epicureans and Stoics—whose views concerning the order of the world appealed to Greek notions of chance and fate—that God was the preserving cause and the governing agent of all creation.[3] By the time of medieval scholasticism, the formulation of divine providence became more teleological in its orientation under the influence of Aristotle's philosophy of causality. In this manner, providence was understood as the divine action whereby God has ordained all things according to his will towards a particular end: God is the first (efficient and formal) and the ultimate (final) cause of all things.[4] Medieval scholastic theologians also appealed to Aristotelian categories to make an ontological distinction between the agencies responsible for primary and secondary causation. This is to say, in relation to providence, that God interacts with creation as the first cause of all things while he brings about his plan for the created realm through the agency of secondary causes.[5] The Reformation brought with it a reinvigorated emphasis on the sovereignty of God, which in turn carried soteriological implications for the understanding of the doctrine of divine providence: God was not only accountable for preserving and governing creation, but he was also the ultimate cause determining the eternal state of every human soul.[6] In continuity with late medieval theology, the

---

3. Louis Berkhof, *Systematic Theology* (London: Banner of Truth Trust, 1959), 180. Though the church fathers emphasized different aspects of the doctrine of providence, and while the doctrine did not receive a sophisticated treatment until Augustine's *City of God*, most patristic theologians concurred that God was the personal agent responsible for the preservation and the governance of creation. V. Loi and H. R. Drobner, *Encyclopedia of Ancient Christianity* (Downers Grove, IL: IVP Academic, 2014), s.v. "Providence"; Elliott, *Providence Perceived*, 8–11, 13. In *Providence of God*, 57, Fergusson concludes that the western Fathers moved their theologies of providence in the direction of Stoic fatalism as a result of their reliance on pagan philosophies. This very same reason leads Fergusson to argue elsewhere that the classical notion of providence suffers from overly deterministic tendencies; see "The Theology of Providence," *Theology Today* 67, no. 3 (2010): 261–78.

4. Thomas Aquinas is an illustration of the above; see Hester Gelber, "Providence," in *The Cambridge History of Medieval Philosophy*, ed. Robert Pasnau (Cambridge: Cambridge University Press, 2009), 2:764. Two aspects of the medieval scholastic notion of providence are noteworthy: (1) the centrality of the doctrine of creation for the doctrine of providence and (2) the tendency of identifying providence as a divine attribute. Fergusson, *Providence of God*, 61; David Burrell, "Providence," in *The Cambridge Companion to the Summa Theologiae*, ed. Philip McCosker and Denys Turner (Cambridge Cambridge University Press, 2016), 156.

5. For a helpful explanation of how Aquinas understood first and secondary causality in the context of divine providence, consult Brian Davies, *Thomas Aquinas's Summa Contra Gentiles: A Guide and Commentary* (New York: Oxford University Press, 2016), 244–62.

6. While some of the magisterial reformers such as Bullinger and Calvin ended up treating providence and predestination separately, the two themes were considered interrelated. Jaroslav

Reformation doctrine of providence retained the language of causality, the concept of double agency and its theological cognate, concurrence, and the teleological nature of divine providence.[7] With the advent of rationalism during the age of reason, the doctrine of providence experienced some significant changes in its material content, primarily due to the fact that Scripture was no longer considered the epistemic foundation for doctrinal formulation. As a result, pantheistic and deistic forms of providence took over more traditional ways of explaining how God was related to creation. In pantheism, the idea of providence became redundant given that God was no longer acknowledged as the preserver and ruler of creation but as creation itself, so providence was understood as something essentially indistinguishable from the order of nature. In its radical form, deism championed the notion that God's involvement with creation was limited to an act wherein the creator originated the universe and bestowed upon it certain natural properties for its survival and maintenance.[8] Consequently, the scope of divine providence was radically constrained to religious and ethical matters as there was no room for supernatural intervention in natural and human affairs as a result of the severe detachment between God and creation.[9]

The beginning of the twentieth century signaled a decline for the doctrine of divine providence. The problem of evil—accompanied by a perceived lack of purpose in personal suffering—a renewed stress on personal freedom and human autonomy, and an energized confidence in scientific naturalism as a metanarrative capable of explaining the most significant questions concerning human existence resulted in the doctrine of providence either being treated marginally or abandoned altogether during the first half of the last century.[10] Revisions characterized by the rejection of the main tenets of classical providentialism took place during the last decades of the twentieth century, most significantly the proposals offered by process and liberal theologians, open theists, and neo-orthodox thinkers.[11]

Pelikan, *The Christian Tradition: A History of the Development of Doctrine*, vol. 4, *Reformation of Church and Dogma (1300–1700)* (Chicago: University of Chicago Press, 1984), 220–21.

7. Fergusson, *Providence of God*, 59.

8. As deism did not comprise a homogenous system of thought, there were an assorted variety of "deistic" views encompassing radical and more orthodox forms. However, deism appeared to be characterized in general by the rejection of revealed theology by an emphasis on natural theology and by its antisupranaturalistic impulses. For more on providentialist accounts of the less strident ilk of deism, consult Fergusson, *Providence of God*, 115–24.

9. Herman Bavinck, *Reformed Dogmatics*, trans. John Vriend, 4 vols. (Grand Rapids: Baker Academics, 2004), 2:598–604.

10. Langdon B. Gilkey, "The Concept of Providence in Contemporary Theology," *The Journal of Religion* 43, no. 3 (1963): 175ff.

11. Fergusson identifies three forms of contemporary revisionism concerning the doctrine of

It is in the context sketched out above that this study takes place. Succinctly, this chapter is an exercise in theological retrieval seeking to rehabilitate a classical explanation of the doctrine of divine providence for the purpose of revealing the identity of the one who directs all things to a determined purpose. Particularly, this chapter appeals to the doctrine of divine providence in the Reformed scholastic tradition as exemplified in the thought of the Puritan theologian Stephen Charnock. In the remainder of this discussion, I will argue that despite contemporary opponents of classical providentialism, Charnock's doctrine of providence remains instructive because the agent responsible for sustaining created reality, acting in all that comes to pass, and ruling over creation is disclosed to be none other than the God of the Scriptures.

STEPHEN CHARNOCK: A REFORMED SCHOLASTIC ACCOUNT OF PROVIDENCE

CHARNOCK: A BIOGRAPHICAL SKETCH

Stephen Charnock was born in St. Katharine Creechurch, London, in the year 1628. At the age of fourteen he was enrolled at Emmanuel College, the Puritan stronghold at Cambridge University during the seventeenth century, where he was awarded a Bachelor of Arts in 1646 and a Master of Arts in 1649. In 1650, he was appointed Fellow of New College at the University of Oxford, and two years later he was incorporated as Master of Arts. Charnock left Oxford in 1655 and went to Dublin, where he became one of the chaplains of Henry Cromwell, chief governor of Ireland. While in Ireland, Charnock was installed Bachelor of Divinity by the University of Dublin, and Cromwell attempted to make him Fellow of Trinity College. As a consequence of the draconian legislation imposed by King Charles II, when he was restored to the throne in 1660, Charnock was forced to abandon his academic and ecclesiastical positions in Ireland and to return to England. Charnock disappeared from public life from 1660 to 1675, during which time he apparently traveled to France and Holland and may have been in contact with continental Reformed theologies. At his return to England in 1675, Charnock was invited to co-pastor a congregation in London, a position he held until his death five years later.[12]

---

providence: (1) "God as Persuasive," (2) "Christological Determinism," and (3) "General Providence Only." In *Providence of God*: 252–95.

12. For more on Charnock's life, consult James M'Cosh, introduction to *The Complete Works of Stephen Charnock*, 5 vols. (Edinburgh: James Nichol, 1864; repr., Edinburgh: Banner of Truth Trust,

Though Charnock is primarily known for his massive work on the existence and the attributes of God, he also discussed a wide assortment of doctrinal subjects that mostly covered soteriological and ecclesiological matters.[13] Charnock's chosen method for conveying his religious ideas were homiletical lectures collected in the form of "discourses." In terms of style, the *Discourses* are theological sermons introduced as lengthy discussions roughly structured according to a defined pattern. Normally, every discourse included a section dedicated to biblical exegesis, followed by a doctrinal formulation—dissected into multiple propositions to be explained and defended—which concluded with a segment devoted to practical application. Regarding content, Charnock's theological sermons, while primarily homiletical in nature, are marked by a level of erudition and detail proper to the scholastic method. The material content deployed in the *Discourses* exhibits many of the same characteristics one may find in other works of the Reformed scholastic tradition. As a representative of the Reformed orthodoxy, Charnock is well-versed in sophisticated methods of biblical exegesis, appeals to medieval rhetoric, seeks to define terms with great precision, and, when advancing an argument for its defense, gives attention to the laws of logic and causality, employs Aristotelian categories, and relies on syllogisms.[14]

CHARNOCK ON DIVINE PROVIDENCE

In general, the specific details about the immediate context and the chronological order of the *Discourses* remain virtually unknown given the scarce information available on their background. Concerning the treatise on *Divine Providence* (1680), we know that it became the first material published after Charnock's death for no other known reason besides that of editorial preference, and we know that it came as a *"prodromus"* to numerous treatises that soon after were made available to the public.[15]

Charnock localizes the starting point of his study on divine providence

---

2010); Richard L. Greaves, *Oxford Dictionary of National Biography* (Oxford: Oxford University Press, 2004), s.v. "Charnock, Stephen (1628–1680)"; J. I. Packer, *Puritan Portraits* (Ross-shire, UK: Christian Focus, 2012), 47–56.

13. Charnock, *Works of Stephen Charnock.*

14. The assertion that Charnock's *Discourses* are scholastic in method and in style of argumentation is the thesis resolved in Julián E. Gutiérrez, "The Lord Reigns Supreme: An Investigation on Stephen Charnock's Exegetical, Doctrinal, and Practical Theology Concerning the Existence and the Attributes of God" (PhD diss., University of St Andrews, School of Divinity, 2017).

15. See "To the Reader," in Charnock, *Works of Stephen Charnock*, 1:3–5. Charnock's entire corpus was published posthumously with the exception of one theological sermon titled *The Sinfulness and Cure of Thoughts*, which has been included in volume 5 of Charnock's *Works.*

in the words found in 2 Chronicles 16:9: "For the eyes of the LORD run to and fro throughout the whole earth, to shew himself strong in the behalf of them whose heart is perfect toward him."[16] As a prelude to the doctrinal propositions that are rendered ahead in the treatise, Charnock exegetes the text carefully by paying attention to the immediate context preceding verse 9, whence he summarizes the plight of the main character of the pericope: Asa, king of Judah, has forgotten that the divine acts of providence have the good of God's people as their aim. By using the anthropomorphism "the eyes of the LORD run to and fro," the biblical author seeks to communicate to his audience that God exercises his providence with care and diligence. This is to say that the acts of providence are both subjective and detailed rather than objective and superficial. Furthermore, Charnock infers from the same opening clause that divine providence is direct, rapid, universal, and efficacious. While the first clause of verse 9 describes providence, the second clause announces its *telos*: its *finis cuius* (i.e., the intention of the moral agent responsible for providence) is "to shew himself strong," and its *finis cui* (i.e., the end of providence itself) is for the benefit of those "whose heart is perfect towards him [God]."[17] The transition from biblical exegesis to doctrinal formulation is marked by three doctrinal points to explore: (1) providence is real, and God is the agent responsible for it; (2) God directs his acts of providence toward the good of his people; and (3) moral creatures are drawn to and appreciative of providence inasmuch as they acknowledge that God is faithful.[18]

Apropos (1): Charnock says that the control and inspection of all created reality are not divine actions effected by some tangential operation but the result of a direct action of God that is mediated by his perfect knowledge of creation. Consequently, Charnock distances himself from pagan accounts of providence by dismissing that the observed order in creation could be produced by *caeco impetu* ("blind impetus") or by fortune.[19] Charnock pre-

---

16. By opening his discourse with a biblical text, Charnock does not intend merely to provide a proof-text in support of his claim; instead, he seeks to identify Scripture as the epistemic basis (*principium cognoscendi*) upon which doctrinal formulation must be established. In addition to the *principium cognoscendi* whence theology derives, Charnock recognizes in God himself a more fundamental principle, an ontological foundation (*principium essendi*) without which theology cannot be. See Charnock, *Works of Stephen Charnock*, 4:491; 2:383; 1:180. For more details on the principles of theology (*principa theologiae*) in Reformed scholastic theology, consult Richard A. Muller, *Post-Reformation Reformed Dogmatics: The Rise and Development of Reformed Orthodoxy, ca. 1520 to ca. 1725.*, 4 vols. (Grand Rapids: Baker Academic, 2003), 1:406–50.

17. Charnock, *Works of Stephen Charnock*, 1:7–8.

18. Charnock, *Works of Stephen Charnock*, 1:8. Interestingly, this discourse (at least in its published form) elaborates only on the doctrinal points (1) and (2).

19. Charnock, *Works of Stephen Charnock*, 1:8.

sents a series of doctrinal propositions that may be organized as a syllogism to indicate the foundation of providence:

A. God has an unquestionable right to govern creation.
B. Only God is qualified for governing creation.
C. There are no reasons to invalidate (A) given (B).
D. Therefore, God is who effectively preserves and governs creation (though in some instances he has appointed secondary causes to do so).

It is worth noting that for Charnock, creative power is both the basis of and the evidence for providence: *virtus creativa est fundamentum providentiae, et argumentum ad providentiam.*[20] Since God is the efficient cause of everything that exists (i.e., he brought reality into being by enacting a decision of his will) and the one who communicates being to all creatures, he has the power to govern and the right to dispose of creation as he pleases. Thus, the divine act of creation and the ontological supremacy of God are the foundations upon which the right to rule creation is incontrovertible. Omnipotence, perfect holiness and righteousness, omniscience, and infinite patience are the qualities whereby God (and no other) is uniquely suited to preserve and govern created reality.[21]

Charnock introduces the notion of double agency in his doctrine of providence by noting that while God is the primary cause accountable for preserving and governing the world, he has appointed the agency of secondary causes to accomplish the purposes he has decreed to come about: "For being the most excellent and intelligent agent, he doth reduce all the motions of his creatures to that end for which he made them."[22] Double causality, in turn, brings into the discussion another aspect of providence besides preservation and government, that is, the doctrine of divine concurrence (*concursus divinus*). For Charnock, concurrence seeks to explain how primary and secondary causality relate to one another, considering that "God as the first cause hath an influence into the motions of all second causes."[23] In this sense, concurrence speaks about the way wherein God acts in correspondence with the acts of his creatures so that it can be said that providence is effected by the eternal determination of the divine will and

---

20. Charnock, *Works of Stephen Charnock*, 1:8.
21. Charnock, *Works of Stephen Charnock*, 1:9.
22. Charnock, *Works of Stephen Charnock*, 1:11.
23. Charnock, *Works of Stephen Charnock*, 2:137.

(at least in some instances), simultaneously, by means of the motions of the creature without hindering God's plan or doing violence to the creature's own inclinations.[24] Or to put it in the lingo of causality, this is to say that the divine will is the efficient cause (*causa efficiens*) of providence, and the motions of the created agent are the instrumental cause (*causa instrumentalis*) thereof.

The problem posed by the existence of evil and sin in the world becomes acute in Charnock's theology of providence for at least two reasons: on the one hand, it is said that the scope of divine providence is universal, which means that it encompasses *all* the actions and motions of the creature, and, on the other hand, by appealing to divine concurrence, it is implied that God concurs with *all* the motions of the creature. On the surface, it logically flows from this scheme of providence that God must be impugned as the agent ultimately responsible for causing evil and sin.[25]

Cognizant of the devastating implications of this inference, Charnock begins to tackle this quandary not by shying away from the claim that the governing and concurrent aspects of providence play a determinant role in the occurrence of all sinful actions in the world but by positing a distinction between God's government by *actio Dei* and God's government by *permissio divina*—the former being God's effectual act of ordering the good through direct mediation (*mediata*) or by means of secondary causes (*immediata*), and the latter being God's sovereign decision in allowing the creature to sin. Charnock thus affirms that God is not the cause of sin *efficaciter*, as if ordering it through an act of efficient causality, but *permissivè*, for he orders it through an act of active permission.[26] Yet that which prompts *permissio divina* is not sin as such, given that it is inherently abhorrent, not *amabile propter se* ("pleasant by itself") and only *honestatur ex fine* ("dignified because of its goal"): "The holiness of God could never intend sin as sin.

---

24. Charnock, *Works of Stephen Charnock*, 1:12.

25. Charnock deals with two other potential objections for the doctrine of providence: one is about the unequal distribution of wealth as observed in society; the other one concerns the apparent delay in executing punitive justice against recurrent evildoers. I have decided to leave aside these two objections considering that the answers Charnock provides do not involve primarily the concept of providence but that of a proper understanding of the divine perfections. For instance, concerning unequal distribution, Charnock's response emphasizes the fact that God is sovereign and that his wisdom and justice makes him suitable to distribute earthly goods as he pleases; meanwhile, when it comes to the urge for immediate punishment for law-breakers, Charnock notes that the issues in this objection concern more with a correct understanding of how the patience of God operates. For more on Charnock's view about the divine attributes of wisdom, dominion, and patience, consult Gutiérrez, "The Lord Reigns Supreme," 156–73, 246–60, 261–71. Cf. relevant sections in Hansang Lee, "Trinitarian Theology and Piety: The Attributes of God in the Thought of Stephen Charnock (1628–1680) and William Perkins (1558–1602)" (PhD diss., University of Edinburgh, 2009).

26. Charnock, *Works of Stephen Charnock*, 1:26.

But the wisdom of God foreseeing it, and decreeing to permit it, intended the making [of] it subservient to his own honour. . . . It [sin] is purely evil, as it is contrary to law; it is good *ratione finis* [in view of its end], as God orders it by his providence; yet that goodness flows not from the nature of sin, but from the wise disposal of God."[27] Hence, one may correctly conclude that in this sort of providentialism, evil is not the direct (absolute) object of God's providence but only the indirect (relative) object thereof.[28]

Though God provides the enabling power for the creature to act sinfully, the creature is moved by God according to his or her nature. This is to say that moral creatures are not externally coerced to commit sin; they sin because God allows the creatures' corruption to run its course while concurring with their own willingness to sin: "God moves the will, which is *sponte mala* [voluntarily evil], according to its own nature and counsels."[29] The difference established between the very act of sinning and the moral deficiency of such act with respect to what is objectively right allows Charnock to claim that God concurs only with the former, while the latter is attributed in its totality to the moral corruption that is inherent in the creature. Consequently, God is properly said to be the deficient cause of sin rather than the origin of immediate efficiency to producing it. In conclusion, God is not the author of sin by ordering it, nor is he morally tainted by concurring with the motions of the creature when she sins.

Apropos (2): Charnock understands that the goodness intended in all the divine acts of providence has one corporate recipient in the church and one individual beneficiary in the regenerate. At this point, Charnock introduces a christological motif in his account of divine providence: Christ becomes the object of providence in the sense that, at one point, the Father orders everything for the purpose of the coming of his Son and the fulfilment of his mission. Ever since, all the actions of providence work toward perfecting the glory of Christ in the church, of whom he is the head.[30]

In brief, Charnock declares that the purpose of divine providence is ultimately for the good of the church and for the glory of God, as is evidenced by the ordering of all things either good (creation, each creature's

---

27. Charnock, *Works of Stephen Charnock*, 1:17, 29. Charnock provides a series of reasons as to why God has ordered sin to enter the world: (1) for his own glory, (2) to bring about temporal mercies, and (3) to bring his justice upon others.

28. Dolf te Velde, ed., *Synopsis Purioris Theologiae: Synopsis of a Purer Theology*, vol. 1 (Leiden: Brill, 2015), 277n22.

29. Charnock, *Works of Stephen Charnock*, 1:27.

30. Charnock, *Works of Stephen Charnock*, 1:62–63. At one point, Charnock describes Jesus Christ as "God's deputy in the providential government" (63).

gifts and common grace, angels) or bad (wicked people and demons, sinful evils and afflictions), by preserving the church through time, and by often revealing his will and entrusting his law to his people.[31]

Theoretical knowledge about the doctrine of providence necessarily brings practical knowledge for the sake of the church. For instance, knowing about divine providence informs us about the perils of neglecting God's governance and advises us about the different forms of denying, abusing, or belittling providence. Knowing about providence also brings comfort as the creature realizes that she is a special object of God's providential care and that God rules over the world not only by his will but also through his fatherly wisdom and goodness. The doctrine of providence also brings exhortation as it prompts the desire for seeking God for daily sustenance, cultivates dependence on God's will, teaches us submission to God's determinations, awakes the desire to study God's providence, and urges us to ascribe glory to God for every one of his acts.[32]

To conclude, Charnock offers an account of divine providence that is structured by the same pattern one finds in most of his remaining *Discourses*. Though rich in theological content, the treatise on providence clearly exhibits the same pastoral concern that is manifested throughout the whole corpus of the *Discourses*. Therefore, Charnock does not seek to offer a systematic account of the doctrine of providence; instead he aims at instructing his audience about the practical implications of knowing about the providence of God. However, this is not to say, as is manifested by the level of sophistication and the complexity of the subjects discussed, that exegetical prowess, doctrinal clarity, and rhetorical style are secondary or inconsequential subjects for Charnock. It simply means that in this literary genre (theological sermons), the primary goal is hortatory rather than merely intellectual. In any case, it is clear that the section dedicated to the "use" of the doctrine (*pars practica*) in the *Discourses* rests upon the findings of a serious investigation of exegetical and doctrinal matters.

DISCLOSING THE GOD OF PROVIDENCE

In the remainder of this essay, I contend that classical providentialism, particularly the kind ascribed to Charnock's theology, presupposes the agency of a personal, transcendent, and self-subsisting being whose nature is

---

31. Charnock, *Works of Stephen Charnock*, 1:64–79.
32. Charnock, *Works of Stephen Charnock*, 1:38–62, 93–120.

characterized by unlimited wisdom and knowledge, infinite power, absolute sovereignty, and unquestionable goodness. I also argue that this being is not simply an abstract idea of divinity but rather that he is the personal God revealed in Scripture. The former proposition is developed by retrieving an account of providence whereby the identity of God is disclosed while recounting the manner in which he executes providence upon creation. The latter proposition is developed in two stages: in the first, it gives an account of how the God of providence disclosed in Charnock's theology does not contradict the image of God revealed in Scripture; in the second, it explains why disclosing the identity of God in classical providentialism is advantageous for contemporary theology.

One might object that by presenting an argument wherein the divine operations are the basis upon which the identity of the agent responsible for these actions is inferred, the role of Scripture as an epistemic principle of theology is being substituted and that such a move could lead to an idea of God devoid of any Christian content. Though the objection is founded upon a legitimate concern, it must be said that the sequential order observed in the line of reasoning of this essay does not necessarily imply a disregard for the foundational role of Scripture in the task of dogmatics. The reason is that this essay retrieves an account of providence (that precisely takes Scripture as its *principium cognoscendi*!) to advance the claim that the identity of the supreme being responsible for the actions of sustenance, governance, and concurrence turns out to be none other than the God of the Bible, a feature lacking in many of the contemporary versions of providence.

PROVIDENCE AND THE IDENTITY OF GOD

In one sense, to speak about God is to speak about his transient and external acts because there is no difference between who God is *in se* and who he is in his *operationes*, as the divine essence does not undergo motion from *potentia* ("power") to *actu* ("act"): God is full and unrestricted actuality: *actus purissimus*.[33] As such, the classical doctrine of providence as exemplified by Charnock speaks not simply about the temporal administration of all

---

33. The underlying assumption for the claim above is that God is devoid of metaphysical composition. Though the *Discourses* do not separately discuss divine simplicity, the latter is foundational in Charnock's conception of the divine attributes. See Gutiérrez, "The Lord Reigns Supreme," 52–55. Cf. Steven J. Duby, *Divine Simplicity: A Dogmatic Account* (London: T&T Clark, 2015), 146. Note also that for the completion of this section, I have adapted material originally written for my doctoral dissertation concerning the relation between the divine attributes and God's providential activity. Gutiérrez, "The Lord Reigns Supreme."

things God has decreed, but it conveys also something objective—though analogical—about the very nature of God. The importance of the doctrine of providence in classical Christian theology is that in it essential features of the one accountable for preserving and ruling created reality are disclosed. More significant is that the author of providence in this narrative turns out to be the God of the Bible and no other.[34] Since the triune God who creates out of nothing is the same one who preserves and governs created reality, a denial of providence is tantamount to a denial of God himself: "He that denies providence denies most of God's attributes, he denies at least the exercise of them. He denies his omniscience, which is the eye of providence; mercy and justice, which are the arms of it; power, which is the life and motion of providence; wisdom, which is the rudder of providence, whereby it is steered; and holiness, which is the compass and rule of the motion of providence."[35]

We now turn to inquire about the nature of the God of providence in Charnock's theology, which will be done by looking in detail at the way such an agent executes his providential activity by considering some propositions (in italics) that represent the thought of Charnock on the matter.

Nothing can depend upon itself in its preservation, no more than it could in its being. If the order of the world was not fixed by itself, the preservation of that order cannot be continued by itself.[36]

From the outset, Charnock's doctrine of providence ascribes to God the unique entitlement, the excellency of being, the inherent ability, and the rightful disposition that is required for upholding creation in existence while preserving the order of nature, for ruling and ordering all creation according to a determined end, and for relating himself with his creatures by enabling them to act while cooperating with the motions of their operations. A Christian doctrine of divine providence operates under the assumption of two general premises. On the one hand, it assumes the existence of creation, for only that which already is in existence can be the

---

34. Cf. John B. Webster, "Providence," in *Mapping Modern Theology*, ed. Kelly M. Kapic and Bruce L. McCormack (Grand Rapids: Baker Academics, 2012), 205: "[A classical] account of providence begins, therefore, by attending to the divine acts of providential care and governance, and by contemplating the agent of these acts."

35. Charnock, *Works of Stephen Charnock*, 1:40. However, this is not necessarily a denial of God's existence (*quoad existentiam*) or a rejection of one or more of the divine attributes (*quoad naturam*) but a form of practical atheism prompted by the rejection of God's providence (*quoad providentiam*) (1:127). Cf. Francis Turretin, *Institutes of Elenctic Theology*, trans. George Musgrave Giger, 3 vols. (Phillipsburg: P&R, 1992), 1:489; Velde, *Synopsis*, 263.

36. Charnock, *Works of Stephen Charnock*, 1:160.

subject of providential care insofar as nothing that receives its being from another can owe its sustenance to itself.[37] On the other hand, logically, it presupposes the existence of a being capable and willing to execute his providential activity over created reality, either directly (as in the case of miracles) or indirectly (as in the case of secondary causality).

Power is the life and motion of providence.[38]

Divine power is essential to the nature of God as no divine action would be possible without it: God acts because he is essentially powerful. Though creation and providence testify about the impressive nature of the power that *is* God in his works *ad extra*, they do not comprehensibly display its full majesty. This means that the power of God is not exhausted by the execution of the works of creation and providence, or, conversely, that the power used for the actualization of the *opera Dei* causes no diminution of the infinite plenitude of power subsisting in God.[39] Furthermore, since the divine life *ad intra* subsists independently from the divine operations *ad extra*, divine power is not made contingent on creation and preservation.

The divine power required for bringing creation into existence is of the same nature as the divine power needed for sustenance and preservation, namely, it is infinite power.[40] However, the God of providence does not act by brute force in executing his providential activity; instead, his power acts according to the eternal disposition of the divine will, which in turn is driven by perfect wisdom and holiness. Though naked power would be enough to enable the motions of providence, it would be insufficient for providing providence with a morally rightful purpose.

[God] governs by his presence what he made by his power.[41]

As it has been noted, the God of providence is essentially infinite in the exercise of his perfections not in terms of magnitude or number but

---

37. Cf. Wolfhart Pannenberg, *Systematic Theology*, trans. Geoffrey W. Bromiley, vol. 2 (Edinburgh: T&T Clark, 1994), 35: "Insofar as God's creative act establishes the existence of creatures, they are referred primarily to God for their preservation in existence."

38. Charnock, *Works of Stephen Charnock*, 1:40.

39. Charnock, *Works of Stephen Charnock*, 1:439.

40. To think of a divine being who is concurrently infinite in his essence and finite in his attributes entails a contradiction that would lead to an irrational notion of God; see Charnock, *Works of Stephen Charnock*, 1:434.

41. Charnock, *Works of Stephen Charnock*, 1:446.

qualitatively. As such, infinity is an excellence that primarily denotes the perfect plenitude of the divine essence in the manifestation of all the divine attributes. This being the case, whatever perfection is predicated of God is by definition infinite given that *esse* ("existence"), *essentia* ("essence") and *attributa* ("attribute") are one and the same in the way God subsists *in se*.

The God of providence is actively present in creation as his acts of preservation and sustenance suggest a continuous activity on his part. This activity is apprehended by the operancy of the divine attributes, which is none other than the divine essence efficient *ad extra*. This means that the presence of God in providence is endowed with the same perfect plenitude that characterizes his attributes, and thus it denotes the infinitude of the divine essence spatially considered; more specifically it indicates the universal presence of God in the entirety of his being.

Since the presence of God in the universe is *repletivè*, filling all places, his providence is accomplished not by the diffusion of divine virtues throughout the created order but rather through the influence of his essential presence.[42] This is to say that God is ubiquitous in acting providentially by virtue of the plenitude of his essence; when God directs providence through his wisdom, enables the creature to act and concurs with their motions by his power, and claims for himself the right to govern upon his sovereignty, he does so essentially. Reasoning from this fact, God's involvement with his creation cannot be taken to be a passive observance of its affairs, but it must be understood as a participation that is operative and morally discernible in the acts of sustenance, governance, and concurrence by virtue of his omnipresence.

Without knowledge, there could not be in God a foundation for government; and without wisdom, there could not be an exercise of government.[43]

To be the agent responsible for providence in the world, God must know himself naturally and necessarily *by* and *from* his own essence.[44] This signifies that knowledge subsists in the life of God as an inherent quality of his being and not as an acquired or learned faculty: God is infinite knowledge always knowing in one indivisible, immutable, eternal act. As God's knowledge

---

42. Charnock, *Works of Stephen Charnock*, 1:436. God's omnipresence does not involve any mixture, division, or multiplication of the divine essence; see Charnock, *Works of Stephen Charnock*, 1:429–30.

43. Charnock, *Works of Stephen Charnock*, 2:18.

44. Charnock, *Works of Stephen Charnock*, 1:465–66.

involves the knowledge of himself, whose nature is infinite, the same knowledge must include a comprehensive understanding of every finite thing. In other words, God knows everything else besides his own being precisely because he perfectly knows himself. Without perfect knowledge of himself, God could not be said to be perfect; ignorance of his own being would contradict his perfect nature, considering that "ignorance of one's self is a greater imperfection than ignorance of things without."[45] As the knowledge God has of himself is essential for the divine life, it is so for assisting in the enacting of the divine operations. Moreover, had God been ignorant of himself, he could not have created the universe because he would have been ignorant of the power residing in his own being. Ignorance of his own righteous nature, as expressed in his holiness and justice, would make God unable to discriminate good from evil, and thus he would not be able to dictate laws of governance.[46]

Just as the God of providence is said to require infinite knowledge in order to know each and every object of his providential care, it also demands from him to be infinitely wise, otherwise he would not be able to direct the knowledge he owns for accomplishing the ends he has eternally established. In this manner, wisdom can be understood as the knowledge of God viewed from an operational or practical perspective: as the infinite knowledge is called omniscience, and the simple knowledge is called universal knowledge, the divine knowledge in regard to acting is called wisdom.[47] The fact that God directs his providential activity to a determined end suggests the operancy of his wisdom, an attribute that comprises three major aspects: (1) to act for a right end, (2) to observe all circumstances for action, and (3) to will and act according to the right reason, according to a right judgment of things. In this construction, wisdom is related to the power of the intellect and to the motions of the will in acting thoughtfully and ethically for an intended end.[48] That God has a determined end for each one of his actions is inferred from the fact that he is infinitely wise. For a perfectly wise agent cannot but act according to a settled purpose, or he would not be perfect, as purposelessness is not a virtue but a vice of the intellect.[49]

---

45. Charnock, *Works of Stephen Charnock*, 1:465.
46. Gutiérrez, "The Lord Reigns Supreme," 137.
47. Gutiérrez, "The Lord Reigns Supreme," 156.
48. Gutiérrez, "The Lord Reigns Supreme," 159.
49. Charnock, *Works of Stephen Charnock*, 2:11–12.

God hath an indisputable and peculiar right to the government of the world.[50]

Only the one who is Lord in the act of creation can be Lord in the act of preservation and government. God is sovereign in creation insofar as the latter is effected by a free motion of the divine will, whereby, by means of God's infinite power, he decrees to bring into existence everything out of nothing and to endow it with life and motion. And since providence is *continuata creatio* (an extension of creation), as it presupposes the operancy of the same divine power and omnipresence working in creation, it follows that the same sovereignty revealed in the free act of the divine will to bring the world into existence operates in the free disposition of the divine will to preserve and govern it. Furthermore, the God of providence cannot be but sovereign for the supremacy of his being is inseparable from the notion of deity. This is to say that God is essentially sovereign, as sovereignty finds its primary foundation in the supreme excellence of the divine essence.[51]

PROVIDENCE AND THE GOD OF THE BIBLE

The study of the biblical names of God played a foundational role in the way Reformed dogmaticians of the orthodox era introduced the *locus de Deo* in their theological systems. Themes such as the existence of God and the divine attributes, as well as the doctrines of creation and providence, were informed by what Scripture had revealed about the divine nature via the divine names.[52] Though without exhibiting the same order and systematic clarity of other theological material of the Reformed orthodox era, the *Discourses* evidence a similar conviction concerning the significance of the biblical names of God. For instance, Charnock says that a denial of divine providence entails a renunciation of God as providential, which is a form of practical atheism: the rejection does not directly involve God revealed as "*Jehovah*, which name signifies the essence of God as the prime and supreme being, but *Elohim*, which name signifies the providence of God, God as rector and judge."[53] This is significant as it gives an indication of the foundational role of biblical revelation as the groundwork for

50. Charnock, *Works of Stephen Charnock*, 1:8.
51. Charnock, *Works of Stephen Charnock*, 2:408–9.
52. Dolf te Velde, *The Doctrine of God in Reformed Orthodoxy, Karl Barth, and the Utrecht School: A Study in Method and Content*, ed. Eddy Van der Borght (Leiden: Brill, 2013), 114–15.
53. Charnock, *Works of Stephen Charnock*, 1:127. Cf. William Ames, *The Marrow of Sacred Divinity* (London: Henry Overton, 1642), 4.13–14: "This *Essence* of God is declared in his Name *Jehova*." See n42 above for clarification about the different forms of denying God.

the doctrine of God in Charnock's theology. This is not to say, however, that metaphysical claims about the nature of God are absent from the discourses on the divine attributes, whence Charnock shapes the material content of his account of divine providence, but that biblical exegesis, not philosophical speculation, is the epistemic principle upon which doctrinal formulation is established.[54]

In his account of providence, Charnock speaks of a living, personal, self-subsistent, and infinite God who rightfully provides for his creation through his unceasing working power whereby he acts—in harmony with his foreknowledge and the counsel of his will—by sustaining everything that exists, operating all that comes to pass, and ordering all things to reach their determined end.[55] In such a description of providence, God could not have been accountable for his providential activities had he not been shown to be in full and immutable possession of the attributes of power, wisdom, knowledge, goodness, and sovereignty, inasmuch as they are indispensable characteristics for preserving, concurring, and governing created reality.

In conformity with the identity of the God of providence, as revealed in Charnock's theology, the Bible discloses that God is a personal being who eternally subsists as Father, Son, and Holy Spirit and whose essence transcends anything in creation, a being in which the operancy of his perfections asserts the ontological supremacy of his existence: "I am the LORD, and there is no other, besides me there is no God" (Isa 45:5).[56] Particularly, Scripture indicates that God is independent in his being, that is, that he subsists by and from himself apart from creation: "For as the Father has life in Himself, even so gave He to the Son also to have life in Himself" (John 5:26). It considers that God is essentially infinite, which means that he is immensurable in his virtues and hence perfect and free from any boundaries spatially or timely considered: "Great is the LORD, and greatly to be praised, and his greatness is unsearchable" (Ps 145:3). It predicates the omnipotence of God signifying that he is capable of accomplishing everything possible that is acquiescent with his nature: "For the Lord our God the Almighty

---

54. Cf. Dolf te Velde, "Eloquent Silence: The Doctrine of God in the Synopsis of Purer Theology," *Church History and Religious Culture* 92, no. 4 (2012): 583. Velde notes in his analysis of the *Synopsis Purioris* that the study of the biblical names of God "not only serves as a linguistic point of entry to the substance of Who God is, but also as an epistemological foundation for the subsequent doctrine of God."

55. Berkhof, *Systematic Theology*, 181. These "acts" of providence should not be understood as if they were different operations in God but as one single and indivisible work that is apprehended as three separate modes of operation.

56. All biblical references for this section are taken from the English Standard Version.

reigns" (Rev 19:6). It declares that God perfectly knows himself and by derivation all things actual and possible, things that have been, are, and will be: "Great is our Lord . . . his understanding is beyond measure" (Ps 147:5). It affirms that God is absolutely sovereign, emphasizing the fact that he has authority and dominion over everything and that he is entitled to act according to the precepts of his will: "Whatever the LORD pleases, he does, in heaven and on earth" (Ps 135:6). It states that God is pure goodness, so it manifests the fact that he always wills and acts that which is objectively good and righteous: "No one is good except God alone" (Mark 10:18). While it is true that the Bible does not develop a systematic explanation of the doctrine of divine providence, it testifies about it by noting the creation's absolute dependence upon God's provision for its preservation (Ps 36:6), governance (Jer 10:23), as well as for its operations (Acts 17:28). The Scriptures also communicate that God's providential activity is universal in scope, including all creatures (Gen 1:30; Job 38:41; Matt 6:26–30), particularly humankind (Ps. 33:12–15) and the people of God (Heb 1:14); it is teleological in character, as it aims for the preservation of the church and the exaltation of God's name (Ps 104:1).

We have seen that in classical Christian theology divine providence is first and foremost a doctrine that reveals who God is in relation to creation. In this sense, providence is understood as being derivative from the doctrine of God insofar as it explains how God acts externally according to what he is essentially.[57] If the doctrine of providence primarily speaks about the nature of God and secondarily about the order established in creation, its material content must take into account what God has freely revealed about himself in Scripture. In consequence, a Christian doctrine of providence must communicate that the God of the Bible, and none other, is the agent who effectively acts in the conservation, sustenance, direction, and guidance of creation.

By establishing that the God of providence is the God of the Bible, classical constructions of providence, of the sort illustrated in Charnock's theology, distinguish themselves from more recent accounts wherein the material content of the doctrine is shaped in ways more palatable to modern sensibilities. These contemporary descriptions of providence are often fashioned by reformulating the doctrine of the divine attributes in partial

---

57. "God's external acts are in accordance with his inner nature; his providence expresses his omnipotent holiness and goodness and wisdom, his infinite resourcefulness in being for us." John B. Webster, "On the Theology of Providence," in *The Providence of God*, ed. Francesca Aran Murphy and Philip G. Ziegler (London: Bloomsbury, 2009), 168.

or complete isolation from Scripture as the epistemic principle for theology. The result is a doctrine of divine providence whose Christian content is deficient given that its doctrinal claims are not inferred from biblical exegesis but rather from philosophical, scientific, or cultural principles. Ironically, such explanations of providence turn out to be ultimately ineffective in accounting for the order of creation, the unfolding of history, and the purpose of evil in the world in the face of its competitors, whether in the form of scientific naturalism, deism, pantheism, or non-Christian religions. On the contrary, classical providentialism offers a more robust explanation of these foundational topics inasmuch as it finds its source and norm primarily in Scripture, from where it can be directed to contemplative exercises on the majesty of God and to engage in reformulations of divine providence that account for the complexities of the doctrine without dispensing with its biblical grounding.[58]

58. Webster, "Providence," 212–13.

CHAPTER 4

PROVIDENCE

A Deflationary Mandate

CHRISTINE HELMER

AS BOTH A LUTHER SCHOLAR and a Lutheran theologian, I have rarely, if ever, had the opportunity to think in a sustained way about divine providence. This doctrine does not figure significantly in Lutheran piety, nor is it helpful in making sense of Luther's God, the *mysterium tremendum et fascinans*.[1] This God is too unpredictable, too indeterminate, too terrifying to be organized or constrained by a theology of providence. Such, in any case, is my guiding assumption. My aim in this essay is to convince my readers that they ought not to think about the doctrine of providence anymore either! I chart an intellectual history of the doctrine in post-Reformation Protestant thought before turning to my Lutheran deflationary intervention.

DOCTRINE AND CULTURE

Why address providence today? A fact of human psychology is that when something becomes a problem, when something is broken, that is when one starts to pay attention. Heidegger begins his famous *Being and Time* from 1927 in this way.[2] A tool is broken; the light switch does not work; the computer

---

1. Rudolf Otto invented this phrase to identify the source of religious feelings of awe and terror in his famous work from 1917, *The Idea of the Holy: An Inquiry into the Non-Rational Factor in the Idea of the Divine and Its Relation to the Rational*, trans. John W. Harvey (Oxford: Oxford University Press, 1958). In chap. 12, "The Numinous in Luther" (on 99–103), Otto admits that he derived this phrase from his earlier studies on Luther, specifically Luther's 1525 text *De servo arbitrio* (*On the Unfree Will*).

2. "In einer Störung der Verweisung—in der Unverwendbarkeit für . . . wird aber die Verweisung ausdrücklich. Zwar auch jetzt noch nicht als ontologische Struktur, sondern ontisch für

program is frozen. In these situations, one notices that something has gone wrong. Under ordinary circumstances, one uses a tool, an object, a thing, in order to get the job done. When the thing does not work, one pays attention. The thing is no longer a tool but a problem that draws attention to itself.

Religion, like tools, betrays this fact of the human psyche. When things go wrong, people pay attention. When someone has a nervous breakdown, that person is made aware of a disharmony in the soul that cries out for resolution. Luther experienced a terrified conscience and overcame his paranoia by putting all his confidence in the *verbum externum*. As an eighteen-year-old student in the Pietist boarding school of Barby, Schleiermacher could not make sense of an abusive father who demanded the death of the son for the salvation of humankind. He wrote a famous letter to his biological father—a military chaplain—and spent the next thirty years working out a doctrine of salvation grounded in the incarnation.[3] Luther and Schleiermacher only took notice of doctrines they had inherited when they became psychological, spiritual, physical, and intellectual problems. When a soul is in crisis, it presses on to resolution. When a doctrine is broken, the theologian becomes aware of it—as a crisis of faith, an intellectual difficulty or a wound in the soul—and begins to query it. Breakdown is the antecedent to breakthrough, as any student of Luther will attest.

Could the thematization of providence in this specific volume from 2019 reveal that this doctrine has become a problem? Could the volume's editors, those responsible for identifying the topic, have experienced a crisis of faith, an intellectual difficulty, a nervous breakdown, that would have led them to problematize this doctrine today? Or could it be that the topic of this volume follows organically from the doctrine thematized in the preceding volume from 2018, namely theological anthropology? Is there a relation between theological anthropology and providence that would explain why the volume's editors chose to address providence here?

In systems of Christian theology, providence is not usually placed after treatments of the human person. Most doctrines have locations set in stone:

---

die Umsicht, die sich als der Beschädigung des Werkzeugs stößt." Martin Heidegger, *Sein und Zeit* (Tübingen: Max Neimeyer Verlag, 1993), 74.

3. The famous letter is dated to January 21, 1787. Schleiermacher writes, "I cannot believe that He, who called Himself the Son of Man, was the true, eternal God: I cannot believe that His death was a vicarious atonement, because He never expressly said so Himself; and I cannot believe it to have been necessary, because God, who evidently did not create men for perfection, but for the pursuit of it, cannot possibly intend to punish them eternally, because they have not attained it." Friedrich Schleiermacher, *The Life of Schleiermacher as Unfolded in his Autobiography and Letters*, trans. Frederica Rowan, 2 vols. (London: Smith, Elder, 1860), 1:46–47.

the doctrine of the person of Christ is always followed by the work of Christ, eschatology is always situated last among the doctrines. A survey of how different theologians have located providence would lead us to think that this doctrine has no fixed place. It is a moveable feast. In the late Middle Ages as questions of nominalism posed the question of human freedom and divine foreknowledge, providence was discussed under the rubric of the doctrine of God. Luther and Calvin agreed. Yet Calvin innovated. He displaced election (or predestination) from its usual connection to the doctrine of God and attached it to "the doctrine of justification by faith and prayer as the principal exercise of faith; there it serves to answer the question why one individual comes to faith, another doesn't."[4] Some theologians in the Reformed tradition worried about the bifurcation between election and soteriology and explicitly made providence a function of Christology.[5] Others saw its usefulness in explicating the extension of the church in the world and located it under ecclesiology.[6] Those theologians particularly anxious about sin and evil located it in relation to eschatology: God is responsible for ushering in the final kingdom.[7] The doctrine of providence, a doctrine that has something for everyone, has no place to lay its head (cf. Luke 9:58). It does not have its own integrity and is usually parasitically related to some other doctrine regarded as more important.

Given that providence can be discussed anywhere in the systematic order of Christian doctrine, let us analyze its movability. The term *providence* is an ancient one. It is bequeathed to us from the Greeks, from, for example, Homer and Plato (as in the term *pronoia*), and the Romans, from Cicero (as in the Latin *providentia*). The term's semantic range includes foreknowledge, foresight, purpose, or plan.[8] Christian theologians appropriated the term to identify the God-world relation as a conceptual frame for particular doctrines. God is related to the world in distinct ways—through creation and redemption—and God governs the world according to specific divine intentions for the world. Different theologians in different epochs of Christian history attended to particular emphases in the

---

4. Dawn DeVries and B. A. Gerrish, "Providence and Grace: Schleiermacher on Justification and Election," in *The Cambridge Companion to Schleiermacher*, ed. Jacqueline Mariña (Cambridge: Cambridge University Press, 2005), 189.

5. A prominent example is Karl Barth.

6. Friedrich Schleiermacher is a case in point.

7. For example, Jürgen Moltmann.

8. On providence in Greek and Roman religion see Hildegard Cancik-Lindemaier, "Providence. II. Greek and Roman Religion," in *Religion Past and Present: Encyclopedia of Theology and Religion*, ed. Hans Dieter Betz et al., 13 vols. (Leiden: Brill, 2007–13), 10:476–77.

God-world relation. Medieval theologians, for example, were interested in how God and the world collaborated in order for the world to reach its divinely appointed destiny. Thomas Aquinas, for example, saw providence in terms of the cooperation between primary and secondary causes that were ordered to a final cause.[9] The Protestant Reformers did not want to identify providence solely in view of final causality. Their emphasis was on the primacy of the divine will to save in Christ without human works. Providence came then to hue more closely to a doctrine of salvation by grace. Whereas providence had in the Middle Ages been conceptualized by an Aristotelian potency-act schema, the doctrine was now firmly related to the divine action of justification of the sinner without works. Divine agency as efficient cause of salvation—God's work of redemption in Christ—was included in providence's purview.

The question of human sin had driven the Protestant Reformation straight to the heart of the divine will for salvation. The human anxiety regarding human merit—or more specifically its insufficiency—before God was alleviated by the theological insistence on God's will to save. The Reformers' emphasis on efficient causality rather than final causality provoked new theological questions, themselves based on new anxieties informed by this emphasis. From the Reformation forward, the doctrine of providence would be implored to soothe personal anxiety over salvation. But it would come to function more universally, eventually becoming the explanatory paradigm for world history. How efficient causality became wedded to final causality is the story of providence in the modern West.

PROVIDENCE IN THE EVERYDAY

The Protestant Reformation was motivated by anxieties concerning the magnitude of sin and the insufficiency of works to merit salvation. The post-Reformation period, too, was characterized by anxiety. Just as particular questions driven by this anxiety in the Reformation led to theological development, so too the anxiety of post-Reformation souls probed new doctrinal conceptualization. Individuals who had been assured that salvation was Christ's free gift became concerned with the speculative question concerning God's foreordained will for personal salvation. Pastors were confronted with the anxiety of individual souls threatening to shipwreck on the question of the divine will. How is God's eternal will to salvation

---

9. Thomas Aquinas, *Summa theologiae* I.22, 105.5.

predisposed to specific individuals? This question is articulated in the post-Reformation context, primarily in the Reformed church, and offers a glimpse into an emerging culture. The question of divine will is relayed in the same semantic field as that of particular interest in personal salvation. The emerging culture of personal interest in salvation will shape the theological development of the doctrine of providence.

Pastors and booksellers took up this new market driven by individual anxiety. They developed tools—readable, practical, tactile—to aid persons as they worked out for themselves a self-understanding of their own relation to God, or more specifically as they sought to discern God's disposition to them. A new industry catered to this emergence of literate individuals anxious to embark on the path of introspection that would give clues to work out the divine disposition. A famous example of the period is *A Golden Chaine* by William Perkins, first printed in 1590. As early modern scholar of English Calvinism Lori Anne Ferrell describes, this bestseller was intended as a personal guide to "ceaseless inquiry . . . by closely observing and analyzing lived experience in order to discern inherent evidence of one's disposition to salvation or damnation."[10] *A Golden Chaine* is a step-by-step manual, complete with flowcharts for the visual learners, worksheets, and pictures to be used, handled, and touched by the anxious soul. The reader is urged to fold and tug at various parts of the paper in order to chart her place and then development on this introspective path. The reader identifies a starting point, a theological term enclosed in a bubble that matches an introspectively identified condition, for example, temporary faith or repentance. Further discernment of one's disposition leads the individual to correlate the diagnosis of her inner state to a theological doctrine. This is done by tracking pre-drawn lines linking the starting point bubble to other bubbles, each enclosing a theological doctrine implied by the starting point, for example, permanent faith or sanctification. Eventually the individual traces a path from bubble to bubble, from doctrine to doctrine, until one has tangibly experienced—through what Ferrell calls a "Protestant kinesthetics"—the "assurance of divine election" at the terminal point of the chart, namely resurrection (or not!). The personal becomes a spiritual laboratory for discerning the divine predestining will. One gains practice in reading the signs of one's life as a code for knowing God.

---

10. Lori Anne Ferrell, "How-To Books, Protestant Kinetics, and the Art of Theology," *Huntington Library Quarterly* 71, no. 4 (Dec. 2008): 600 (article on 591–606); see also Lori Anne Ferrell, "Transfiguring Theology: William Perkins and Calvinist Aesthetics," in *John Foxe and His World*, ed. Christopher Highley and John N. King (New York: Routledge, 2002), 160–82.

From *A Golden Chaine* by William Perkins

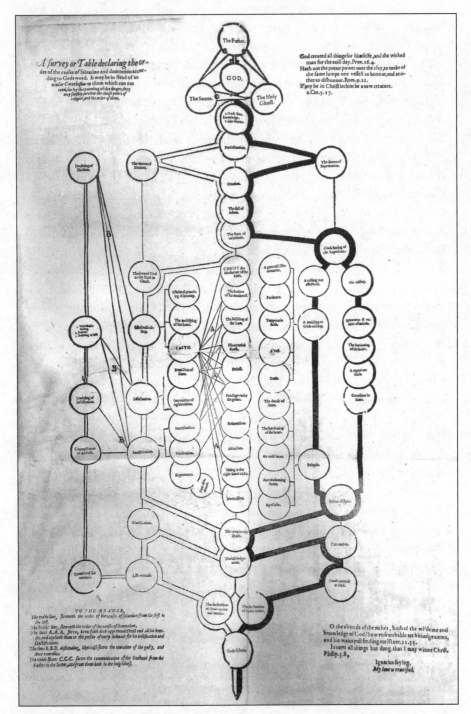

The turn to individual piety in the post-Reformation Protestant context is particularly compelling. It represents an empirical turn. The path to self-knowledge involves learning to read, daily practice guided by manuals, and an increasing constancy of attention to the state of one's soul. The turn to the subject—exacerbated by the anxiety surrounding predestination—urges on a development of the self that will eventually be called "modern." The modern self, motivated by anxiety and doubt, presses on to self-awareness, self-discovery, and self-knowledge in relation to the knowledge of God that remains the heart of Christian theology and worship. The modern self is shaped by a distinctive technology of piety through spiritual aids that address anxious questions. An empiricism of the self emerges as God's predestining will is sought through the introspection and spiritual aids.

Matthew Henry's *Method on Prayer*, like Perkins's *A Golden Chaine*, was an extraordinary personal resource for spiritual formation in the post-Reformation period. Henry wrote and organized this volume for daily biblical study, contemplation, and devotion that has been formative for Protestant piety since it was first published in 1710.[11] Henry's aim is distinctive—to provide a resource for individuals and families as they negotiate their everyday experience in relation to God.[12] God is concerned with the everyday, the ordinary ebb and flow of daily existence, as Henry gives examples from the everyday stresses of his parishioners. There are examples of prayers for his parishioners in their personal lives, women fearing imminent childbirth, parents who have difficult children, and those near death who require comfort. There are prayers for those exercising public vocations, for example, sailors who depend on good weather, traveling merchants who hope for safe passage, and farmers who rely on rain at the right time. There are prayers for prisoners in need of spiritual renovation, and prayers for the ordinary worker who is concerned that he will not get paid.[13] Individual needs are transposed into prayer—petitions and thanksgiving demonstrate the appropriate literary forms framing this transposition of personal concerns before the divine. By guiding his readers through concrete examples, Henry teaches individuals and families that God is concerned with the everyday. There is no need to hesitate in

---

11. Matthew Henry, *Method for Prayer*, ed. Ligon Duncan and William McMillan, http://www.matthewhenry.org/.

12. See my article, "Prayer and Providence: Matthew Henry and the Theology of the Everyday," in *Matthew Henry: The Bible, Prayer, and Piety: A Tercentenary Celebration*, ed. Paul Middleton and Matthew A. Collins (London: T&T Clark, 2019), 189–202.

13. See examples under section 8, "Occasional Addresses," at http://www.matthewhenry.org/.

bringing mundane anxieties and concerns before the divine throne. God is concerned with them all.

Prayer, like how-to spiritual guides, was a practical source for everyday Christians in orienting their lives to God's will. The practice of prayer shapes a distinctive religious sensibility. It is, first and foremost, attuned to the Bible. Individual concerns lead to searches for biblical precedents that are then woven into petitions. Prayer triggers the religious imagination to connect individuals with God's concern for the everyday. The person cultivates attention to details and relates them to God. Through this daily practice of relating self to God, the individual grows in knowledge of both self and God, and specifically, the nature of God's concern for providing sustenance, resolving difficulties, healing illness, protecting travelers, and administering rain and sun for successful crops. Through the practice of prayer, individuals add content to the doctrine of providence in terms of God's sustaining will in the everyday. This learning, in turn, shapes one's spiritual disposition to the self and world. All things can be known as objects of divine concern.

The exercise in a spirituality of providence cannot be restricted to Calvinist and Puritan circles. The concern with God's governance became particularly significant in Germany during the Thirty Years' War, which witnessed massive loss of human life and destruction of land, animals, and infrastructure. In this context of war, Lutheran hymn compositions give evidence for a heightened spiritual attention to God's governance of the political situation. Lutheran composer and organist at the Saint Nicolai Church in Berlin, Paul Gerhardt, for example, composed the moving twelve-strophe hymn "Befiehl Du Deine Wege" ("Entrust Your Way") on Psalm 37—used by Johann Sebastian Bach in two of his cantatas—that articulates a theology of hope in the goodness of divine governance, even in the aftermath of the war and Gerhardt's dismissal from his church post.[14] Pietism, a movement for spiritual and church reform that swept Europe during this time, contextualized recommendations for regeneration of personal and communal piety in relation to the "hope for better things," as Frankfurt Lutheran pastor Philip Jacob Spener claimed.[15] Even as Pietist

---

14. The English translation by Francis Brown in 2006 for the first strophe is: "Entrust your way and what grieves your heart to the most faithful care of him who governs heaven! He who gives to the clouds, air and wind their way, course and path will also find a way where your feet can go." Online http://www.bach-cantatas.com/Texts/Chorale066-Eng3.htm.

15. This phrase is attributed to Philip Jacob Spener, *Pia Desideria*, trans. Theodore G. Tappert (Philadelphia: Fortress, 1964), 76 ("the possibility of better conditions in the church"). See Johannes Wallmann, *Der Pietismus* (Göttingen: Vandenhoeck & Ruprecht, 1990), 26. Wallman

conventicles were persecuted by Landeskirchen throughout Germany, except for southwestern Württemberg, Pietists oriented their spiritual practices of Bible reading, devotions, prayer, and moral rigor to the divine plan that would turn persecutions into blessings, evil into good (as in Gen 50:20, applied to Rom 8:28). God is concerned with the everyday as well as with the final outcome.

The early modern period, also extending into the Enlightenment, can be seen as the emergence of a new awareness of the self through the practice of spiritual technologies that were put into place by religious leaders who attempted to resolve anxieties exacerbated in the post-Reformation world. The theological topic of the God-world relation became the conceptual frame in which the anxieties were articulated and solved. God's electing will inspired technologies of empiricism—whether introspection or science or global expansion—that secured the individual quest for discerning the divine will by engaging in spiritual practices. Providence was dislocated from a fixation on the eternal decree to the discerning of God in the everyday through prayer, devotion, and hymnody that in later Pietist development became concerned not only with the efficient cause of predestination but with final causality—the final revelation of God's plan for blessing. From personal to social, providence and its implications for the modern subject became embedded in the broader interests of European culture that ricocheted around the globe in terms of scientific developments and global expansion. It is now to the move from personal to social and ultimately political and economic that I turn in order to show just how perniciously providence permeated modern self-understanding.

FROM PERSONAL TO UNIVERSAL

Human nature is to exist with others, to be aware of one's shared consciousness as participants in the same species. With the evolution of the modern self and its preoccupation with the personal development of the God-self relation, we also see the evolution of new forms of human community. The question of how modern selves form relations so as to constitute communities is central to the development of the doctrine of providence, and specifically to its displacement as a doctrine allied with the divine predestining will before time to the rubric of final causality. The individual

---

relays that Spener's idea of a future hope for inner worldly kingdom of peace is tied to the return of Christ in this world.

is situated in a nexus of intersubjectivity. Individual development occurs together with the emergence of new forms of social cohesion in churches, moralities, political forms, and forms of economic exchange. As such, new ways of articulating emergence in terms of social purpose—the highest good so to speak—begin to occupy the theological and philosophical imagination.

Henry's method already reveals a growing awareness of final causality. While specific petitions are articulated in view of God's interest in the everyday, Henry incorporates self and world under the purview of divine providence. One example of the relation between specific petition and the awareness of an overarching divine intention is Henry's morning devotion for the family. He suggests the following prayer:

> Our bodies and all our worldly affairs we commit to the conduct of the wise and gracious providence, and submit to its disposals. . . . O give us grace to do the work of this day in its day, according as the duty of the day requires; and to do even common actions after a godly sort, acknowledging thee in all our ways, and having our eyes ever up to thee, and be thou pleased to direct our steps.[16]

Henry deliberately sets specific concerns of the self in relation to God's concern for the world. Body and work are given over to God's care; the praying person requests God to help with work done to the best of one's ability. The self's concern with the personal sphere ultimately gives way to a view of God's interest in the whole of creation. The human has a responsibility to conduct personal and worldly affairs in attunement to providence. All creatures and the whole world are ultimately dependent on God for life, sustenance, and prospering. The self acknowledges that personal contribution to these affairs is situated in view of a larger rubric, the plan of which only God knows. In prayer, the individual works out the specificities of everyday life in relation to God's providential care for the world. The individual's attention is directed to the whole.

Not only pastors but philosophers during this post-Reformation period appeal to providence in terms of final causation. This philosophical development shows a broader cultural interest in locating personal introspection in universal structures of meaning. The evolution of modern consciousness can be observed in theological and philosophical considerations in connecting

---

16. See "Morning Prayer for a Family," no. 4 under section 9, "Short Forms of Prayer," 238, http://www.matthewhenry.org/.

personal awareness to broader ethical, social, and political theories that imbue the personal with a sense of purposive living in the modern world.

Adam Smith (1723–1790), the Scottish moral philosopher, is an example of a post-Reformation thinker who relates individual economic concerns to a broader theory of economic exchange that, ultimately, is situated in view of the divine. Smith's work *The Wealth of Nations* from 1776 is famous for the oft-quoted phrase regarding the invisible hand of the market.[17] Also an author of works on education and the university, Smith became interested in policies to promote a nation's wealth in the context of the Industrial Revolution and his observations of poverty in France. Smith works on the basis of theological anthropology, which heavily echoes his earlier work in *The Theory of Moral Sentiments* from 1759 and explains how a community of rational human beings can be constituted on the basis of self-interest. He finds that, unlike Hobbes's fears of "nature red in tooth and claw," people will generally create divisions of labor which allow them to work productively.[18] Smith's idea of a community is an association of adults who have each divided themselves into some unique occupation where they are the experts. The citizens of the community are defined by what they make and what they want: the breadmaker who likes fresh fish, the woodworker who has a steak for dinner every night, the doctor who buys the newspaper every day. These people create wealth, and occasionally collaborate in creating wealth, in order to carry out exchanges for mutual benefit.

Smith's idea of moral behavior is fundamental to his idea of an orderly society, which is the topic of his *Theory of Moral Sentiments*. Smith believes wealth comes from interactions and exchange—for this, we need a society which practices justice.[19] There are dispositions that inevitably orient individuals to others. Smith argues that sympathy grounds the human orientation to community; people naturally experience a resonance between their emotions and those that they observe in others.[20] The material observation of another person's conditions leads us to imagine ourselves "in their

---

17. When I taught this book during the spring quarter of 2017 in a class at Northwestern University titled "Economics and Religion in German Culture," the undergraduate students, many of them majoring in economics, supposed that the "invisible hand" referred to the market's capacity for self-regulation.

18. Adam Smith, "The Wealth of Nations," abridged in *The Essential Smith*, ed. Robert L. Heilbronner, with the assistance of Laurence J. Malone (New York: W. W. Norton, 1986), 168–72.

19. "But that, somehow or other, we feel ourselves to be in a peculiar manner tied, bound, and obliged to the observation of justice." Adam Smith, "Theory of Moral Sentiments," abridged in Heilbronner, ed., *Essential Smith*, 93; "justice, on the contrary, is the main pillar that holds up the entire edifice" (97).

20. Smith, "Theory of Moral Sentiments," 101.

shoes." The empathic sentiment is itself not morality, but it encourages the explicit development of morality that is required for any social cohesion. Smith develops a theory of the "impartial spectator," the individual who pays attention to sympathy that extends attention beyond immediate self-interest.[21] The impartial spectator is one who has overcome bad behavior by the inner voice that encourages self-loathing in those who act badly. This spectator then learns to embody particular virtues that are beneficial to reciprocal obligations and managing moral impulses. Virtues constituting such a society that thrives on exchange are prudence, beneficence, and self-command,[22] which combine to motivate an individual who respects the rights of others.

Smith reflects on how individuals must be formed to act in groups. Individual empathy and moral virtue are necessary for social well-being as it is constituted by the reciprocity of exchange. The government must facilitate these exchanges by establishing structures, like schools and roads. But for Smith, the entire process of moral formation, political process, and economic exchange is referred to a force which he views as external to society and which governs the world rationally.[23] Smith makes very few references to this external cause in his work. Yet two explicit references disclose the theology of providence he presupposes. Smith mentions "the invisible hand of the market" in view of what he considers the divine providence that assures an orientation of economic exchange—driven of course by moral virtue—to a particular end. As Smith writes about an individual who might not be entirely motivated by virtue, yet "he is in this, as in many other cases, led by an invisible hand to promote an end which was no part of his intention."[24] This end, as Smith mentions in another passage, is "the great, benevolent and all-wise Being, who directs all the movements of nature; and who is determined, by his own unalterable perfections, to maintain in it, at all times, the greatest possible quantity of happiness."[25] Self-interest that is overcome through moral virtue and social cohesion that is motivated by virtue exemplify a market that is ordered by divine

---

21. "But, in order to attain this satisfaction, we must become the impartial spectators, of our own character and content." Smith, "Theory of Moral Sentiments," 103.

22. Smith, "Theory of Moral Sentiments," 133–40.

23. "He should, therefore, be equally willing that all of those inferior interests should be sacrificed to the greater interest of the universe, to the interest of that great society of all sensible and intelligent beings, of which God himself is the immediate administrator and director." Smith, "Theory of Moral Sentiments," 141.

24. Smith, "Wealth of Nations," 265. This is the only place in "Wealth" in which Smith explicitly refers to the "invisible hand of the market."

25. Smith, "Theory of Moral Sentiments," 141.

providence. Through the concept of providence, Smith directs the market to a universal eudaemonistic end. The purpose for the exercise of virtue in the reciprocity of economic exchange (in which the government too participates) is the realization of the divine end, or final cause, for human society, namely creaturely happiness.

Smith, like Henry, develops his ideas about the individual as modern agent in relation to an emerging theology of divine providence. As Christians pray, they become attuned to God's concern for them. As they become aware of divine providence, they extend their understanding of divine concern from individual to community. They learn that all areas of human flourishing—individual, social, economic, and political—are grasped by the invisible hand's determination. The story about the development of the doctrine of providence in the post-Reformation period is the story of how the modern subject takes shape together with emerging social, cultural, and political forms. While providence began its humble journey into modernity by accessorizing the doctrine of predestination, it soon became the master template of modernity.

PHILOSOPHY OF HISTORY

Providence has been a remarkably resilient doctrine in modern times. From the personal to the social, from the family to the "big picture," the doctrine functioned in piety and theology as a motor of the emergence of the modern self and modern social organization. Its utility was framed in terms of efficient and final causality. The quest for individual meaning led to probing the divine disposition in terms of efficient causality; God's will was discerned in an individual's self-constitution in the everyday. The quest for universal meaning led to questions regarding final causation. God's plan for society, politics, and history were determined as benevolent and just.

The story of divine providence in the modern world has one more chapter. With the rise of German historicism in the eighteenth century, providence found a providential landing pad. In its culmination in the systematic philosophical theology of the early nineteenth-century German Idealists, providence became the explanatory paradigm for God's relation to all of human history. A modern understanding of history would be underpinned by providence. Two early nineteenth-century Protestant thinkers, the Lutheran philosophical theologian Georg Wilhelm Friedrich Hegel and the Reformed theologian and pastor Friedrich Daniel Ernst Schleiermacher, succeeded in relating the entire realm of historical agency to divine determination.

The explication of the meaning of world history identifies the systematic aim of both Hegel and Schleiermacher. These thinkers sought to conceptualize world history in view of divine necessity. They transformed God's providence into a metaphysic of history. Hegel located the rationality of historical contingency in the divine eternity; the rational became real in and through human history. Even evil was absorbed into and explained by divine necessity. Schleiermacher was not as certain as Hegel that the reality of world history could be ascertained by rational philosophical tools. Rather his theological perspective restricted providential meaning in specific ways. Yet as we will see, Schleiermacher, like Hegel, represents the culmination of a conceptualization of providence as a metaphysic of history.

Schleiermacher begins his account of providence where a Reformed theologian would come to expect it: under the doctrine of creation. Yet he immediately qualifies his discussion by considering the exegetical role of Genesis 1–2 in the doctrine. He contests the historical interpretation of the story of creation at the beginning of the Christian Bible that he claims led to a theological distinction between creation and preservation.[26] Concerned with coherence and the prohibition of erroneous distinctions, Schleiermacher relegates creation under preservation. The meaning of the biblical account of creation and fall is the universality of human fallenness. Any speculation concerning historical cause is prohibited. Theology begins "in the middle," namely with the consideration of the world as fallen.[27] Divine preservation, not creation, must properly be deemed the doctrine relating the fallen world to God. Preservation, not creation, thematizes ongoing divine causal activity that prevents the world from sinking into nothingness.[28] Schleiermacher even prefers the term *preservation* to *providence*, as the meaning of the term *preservation* is more closely aligned with the Roman confession that identifies God as "pantocrator," or almighty. The determination of the content of the "Whence" of the feeling of utter dependence is precisely God as almighty. The way in which God's almighty world governance (*Weltregierung*) is explicated under the rubrics of wisdom and love is "self-imparting deity," meaning God directs the world's formation toward the kingdom of God.[29]

---

26. Friedrich Schleiermacher, *Christian Faith: A New Translation and Critical Edition*, trans. Terrence N. Tice, Catherine L. Kelsey, and Edwina Lawler, 2 vols. (Louisville: Westminster John Knox, 2017), 1:205–7 (§36). Subsequent references to *Christian Faith* are abbreviated as CF.

27. I characterize Schleiermacher's theological method as beginning "in the middle," an approach that situates him in conversation with the Romantics in Berlin around 1799.

28. CF 1:213 (§38).

29. The term "self-imparting deity" is Schleiermacher's designation for the revelation of the

Two ideas are important for understanding Schleiermacher's concept of providence as an all-encompassing divine causality that directs the world to its realization of the kingdom of God. The first is Schleiermacher's indebtedness to the work of Lutheran pastor Johann Gottfried Herder. Herder took up the notion of *Bildung* from seventeenth-century Pietists to describe the growth or development of an individual that takes place in relation to the whole. *Bildung* was an important Pietist notion that had its biblical basis in Genesis 1:26: the *Bild* is the image of God in humans.[30] As developed by Pietists with their formation of notions of the modern self in the culture of the Enlightenment, the concept of *Bildung* grew to become one of the most important ideas of German intellectual circles in the eighteenth century. Significant to the concept is that the self cannot be imagined as an autonomous individual capable of independent growth. Rather the self exists intersubjectively and develops only in reciprocal interactions with the community. The *Bildung* of the individual requires the *Bildung* of society, as evidenced in art, education, morality, politics, philosophy, and theology.[31] Herder locates *Bildung* as overarching social concept to providence as its divine correlate. He writes,

> Every creature in the universe is to be simultaneously means and end: a tool in the hands of providence, but also a universe all of its own. . . . Behold the entire universe from heaven down to earth—what is a means, what is an end? Is not everything a means towards a million ends, everything an end by a million means? The chain of omnipotent, omniscient Good contains thousands of entwined meshes: every link of this chain hangs in its proper place as a link, yet none can see where the chain as a whole hangs in the end.[32]

The significance of Herder's conception is that it secures the divine attributes of omnipotence and omniscience to determine providence as well as a prerogative of goodness in order to guarantee that this concept of providence orients the individual within all of culture to the unified development of the whole.

---

divine attributes of love and wisdom in and through world history. For a detailed explanation of this idea, see DeVries and Gerrish, "Providence and Grace," 191.

30. For details on the concept of *Bildung* in Pietism, see Ruth Jackson, *The Veiled God: Friedrich Schleiermacher's Theology of Finitude* (Leiden: Brill, 2019), 126–30.

31. Jackson, *Veiled God*, 130.

32. Johann Gottfried Herder, "Another Philosophy of History for the Education of Mankind," in *Another Philosophy of History and Selected Political Writings*, trans. Iohannes D. Evrigenis and Daniel Pellerin (Indianapolis: Hackett, 2004), 72.

Inspired by Herder, Schleiermacher establishes the basis of his theological system not on the question of being but on the question of human freedom. Human freedom, limited by dependence on others, is the finite cause of actions that are directed in spacetime reality. The transcendental cause for human freedom cannot be identified with a distinct creative act. Rather the transcendental cause is the divine causality that is responsible for the existence of the entire causal nexus in which finite freedom is located. The Whence of the feeling of absolute dependence—and by this Schleiermacher insists that the feeling of absolute dependence is established on the basis of an awareness of the self's unity with the whole—is the divine causality.[33] It is the ground of finite freedom, directed toward the whole as purposive teleology.[34] With Schleiermacher a compatibilist view of freedom enters the notion of preservation. Divine causality is not in competition with finite causality but unconditioned, absolute, and nonreciprocal. God sustains the powers of finite causality as omnipotent without competing with them. Transcendental freedom secures freedom for finite agents. God is active, almighty, and omnipotent within everything, but—as absolute causality directed to the whole—in a way that differs from finite causality in the social and natural world.

The crucial move that Schleiermacher makes in view of the divine causality is that there is one intention directed to the whole of human history embedded in the worldly causal nexus. Because divine causality is the transcendental cause for finite freedom, its condition as the unconditioned cannot be divided up into temporal, discrete units. Spacetime discrete units are all reciprocally related to each other as a whole, and as such, the whole is the object of God's plan. Divine causality as the ground of spacetime units reciprocally related to each other within the whole commits Schleiermacher to the theological notion of God's governance of the world as a unity directed toward a single goal, namely the realization of the kingdom of God in the world through the mediation of the church. Any theological distinction, such as that in Protestant orthodoxy distinguishing between general, special, and most-special providence implies division in the one divine plan, which is illegitimate on philosophical-theological grounds and on the grounds of piety.[35] It is erroneous, according to Schleiermacher, to assume that for the individual there is a special divine causality somehow

---

33. See CF 1:24–27 (§4.4).
34. CF 1:251–53 (§46.2).
35. CF 1:253–57 (§46, postscript).

separate from the connection with the whole. It must be underlined that on this point Schleiermacher is not heterodox. In support of his position he cites Lutheran orthodox theologian Johann Quenstedt in saying that all the strictest dogmaticians have understood divine preservation and natural causation as one and the same thing, though from different perspectives.[36] Divine preservation is clearly and simply the upholding of the entire causal nexus.

The theological contribution Schleiermacher makes to the doctrine of providence—or more aptly preservation—is twofold. First, as a theologian engineering the first ecumenical alliance between Lutheran and Reformed Churches, he was able to bring together the seventeenth- and eighteenth-century Lutheran notion of relative freedom with a metaphysics of causality.[37] Second, he detracted any personal anxiety regarding predestination by bringing providence into the realm of divine causality directed to the whole. He theologically determined this metaphysical claim by focusing on divine election as the one divine decree made available in Christ, namely redemption of the whole through the particular mediation of Jesus of Nazareth.[38] While Schleiermacher's model uses providence to solve the problem of freedom in relation to the unconditioned, it is christologically directed: the redemption in Christ that is brought about historically by the church, and then eschatologically in universal redemption, reveals the essence of divinity as wisdom and love.[39] The anxious pangs of an individual's conscience are assuaged by a theology in which providence is oriented as one divine decree to Christ's person, who is identical with the work of transforming lives and communities in order to actualize the kingdom of God. The entire project of the causal nexus is designed for redemptive success—oriented by the divine attributes of love and wisdom as becoming more and more present to and in creation. In Christ, God's vision for humanity and world becomes real. Schleiermacher's philosophy of history is ultimately a theology of providence that is driven by the revelation of the divine attributes as the church extends its expression of Christ throughout the world.

---

36. CF 1:255 (§46, postcript).

37. Annete I. Hagan explicates this point in detail in her book *Eternal Blessedness for All? A Historical-Systematic Examination of Schleiermacher's Understanding of Predestination* (Eugene, OR: Pickwick, 2013).

38. Schleiermacher explicates this theological determination of God's providential plan in Jesus in his treatise *On the Doctrine of Election with Special Reference to the Aphorisms of Dr. Bretschneider*, trans. Iain G. Nicol and Allen G. Jorgenson (Louisville: Westminster John Knox, 2012).

39. See CF 2:1002–4 (§165).

Schleiermacher's vision resonated powerfully in the tradition of German theology. Late nineteenth-century Lutheran theologian Albrecht Ritschl framed his theory of justification with reconciliation as community oriented to the highest good.[40] Karl Barth appropriated Schleiermacher's concept of the one divine election in Christ as his own.[41] Wolfhart Pannenberg used the historical paradigm to make a case for its theological revelatory significance.[42] Schleiermacher is exemplary for modern theology for using the doctrine of providence to unite all of world history under the aegis of the divine will to redeem. With the rise of modern historicism as explanatory paradigm for human agency, the doctrine of providence achieved pride of place in the modern worldview. No longer limited to a theology of everyday piety, Schleiermacher elevated providence to a metaphysics of history, securing human freedom as compatible with divine omnipotence, guaranteeing a successful outcome with first fruits in Christ, and claiming that all of history charted the progress toward final cause. What had started as an anxiety-producing idea for Calvinist Christians in the early modern world ended up framing an entire modern worldview. A doctrine that had been born in the post-Reformation anxiety about the future became the confident symbol of modern history in its teleologically directed formation. Providence had come to stand for the progress of humanity toward its highest good. Theology's doctrine of providence, which had not found a permanent resting place in the pantheon of Christian dogmatics, ended up ruling over them all.

To underscore this claim, providence was instrumental in shaping modern identity by the creation of a historical narrative of modernity. The "linear progress narrative," as American scholar Michelle Wright claims, is "what organizes most of our knowledge and knowledge production in the West. Today across the natural sciences, social sciences, and humanities, we organize most of our epistemologies according to this spacetime teaching and arguing that our current knowledge is the result of or based on previous achievements and that we are more 'advanced' than previous generations of scholars and practitioners—that word itself presuming a linear movement forward."[43] Providence shaped a metaphysic of history with its

---

40. In English translation, see Albrecht Ritschl, *The Christian Doctrine of Justification and Reconciliation: The Positive Development of the Doctrine*, trans. H. R. Mackintosh and A. B. Macaulay (Edinburgh: T&T Clark, 1900).

41. Karl Barth, *Church Dogmatics* II/2, trans. G. W. Bromiley and T. F. Torrance (Edinburgh: T&T Clark, 1957).

42. Wolfhart Pannenberg, "Heilsgeschehen und Geschichte," *Kerygma und Dogma* 5 (1959): 259–88.

43. Michelle M. Wright, *Physics of Blackness: Beyond the Middle Passage* (Minneapolis: University

historiographical, economic, political, ethical, and religious commitments. A doctrine that rose contiguously with the emergence of the modern subject ended up making modernity.

CRISIS OF DOCTRINE, CRISIS OF MODERNITY

Let us return to our initial question: Why is providence thematized in this book? What is the problem with providence? We have traversed the history of the doctrine as it has come to represent the modern worldview. In order to answer our question, let us look at the reality produced by the doctrine. Let us look at the modern world. What do we see?

We see 50 percent of the world's population traumatized by the misogynist effects of the patriarchy. Hundreds of young women recently gave impact statements in a Michigan courtroom on the explicit sexual violence they experienced at the literal hands of an imposter doctor aided and abetted by the most powerful governing bodies in the sports arena. We see and hear women talk (or, if they were murdered, their grieving relatives) of the myriad inventive ways the patriarchy deploys to diminish, harass, sexualize, underpay, overwork, silence, ignore, humiliate, exploit, beat, rape, and murder girls and women—because they are women.

We see African Americans traumatized by a pernicious system of racism established by slavery and legitimated by the current legal system. Young black men are assassinated by police officers simply for wearing a hoody. Mass incarceration is a reality for black and brown bodies. Predominantly black neighborhoods are redlined by city officials and bankers to prevent affordable housing and to promote life in poverty. A football player who risks his career by taking a knee becomes the target of a swift outcry. We see people in the name of nationalism disown responsibility to brown Catholic bodies at our border. Toddlers, women, and men are desperate for refuge in a country that has precipitated unrest in their countries of origin in the first place. On the global scale, we see sixty-five million refugees fleeing war, climate catastrophe, and political persecution in one year, as the 2017 film "Human Flow" by the Chinese activist Ai Wei displays. This is how most people experience the modern world.

What about the worldly casual nexus? The casual nexus does not speak for itself. There are, however, scientists who are trained to see the evidence and draw scary conclusions. Scientists talk about creation in distress, oceans

---

of Minnesota Press, 2015), 16.

choking on plastic waste, microorganisms invaded by microplastics. They measure the rising of surface temperatures and the melting of the polar caps. They warn of an insect apocalypse and a sixth great extinction. All of creation is groaning (Rom 8:22) because humans insist on an unsustainable lifestyle fueled by the bones of dinosaurs. The entire casual nexus, from microscopic to macroscopic levels, is on the brink of a point beyond which nature will not recover. The planet is supersaturated with carbon's heat—the avalanche to apocalypse is the result of our making.

The crisis of modernity is evident around us. The avatars of death have charted the next phase in the linear progress narrative. With modern reality spiraling out of control, the doctrine that created it in the first place has become a theodicy. The doctrine once used to uphold God's sovereignty has become misused to legitimate the progress of history with its nationalism, white supremacy, sexism, and economic colonialism. Providence has become dystopic, the final act of the human drama.

Now, finally, we can see the wisdom of the book's editors in soliciting articles on the doctrine of providence at this time in human history. The answer to the question, "Why providence now?" can be discerned by looking at the reality of the modern world. We are fundamentally anxious about the doctrine because it has invaded and seeped into all nooks and crannies of the modern worldview. We are much too slowly realizing that this modern worldview is catapulting toward death. The doctrine of providence is in crisis because modernity is in crisis. Humans have created the modern crisis—not God—and theologians have legitimated this development by appealing to providence. At the end of modernity, humanity is itself in jeopardy and with it the world. Providence is the problem of an entire worldview—the modern worldview projected onto providence. The anxiety underlying this volume is that both together have failed.

INTERVENTION

The diagnosis demands a prescription. The prescription must be swift. We have twelve years according to scientific calculation to get our act together, economically and politically, to prevent the worst of irreversible effects of climate change.[44] The prescription must be surgically precise. There is no

---

44. See, e.g., Jonathan Watts, "We Have 12 Years to Limit Climate Change Catastrophe, Warns UN," *The Guardian*, October 8, 2018, https://www.theguardian.com/environment/2018/oct/08/global-warming-must-not-exceed-15c-warns-landmark-un-report.

time for trial and error. There is no time to test out a malleable doctrine that can be bent like a waxen nose to suit human ideological interests. The prescription must be sufficiently countercultural. It must turn away from human delusion to the reality of God.

At this point I turn to Luther—a theologian not seduced by the linear progress narrative but one whose theological sword can be used to slice through the human inventions that have made modernity what it is, including the doctrine of providence, in order to get to the heart of the matter: the reality of the living God. Luther's God is the one required for such an enormous intervention. His God cannot be strung along a history of progress legitimating human tradition by appeal to a providential plan. Luther's God is the one who unmasks providence as a theological delusion. The intervention we need to learn from Luther is that we need to get theologically real.[45]

The reality of Luther's God, the one who resists all efforts of theological legitimation, is the God who is hidden. The hidden God is the divine majesty. The God who is hidden has no determination. Luther can describe this God as either God or the devil; without determination by revelation, there is no way of telling the difference. Because God is hidden, humans have no categories to penetrate the divine opacity and make any sense of God. The God above God—as Luther formulated it—refuses to be known or determined in any way.[46] God defies humans. God maintains the prerogative to remain hidden or to reveal. This undetermined God is the God that humans have no business seeking. As Luther writes in the compelling phrase he borrows from Erasmus of Rotterdam, "quae supra nos nihil ad nos."[47] What is above us has nothing to do with us. When God is sovereign, we do not even want to know what that looks like.

Luther's concept of the hidden God is an apt intervention for a doctrine that has misused the idea of sovereignty to legitimate modern progress. The hidden God defies the human capacity to know. This God—the one that humans want to use to justify their lives and histories, political policies, and pedagogical plans—is the one from whom one must flee. That God is the God apart from any revelation or any determination. In fact, the divine

---

45. For a detailed account of the importance of a realist perspective in theology, see my book *Theology and the End of Doctrine* (Louisville: Westminster John Knox, 2014).

46. Martin Luther, *D. Martin Luthers Werke: Kritische Gesamtausgabe*, 121 vols. (Weimar: H. Böhlau et al., 1883–2009), 18:685–86 (*De servo arbitrio*).

47. Still the best explication of Luther's phrase on the hidden God is Eberhard Jüngel, "Quae supra nos, nihil ad nos: Eine Kurzformel der Lehre vom verborgenen Gott im Anschluß an Luther interpretiert," in *Entsprechungen: Gott—Wahrheit—Mensch* (Munich: Chr. Kaiser, 1980), 202–51.

majesty defies the human desire to know. The divine retains the prerogative for unknowability precisely because of divinity. The intervention for providence is accomplished by pointing to the hidden God who resists human legitimation and refuses human control.

This is not the whole picture of Luther's God. To find the God who has definitively revealed the divine self to the world, one has to look in the world, to the God hidden in humble humanity—a Jewish baby in a manger because there was no room for him in the inn (cf. Luke 2:7);[48] the gracious preacher who healed those who had been abused by the system; who was compassionate to the intense suffering he encountered; the one who, even when exhausted, stopped to listen; the one persecuted by jealousy and killed by crucifixion. Divinity is veiled in compassion; grace is bestowed through death.[49] The eternal mystery of God is determined by embodiment. The incarnation is the self-determination of God who is interested in saving in ways that are unpredictable, uncanny, and downright scandalous. It is this God who insists, "Follow me" (cf. Matt 16:24).

A theological intervention requires pondering and following this one, who will one day ask, "Where were you when I was killed by a police officer, when I was thrown into prison without a trial, when I was beaten by my partner, when I was alone and dehydrated at your border, when I was diminished because I was different, when I became extinct because you didn't care, where were you?" (cf. Matt 25:34–35). This question is not the revelation of the God of providence, who will rescue us from man-made modernity. This is the God who reveals the divine self in a demonstration of true humanity. Among the shards and laments of modernity, this God is still present, insisting that persons transform their delusions of who God is and follow the wounded one who leads into the mystery of graced life. Theology is about God, the reality of God in the present day—not the God of providence but the providential God.

---

48. A delightful composite of Luther's different writings on Jesus's birth and infancy is Roland H. Bainton, ed., *Martin Luther's Christmas Book* (Minneapolis: Augsburg, 1948).

49. This is, of course, the quintessence of Luther's theology of the cross as succinctly formulated in thesis 20 of the *Heidelberg Disputation*: "The person deserves to be called a theologian, however, who understands the visible and the 'back side' of God [Exod. 33:32] seen through suffering and the cross." Martin Luther, "Heidelberg Disputation," in *The Annotated Luther*, vol. 1, *The Roots of Reform*, ed. Timothy J. Wengert (Minneapolis: Fortress, 2017), 99.

CHAPTER 5

DIVINE PROVIDENCE'S *WETENSCHAPPELIJKE* BENEFITS

A Bavinckian Model

NATHANIEL GRAY SUTANTO

IN 1876, A HIGHER EDUCATION ACT in the Netherlands effectively reconfigured the theological faculty in the Dutch universities into departments of religious studies. A seemingly inevitable consequence of a series of philosophical shifts within modern thought that questioned the legitimacy of theology as an academic discipline, two issues, broadly considered, fueled this reconfiguration. First, theology was increasingly considered to be a private matter that could not be empirically or objectively verified. In other words, though it might be conceded that theology could be beneficial for ethical or devotional purposes, it was unclear whether it could be subjected to or improved by scientific (*wetenschappelijke*) inquiry. Second, there was an ever-increasing divide between the church and the academy. The church and her seminaries justified their existence on the basis of the private piety of faith and the formation of ethical principles. The universities, on the other hand, investigated those fields of knowledge with methods of investigation that were purportedly neutral and purely rational in character. With this dichotomy in place, there seemed to be no need for theology within the university. How can such a faith-based discipline contribute to the other fields of inquiry within higher education?

The neo-Calvinist dogmatician Herman Bavinck responded to these issues with acute urgency. Indeed, one might say that a large motivation behind all of his writings was the endeavor to demonstrate that (1) theology is indeed scientific, because God has revealed himself, and (2) this same revelation is the "secret" behind every facet of human culture and intellectual investigation and thus ought to be investigated as a means of servicing the other academic disciplines.[1] Theology is and remains the queen of the sciences not simply because her subject matter transcends all others but because theology explores the divine realities that undergird and make possible all scientific pursuits. "The deeper science pushes its investigations, the more clearly will it discover that revelation underlies all created being."[2]

For the interests of this chapter, more specifically, Bavinck turned to the doctrine of divine providence frequently in order to respond to these intellectual shifts. Deploying divine providence was seen by Bavinck to be a means of vindicating theology's place within the university as a science in itself that contributes to other sciences. As he says very specifically, "All science (*wetenschap*) rests on the assumption that reality is not coextensive with phenomena but contains a kernel of divine wisdom, being the realization of the decree of God—insofar as the truth is bound to reality and finds its criterion in correspondence with reality."[3]

This essay explores what Bavinck means by this and retrieves his organic model of divine providence and elaborates on the ways in which he thought that divine providence contributes intellectually to two academic sciences (*wetenschappen*): the disciplines of natural science and history. Hence, this chapter's contribution is twofold. First, there is the obvious historical-theological yields of attending to how one dogmatician deployed a key Christian doctrine in a modern context. Second, Bavinck's approach could be seen as a fresh way of preserving the doctrine of meticulous providence in light of contemporary challenges, as a performative account that models the dogmatic and *wetenschappelijke* fruits of affirming such a model.[4] This is so

---

1. "The world itself rests on revelation; revelation is the presupposition, the foundation (*grondslag*), the secret (*geheim*) of all that exists." Herman Bavinck, *Philosophy of Revelation: A New Annotated Edition*, ed. Cory Brock and Nathaniel Gray Sutanto (Peabody: Hendrickson, 2018), 24.

2. Bavinck, *Philosophy of Revelation*, 24.

3. Bavinck, *Philosophy of Revelation*, 68.

4. Andrew McGowan had already argued that Bavinck's doctrine of divine providence was particularly amiable to a "productive relationship" with the empirical sciences, ecology, and culture, because he considered common grace to be a subset within it. However, McGowan did not elaborate on how Bavinck himself drew out that relationship. See Andrew McGowan, "Providence and Common Grace," in *The Providence of God*, ed. Francesca Aran Murphy and Philip G. Ziegler (London: T&T Clark, 2009), 109–28 (121). Common grace (and the underlying antithesis that common grace suspends in the current redemptive-historical age) is commonly regarded to be a distinctive emphasis

in distinction from some contemporary approaches that seek to defend this doctrine by retrieving neglected scholastic distinctions that might illumine the intelligibility of affirming such a model,[5] or by articulating its ability to reckon with the problem of evil,[6] or by drawing out its implications for religious piety.[7] Stated in another way, while contemporary retrievals of classical models of divine providence had been by way of *expositio*, clarifying the dogmatic place and material of this revealed Christian doctrine, this essay focuses on Bavinck's writings that were characterized by *disputatio*, honing in on the polemical and explanatory powers that divine providence might provide for other areas of scientific inquiry in a way that avoids the temptation unduly to project divine purposes unto historical movements.

The rest of this paper proceeds in three steps.[8] First, I sketch Bavinck's doctrine of divine providence from his *Dogmatics*. Second, I show the ways in which Bavinck deployed divine providence as an aid for the natural and historical sciences. Finally, I summarize Bavinck's model of displaying divine providence's *wetenschappelijke* benefits by four predicates: that it is inductive, closely textual, revelational, and organic.

BAVINCK ON DIVINE PROVIDENCE AND THE ORGANIC MOTIF

It is important to clarify that Bavinck did not construct a doctrine of divine providence in a manner that acquiesced to or was determined by

---

of the Dutch neo-Calvinistic tradition. See also James Eglinton, *Trinity and Organism: Towards a New Reading of Herman Bavinck's Organic Motif* (London: T&T Clark, 2012), 37–44.

5. See, for example, the recent and helpful writings by Steven J. Duby, "Divine Immutability, Divine Action, and the God-World Relation," *International Journal of Systematic Theology* 19 (2017): 144–62; "Divine Action and the Meaning of Eternity," *Journal of Reformed Theology* 11 (2017): 353–76. See also his *Divine Simplicity: A Dogmatic Account* (London: Bloomsbury, 2016).

6. E.g., David E. Alexander and Daniel M. Johnson, eds., *Calvinism and the Problem of Evil* (Eugene, OR: Pickwick, 2016). For a recent, popular, and accessible treatment, see Greg Welty, *Why Is There Evil in the World (and So Much of It?)* (Fearn: Christian Focus, 2018).

7. Guillaume Bignon, *Excusing Sinners and Blaming God: A Calvinist Assessment of Determinism, Moral Responsibility, and Divine Involvement in Evil* (Eugene, OR: Pickwick, 2017). These emphases on divine providence confirm Charles Wood's observation that religious communities primarily invoke the doctrine to encourage "the counsel of patient acceptance and endurance" within whatever circumstances of life befalls the believer. "Providence," in *The Oxford Handbook of Systematic Theology*, ed. Kathryn Tanner, John Webster, and Iain Torrance (Oxford: Oxford University Press, 2007), 97.

8. The works I cite below are from Herman Bavinck, *Christelijke wetenschap* (Kampen: Kok, 1904); *Christelijke wereldbeschouwing*, 3rd ed. (Kampen: Kok, 1929); and *Philosophy of Revelation*. Translations from *Christelijke wereldbeschouwing* are from a pre-print of our forthcoming Herman Bavinck, *Christian Worldview: An Annotated Translation*, ed. and trans. Nathaniel Gray Sutanto, James Eglinton, and Cory C. Brock (Wheaton: Crossway, 2019). The page references are still from *Christelijke wereldbeschouwing*.

the intellectual challenges of his day. Rather, his method was that of apply-ing and responding to those challenges with what is firstly and properly received as revealed doctrine. Indeed, this order is irreversible. Bavinck strongly affirmed that God's revelation should shape and motivate the dogmatic material, and hence that polemical tasks must depend upon a prior reception of revealed doctrine. In this, Bavinck would agree with John Webster's claim that "*disputatio* is subordinate to *expositio*."[9] Thus, it is important to note that our focus on Bavinck's later texts presuppose his earlier exposition of divine providence in the *Reformed Dogmatics*.

Before attending to the specific *wetenschappelijke* benefits of divine prov-idence, then, a brief dogmatic sketch of Bavinck's treatment of providence is in order. In this sketch, I attend to four features of divine providence in Bavinck's *Dogmatics*: its all-encompassing scope as preservation, concurrence with secondary causes, teleological governance of creatures, and dogmatic relation to God's triune being and creation, especially in light of the organic motif. Providing this sketch also anticipates the ways in which Bavinck deployed providence to illumine and aid the other sciences.

First, then, on its scope. Bavinck begins his chapter on providence by attending to the Scriptural language on the matter. God's preservation of his creatures is never idleness, for creatures can have no existence apart from God's active preservation.[10] Scripture admits of no independent creatures, as "independence is tantamount to nonexistence."[11] God's providence is extensive in scope, including within it the entirety of all that exists outside of God, but it is also intensively focused on God's people, the object of God's fatherly care. After discussing some classical distinctions with respect to divine providence—that it is a divine act distinct from the plan of God and that it is more precisely delineated as God's preservation and governance of the world—Bavinck argued that the Christian doctrine of divine providence provides a stark alternative between pantheism and deism. Providence dis-tinguishes between God and creatures but maintains that creatures remain

---

9. John Webster, "On the Theology of Providence," in Murphy and Ziegler, eds., *Providence of God*, 161. Webster proceeds, on the same page: "Dogmatics has a twofold task: an analytic-expos-itory task, in which it attempts orderly conceptual representation of the content of the Christian gospel as it is laid out in the scriptural witness; and a polemical-apologetic task in which it explores the justification and value of Christian truth-claims." It is worth emphasizing, however, that Bavinck's goal isn't reducible to apologetics, nor is he merely exploring the value of Christian truth claims. His goal was in a sense more ambitious: he attempted inductively to illustrate the persistency and inevitability of Christian claims—one can't get away from those claims, even in the so-called nondogmatic sciences.

10. Herman Bavinck, *Reformed Dogmatics*, vol. 2, *God and Creation*, ed. John Bolt, trans. John Vriend (Grand Rapids: Baker Academic, 2004), 592. Hereafter *RD*.

11. Bavinck, *RD*, 2:592.

related to and dependent on God.[12] Indeed, providence refers to the "entire implementation of all the decrees that have bearing on the world after it has been called into being by creation."[13] It is the work of God in preserving and governing all that exists outside of God, whether in the economy of nature or grace. As such, it is an all-encompassing doctrine, the implementation of God's freely known decree in time. "All the works of God *ad extra*, which are subsequent to creation, are works of his providence."[14]

Second, divine providence establishes rather than diminishes creaturely causes. "Every creature received a nature of its own, and with that nature an existence, a life, and a law of its own."[15] God sustains all that is outside of God moment to moment in a manner concurrent with their natures, which preserves the integrity of secondary causes.[16] As the unfolding of God's wise plan *ad extra*, God's providential ordering of all things exhibits the diverse perfections of his being as creatures function in accordance with their imbued natures. "All things are based on thought," Bavinck wrote, appealing to Augustine's understanding that God had implanted "hidden seeds," "seminal reasons," and "original principles" into his creation.[17] This includes all of the "interconnected" orders that bind the manifold "laws and relations" that exist "in every sphere" of created existence: "the physical and the psychological, the intellectual and the ethical, the family and society, science and art, the kingdoms of earth and the kingdom of heaven."[18] Hence, while God is free from external causes, creaturely things "do depend on one another" in a complex nexus of interlocking relations.[19]

---

12. Bavinck, *RD*, 2:594–604.

13. Bavinck, *RD*, 2:604.

14. Bavinck, *RD*, 2:604.

15. Bavinck, *RD*, 2:609.

16. Bavinck, *RD*, 2:606–9. Hence, Bavinck explicitly rejects occasionalism: "Creation and providence are not identical. If providence meant a creating anew every moment, creatures would also have to be produced out of nothing every moment. In that case, the continuity, connectedness, and 'order of causes' would be totally lost, and there would be no development in history." *RD*, 2:607.

17. Bavinck, *RD*, 2:609. Earlier, Bavinck argued that God's "decree is the 'womb' of all reality." *RD*, 2:373. In another place, Bavinck further demonstrated that his understanding of divine providence is firmly rooted in the classical doctrine of divine ideas as the exemplary causes of created things: "The word must be joined by the deed, generation must be joined by creation, wisdom must be joined by God's decree, in order to grant a real existence to what existed eternally in the Divine consciousness as an idea." Bavinck, *Christelijke wereldbeschouwing*, 56. In the next page, Bavinck argued that the older saying *forma dat esse rei* ("the form gives existence to the thing") must be understood biblically and not Hellenistically, as forms have no independent existence and cannot serve as the efficient cause of created things but rather are brought into existence solely by the will of God. On this, he cites Johann Heinrich Alsted, *Encyclopaedia septem tomis distincta* (Herbonae Nassoviorum: Corvinus Erben, 1630), 1:615.

18. Bavinck, *RD*, 2:610.

19. Bavinck, *RD*, 2:610.

Providence orders the multiplicity of created natures into a unity, and concurrence "is the reason for the self-activity of the secondary causes, and these causes, sustained from beginning to end by God's power, work with a strength that is appropriate and natural to them."[20]

Third, providence guides the universe toward a particular *telos*. In Bavinck's discussion, governance is not a third thing alongside preservation and concurrence but rather a consideration of God's providence within a teleological perspective.[21] Governance expresses the kingship of God, highlighting his rule in relation to sin and the redemption wrought by Christ. In the cross, Christians witness the sovereignty of God over evil and the victory and wisdom of his purposes. It comforts those in affliction and points them to the establishment of God's kingdom. Providence, then, has a specific historical focus on Christ's redemption, along with a pastoral focus for the comfort of God's people.[22]

Finally, to further appreciate the dogmatic shape of Bavinck's account of providence, one ought to situate his treatment within its textual location in the *Dogmatics*. As we have seen, providence sustains and directs God's creation, which is itself the bringing about of the product of God's divine counsel *ad extra*. As such, a treatment of providence is properly located after a consideration of God's triune being, the divine counsel, and creation.

Bavinck took pains to warn against understanding providence and its outworking within creation as "mechanical," which is a reductionist tendency of materialist worldviews.[23] This is because of Bavinck's prior argumentation on the triune God and creation. Echoing the classical and Reformed orthodox tradition, the three persons share the same divine essence and enjoy an equality in glory, power, and divinity. The divine essence is simple. God is not composed of parts—he is unchangeable, *a se*, possesses life in and of himself, and is thus utterly self-sufficient.[24] The three persons are thus distinguished only by the proper relative properties belonging to each: unbegottenness and paternity to the Father, eternal generation and filiation to the Son, and the Spirit's procession from the Father and the Son. While these classical confessions on the divine nature emphasize God's utter otherness as distinct from all creaturely beings,

---

20. Bavinck, *RD*, 2:614.
21. Bavinck, *RD*, 2:615.
22. Bavinck, *RD*, 2:618.
23. Bavinck, *RD*, 2:610.
24. I provide a sketch of the classical countours of Bavinck's doctrine of God in chap. 2 of my God and Knowledge: Herman Bavinck's Theological Epistemology (London: Bloomsbury, forthcoming).

Bavinck had also argued that the confession of God's triunity requires us to see creation anew. The confession of God's triune being has both doxological and creational implications.

Creation bears the imprints of God's self, as creation arises out of "all the ideas that are included in the divine decrees," which themselves stem from the fullness of God's self-knowledge.[25] As such, "all of the works of God *ad extra* are only adequately known when their trinitarian existence is recognized."[26] How, then, does creation display a "trinitarian existence"? Bavinck's answer is that creation, read in light of Scripture and spiritual illumination, displays "vestiges" of the Trinity and that the "higher a thing's place in the order of creation, the more it aspires to the triad."[27] This affirmation of the vestiges of the Trinity and the aspiration of higher orders of creation to form triads does not, however, lead Bavinck into a quest to find fixed triads that mirror God's being. For Bavinck, the triune God alone enjoys an absolute three-in-oneness, and creation displays its triune shape not by exhibiting precise triads but by its *organic* character.[28] God's absolute three-in-oneness is reflected by creation's many unities-in-diversities. The organic shape of creation becomes an ongoing motif used by Bavinck throughout his writings to communicate the distinctiveness of the Christian worldview. A significant passage on this is as follows:

> Scripture's worldview is radically different. . . . Everything was created with a nature of its own and rests in ordinances established by God. Sun, moon, and stars have their own unique task; plants, animals, and humans are distinct in nature. There is the most profuse diversity, and yet, in that diversity there is also a superlative kind of unity. The foundation of both diversity and unity is in God. It is he who created all things in accordance with his unsearchable wisdom, who continually upholds them in their distinctive nature, who guides and governs them in keeping with their own increated energies and laws. . . . Here is a unity that does not destroy but rather maintains diversity, and a diversity that does not come at the expense of unity, but rather unfolds it in its riches. In virtue of its unity, the world can, metaphorically, be called an organism, in which all the parts are connected with each other and influence each other reciprocally.[29]

---

25. Bavinck, *RD*, 2:342.
26. Bavinck, *RD*, 2:333.
27. Bavinck, *RD*, 2:333.
28. See Eglinton, *Trinity and Organism*, 89. On the implications of this claim to the doctrines of original sin and the image of God, see Nathaniel Sutanto, "Herman Bavinck on the Image of God and Original Sin," *International Journal of Systematic Theology* 18 (2016): 174–90.
29. Bavinck, *RD*, 2:435–36.

The key moves in Bavinck's treatment of how providence particularly benefits the sciences are present in this passage. An organic worldview maintains both unity-and-diversity in a way that resists the tendency of reductionism that fails to do justice to the manifold ordinances within creation. Said in another way, reading creation as the ordained manifestation and ectypal reflection of God's triune being disciplines Christians to be holistic thinkers—to take into account all of the relevant phenomena and patiently to trace the connections between them until an explanatory account emerges that does justice to the diversity and unity of creation. This is a clear advantage that an organic worldview has over a mechanical one: "It is only when we exchange the mechanical and dynamic worldview for the organic that justice is done to both the oneness and diversity, and equally to being and becoming," refusing then a "one-dimensional" view of the world.[30] If the mechanical worldview is "exclusive" (*exclusief*), the organic view recognizes the proper place of mechanical explanations but refuses to reduce "life, consciousness, freedom, and *telos*" ("*leven, bewustzijn, vrijheid, doel*") into mechanistic realities.[31]

With this sketch in place, one can now come to grasp why Bavinck specifically applied divine providence to the discussion of natural science and history.[32]

PROVIDENCE AND NATURAL SCIENCE

The connection that I draw here between Bavinck's discussion of providence and the academic discipline of the natural sciences is one that Bavinck himself explicitly makes at the end of his formal discussion of providence in the *Dogmatics*. There, Bavinck cites approvingly the judgment of the German physiologist Emil H. Dubois-Reymond that Christianity had made science—"specifically natural science—possible and prepared the ground for it."[33] Due to Christianity's doctrines of God, creation, and

---

30. Bavinck, *Christelijke wereldbeschouwing*, 50.
31. Bavinck, *Christelijke wereldbeschouwing*, 50.
32. For a brief summary of Bavinck's understanding of the relationship of Christianity, science, and the organic worldview, especially with reference to the question of evolution, see Abraham Flipse, *Christelijke wetenschap: Nederlandse rooms-katolieken en gereformeerden over de natuurwetenschap, 1880–1940* (Hilversum: Verloren, 2014), 97–103, and his "The Origins of Creationism in the Netherlands: The Evolution Debate among Twentieth-Century Dutch Neo-Calvinists," *Church History* 81 (2012): 104–47 (esp. 112–16). Unlike Flipse's more historically oriented contributions, however, this essay focuses more specifically on Bavinck's use of the doctrine of providence.
33. Bavinck, *RD*, 2:611. Bavinck referred to E. H. Dubois-Reymond, *Culturgeschichte und Naturwissenshchaft* (Leipzig: Veit, 1878), 28.

providence, which distinguished God from nature in a manner that preserved the link between the two, nature could then be studied without fear of violating some divine force within it. Further, as Christianity taught that nature was grounded in the "harmony and beauty of the counsel of God, and hence the unity of the cosmic plan," an "order" of nature came into view, which recognized "a wide range of ordinances and laws for created things."[34] Hence, there was never a real conflict between Christianity and natural science. Bavinck argued that the history of the debates reveal that the two sides were never that of Christianity *versus* natural science but Christians on both sides hypothesizing conflicting answers on particular scientific questions. In this regard, Bavinck pointed specifically to how Christians in the past wedded themselves either to an Aristotelian-Ptolemaic or a Copernican worldview when they debated heliocentrism, as one example.[35]

Apart from these brief comments on how providence invigorates natural scientific investigation, however, Bavinck does not detail specifically *how* Christian theism actually aids this empirical project in his *Dogmatics*. For this, we need to turn to his later works, and for interests of space, I'll focus my attention mostly on the main arguments of his *Christian Worldview* and his Stone Lectures, where he arguably gives the most sustained reflections on this issue. [36]

An adequate grasp of Bavinck's argument requires following the grain of his text. It's important to note that Bavinck does not superimpose beforehand the doctrine of divine providence into the debates that he is exploring. His method is strongly textual and inductive—he immerses himself into the current scholarship before reaching into this doctrine and then presents the doctrine in a way that doesn't negate the best results of that scholarship but rather seeks to *accommodate* those insights. As we proceed, the earlier themes that emerged from his doctrines of creation and providence will

---

34. Bavinck, *RD*, 2:612.

35. Bavinck, *RD*, 2:612n80, pointing to the discussion of the debate on heliocentrism in *RD*, 2:483–84.

36. The arguments of these two works are discursively and materially related, as Bavinck regarded the latter to be a kind of sequel to the former (Bavinck, *Philosophy of Revelation*, 23n61). Bavinck treats the topic of natural science and Christian faith in numerous places. His 1911 Parliament address "Christianity and Natural Science" repeated the point that science was freed by Christianity and needs divine revelation, but its politically tinged context did not allow Bavinck to provide many specific examples of how this was so. Herman Bavinck, "Christianity and Natural Science," *Essays on Religion, Science, and Society*, ed. John Bolt, trans. Harry Boonstra and Gerrit Sheeres (Grand Rapids: Baker Academic, 2008), 81–104. See also the essay "Evolution" in the same volume (105–18) and Herman Bavinck, "Christendom en Natuurwetenschap," in *Kennis en leven: Opstellen en artikelen uit vroegere jaren*, ed. C. B. Bavinck (Kampen: Kok, 1922), 184–202.

resurface: a focus on unity-in-diversity and thus a desire for holism and nonreductionism.

Two issues that arise from the contemporary scientists on the nature of nature drive Bavinck's concerns: that of nature's most primitive material and that of nature's development.

One central question on the object of study in empirical investigation is the nature of what is studied itself: what unifies the diverse phenomena of matter and motion and the seeming regularity that governs what we see before us? How do atoms, which seem to lack consciousness, relate to one another? How does the lifeless relate with life itself? What comes first—matter or energy, and how do these two basic ingredients relate? Two broad trends arose in Bavinck's day on the nature of nature: materialism and dynamism: "While materialism regards matter as an eternal substance and energy as pertaining to it, dynamism to the contrary sees energy as original and material as derivative."[37]

Thinkers who espoused the materialist view, represented by the German biologist Ernst Haeckel (1834–1919), denied that appeals to extraphysical realities were scientific or helpful to the empirical enterprise and argued that at best dynamism was a "fruitful cerebral epidemic" (*fruchtbare cerebrale Epidemie*) that would "quickly pass."[38] Reality is one large machine, they thought, and the unity of the whole is reducible to an aggregate of material parts.

In contrast, proponents of dynamism argued that mechanical explanations lacked the ability to account for the origins of life and the rational order that seems to govern natural laws. Cells come from preexisting cells, and the lifeless cannot produce life, and thus they concluded that there must be a more primordial power behind the material world. But dynamism, while correctly demonstrating the inadequacies of materialist worldviews, is vulnerable as well, for it seems "impossible to form a clear concept or representation of these primordial elements of things."[39] What exactly is this energy or law that drives matter? From where does it arise? Eduard von Hartmann (1842–1906), a German representative of dynamism, argued that "activity without an active element" (*Thätigkeit ohne ein Thätiges*) cannot

---

37. Bavinck, *Christelijke wereldbeschouwing*, 41.
38. Bavinck, *Christelijke wereldbeschouwing*, 39. Bavinck is citing Ernst Haeckel, *Die Welträthsel* (Bonn: E. Strauss, 1899), 444. On page 73 of *Philosophy of Revelation,* Bavinck writes that "Haeckel goes even so far as to claim that everyone who still believes in a soul, or a principle of life, deserts the domain of science and seeks refuge in miracles and supernaturalism." Bavinck cites *Die Welträthsel,* 209.
39. Bavinck, *Christelijke wereldbeschouwing*, 41.

exist and inferred that there is some absolute substance behind all matter—but this seems simply to replace materialism with pantheism.[40] Wilhelm Ostwald (1853–1932), a dynamist who argued that mechanical-materialism was "a mere delusion," merely hypothesized the existence of energies from material being without actually shedding light on how matter and energy relate or what these energies actually are.[41] It is also difficult methodologically to justify the inferences of the dynamists, for they seem suspiciously to be nothing but speculative judgments.

Both materialists and vitalists, at the end of the day, resort to metaphysical and worldview judgments, tempted as they are to make these totalizing claims that transgress into other disciplines due to the relative success they've enjoyed in their realm of the natural sciences.[42] Both, too, seem to reduce the phenomena that the other investigates: materialists deny the existence of nonphysical forces, and dynamism, with its talk of energies, can't seem to make sense of "impermeabilty, mass, intertia, expansion, and visibility."[43] As Bavinck summarized,

> Mechanism and vitalism stand here in bitter opposition, and the neo-vitalists are at war among themselves on the question whether the cause of life is to be sought in a special force of the organism, or rather in an idea or form dominating and governing this organism. And thus riddles increase step by step, as science penetrates more deeply into the essence of things or rises higher in the ascending scale of creation. . . . Everywhere in creation we face an endless differentiation, an inconceivable multiformity of creation, an inexhaustible wealth of essence and life.[44]

The second issue that arises in empirical investigation is the question of development. Mechanical explanations cannot accommodate true development in the sense of "progress and perfection" (*vooruitgang en volmaking*), for all differentiation is reducible to accidental changes.[45] Progress presupposes notions of goals, plans, and purposes, of will and intelligence, of "*principia and radix*"—and no shuffling of accidental material can cause these notions to arise.[46] Furthermore, the changes that a combination of material parts bring about are often not merely a new relation between those parts but

40. Bavinck, *Christelijke wereldbeschouwing*, 42.
41. Bavinck, *Philosophy of Revelation*, 73–8; *Christian Worldview*, 43.
42. Bavinck, *Philosophy of Revelation*, 73, 75, 76.
43. Bavinck, *Christelijke wereldbeschouwing*, 44.
44. Bavinck, *Philosophy of Revelation*, 94.
45. Bavinck, *Christelijke wereldbeschouwing*, 58.
46. Bavinck, *Christelijke wereldbeschouwing*, 58; *Philosophy of Revelation*, 82.

results of a higher and different order.[47] If simple elements like water and sulfuric acid already possess "properties different from those of the elements themselves" that are impossible to explain by way of a necessary, rational principle, then how much more so for higher organic life?[48] One might predict the new phenomena that arise when certain elements are brought together and thus draw a range of variability, but such phenomena show that higher forms cannot be explained by the mere addition or a rearrangement of material parts. In other words, Bavinck is forming something like an *a fortiori* argument. If simple developments cannot be explained by some rational principle or by an appeal to an inherent property of the more primal material element themselves, then how much more intractable would the unity and progress of the entire cosmos be to us?

It is precisely after Bavinck had explored these results within the scientific communities that Bavinck argued that the natural sciences require aid from Christian metaphysics. In contrast to the desire for explanatory and metaphysical uniformity—of reducing nonphysical forces to matter or of reducing matter to some absolute unconscious substance—"the full truth is first presented to us in Scripture, when it teaches that things have come forth from God's manifold wisdom (πολυποιχιλος σοφια), are mutually distinguished by a common character and name, and teaches that in their multiplicity they are one, and in their unity they are still distinct."[49] In contrast to both mechanism and vitalism, Christian theism presents an organic worldview, which recognizes that nature "is much more capacious and richer than the concept that dominates current day natural science" and yet simultaneously accommodates the insights of "the mechanical explanation for phenomena."[50] What it *does* deny is the right of mechanical or vitalist explanations to become unlimited, transgressing beyond its spheres and reducing all other fields of inquiry under its own terms and methods. Christian theism, declaring that the universe is an organism because of its origin in God's triune wisdom, can accommodate both materialist and vitalist insights while simultaneously keeping both in relation, hence resisting dualism: "The organic view thus acknowledges and proceeds from the

---

47. Bavinck, *Christelijke wereldbeschouwing*, 63. In *Philosophy of Revelation*, 82, Bavinck reiterates the same examples of water and sulfur.

48. Bavinck, *Philosophy of Revelation*, 82. Bavinck used the same example of water and sulfuric acid in *Christelijke wereldbeschouwing*, 63: "Water is essentially distinguished from hydrogen and oxygen, taken on their own. Sulfuric acid is something different to sulfur or oxygen."

49. Bavinck, *Christelijke wereldbeschouwing*, 45.

50. Bavinck, *Christelijke wereldbeschouwing*, 45–46.

multiplicity of creations, just as nature itself shows us."[51] Matter and spirit can thus be related as distinct parts of creation: "All things are knowable because they were first thought. And because they are first thought, they can be distinct and still one. It is the idea that animates and protects the organism's distinct parts."[52]

Bavinck argued that it was insufficient, however, merely to ground the universe in the divine intellect and wisdom—it was also brought into being by the divine will. Herein is the answer to the question of development. Citing Johann Alsted again, Bavinck argues that all things are imbued by divine wisdom with a particular form (*forma*) that moves them internally toward one direction or another. God's power bears all of creation, directing them by ordinances that do not violate nature but are intrinsic to its diverse parts.[53] Moreover, the Christian worldview reveals a "divine thought that must be realized in the passing of time" and thus bears an inherently teleological character.[54] Divine providence is not an unconscious or random governance of all things (*contra* Von Hartmann) but the implementation of a wise decree with a beginning and end. "All of these different created things, with their different substances, ideas, powers, and laws are—according to the organic view—taken up in one great whole, and are subservient to a highest end. There is finality everywhere, in the inorganic and in the organic."[55]

PROVIDENCE AND THE DISCIPLINE OF HISTORY

Modern and ancient accounts of the relationship between providence and history alike tended to wed divine purposes with one nation, political movement, or economic process in an attempt to justify specific imperial expansions and capital ambitions.[56] Bavinck's application of the divine counsel to the historical sciences, however, is in keeping with his emphasis on its explanatory powers for the sciences.[57] Two issues arise in the schol-

---

51. Bavinck, *Christelijke wereldbeschouwing*, 51.

52. Bavinck, *Christelijke wereldbeschouwing*, 52. See also the parallel in Bavinck, *Philosophy of Revelation*, 79.

53. Bavinck, *Christelijke wereldbeschouwing*, 59.

54. Bavinck, *Christelijke wereldbeschouwing*, 60.

55. Bavinck, *Christelijke wereldbeschouwing*, 66.

56. On this, see David Fergusson, "Divine Providence," in *The Oxford Handbook of Theology and Modern European Thought*, ed. Nick Adams, George Pattison, and Graham Ward (Oxford: Oxford University Press, 2013), 655–72; and Brenda Deen Schildgen, *Divine Providence: A History* (London: Bloomsbury, 2012).

57. Bavinck acknowledges that the Christian worldview in general and God's providence in particular are more directly and significantly related to the historical disciplines. See *Christelijke*

arly literature that Bavinck addressed in the discipline of history: (1) the seemingly irreconcilable tension between necessary truths and contingent history and (2) the scholarly attempts to explain history under a singular cause or a grand narrative of successive phases untethered from divine action. Bavinck's argument here matches his discussion on the natural sciences—God's providence and divine counsel preserve unity-in-diversity.

Bavinck treats the first tension in his *Christian Worldview*. In Kant's ethics there is the paradigm that represents the ideal view of ethics and reason—ethical norms are absolute ideals untouched by the ebbs and flows of history. These norms, however, are untethered from the classic ideas of God and known only by way of practical reason. Hence, despite performing "an outstanding service for morality in his day," Kant's views were immediately vulnerable to criticism from the emerging historical consciousness that sought to take seriously the empirical facts of human development.[58] Paying strenuous attention to the concrete histories and developments of religious societies and cultures had yielded enormous insights on various people groups—specificities and details that would remain veiled were one to stay within the realm of noumenal abstractions.

Yet this historicism also led quickly to a kind of identity politics and epistemological and religious relativism. Soon, the "norm was sought in the historical, the ideal identified with reality, the relative exalted to the rank of this absolute."[59] Each people group had a right to their own religious founders: "the Persians had their Zarathustra, the Greeks their Homer, the Arabians their Mohammed."[60] With haunting prescience, Bavinck observed the emergence of the argument that presented Aryan Germans as the people group which achieved the pinnacle of historical progress. Christ was thus not a Jew but an Aryan man. "Relativism appears then to be impartial, as it wants to know of no fixed norms, and claims only to be concerned with, and to speak of, the concrete, the historical. But it makes the relative itself into the absolute and, therefore, exchanges true freedom for coercion, real faith for superstition."[61] This historicist-relativistic view is then caught in a bind: while claiming that absolute ideals cannot exist, it makes normative claims about progress and prescribes ethical imperatives. This is

---

wereldbeschouwing, 94. "The indispensability and significance of revelation appears in history in an even higher and richer measure than in nature." *Philosophy of Revelation*, 92.

58. Bavinck, *Christelijke wereldbeschouwing*, 73.
59. Bavinck, *Christelijke wereldbeschouwing*, 76.
60. Bavinck, *Christelijke wereldbeschouwing*, 76.
61. Bavinck, *Christelijke wereldbeschouwing*, 77.

also typified clearly, Bavinck thought, in the philosophy of Karl Marx and Friedrich Engels, who seemed to make absolute judgments on capitalism while endeavoring zealously for their own utopian society, despite claiming that ethics were merely the "products of economic development."[62]

These observations led Bavinck to conclude that humanity cannot escape ideal norms. These norms, however, are encountered not by theorizing but *in* concrete reality itself. "In practice, they apprehend us in every moment," showing that "the work of the law is written on [our] hearts" in a manner no less objective than what is perceptible to the senses.[63] Concrete history, then, somehow discloses to us transcendent realities.

If in the *Christian Worldview* Bavinck addressed the modern attempts either to evacuate norms from historical phenomena or to absolutize history into some absolute standard itself, his 1908 *Philosophy of Revelation* expanded the argumentation to investigate the attempts to explain history under a "monistic doctrine of causality" and a "monistic-evolutionary conception."[64]

Bavinck began his lecture on revelation and history by surveying the ways in which scholars sought to explain history under a singular cause. Some argue that "the ultimate and principle causes of historic events" are found in the physical environment, others in "psychology and social circumstances" or natural selection. Still others, like Marx, locate it in class and economic conflict, or with Karl Lamprecht, in some folk-soul (*volkziel*)—the developments of a collective social consciousness. Likewise, attempts to explain history under a single narrative of successive phases of evolutionary development run into significant problems. The application of the term *evolution* to the discipline of history, Bavinck argued, was an instance of the Baconian fallacy of *idolum fori* (idol of the marketplace). While Bacon used this term to critique the transposing of common social terms to nature, Bavinck was arguing in the opposite direction. Those who described history in nontheistic, evolutionary ways were unduly transposing a concept that belonged to cellular organisms to the history of humanity. But whatever unity or development that can be ascribed to human history was utterly different from that of cellular organisms, for this unity was born not simply out of internal growth but also out of freedom and ethics. "Monism overlooks the difference between a biological, a psychical, and an ethical organism, just as it does that between an organism and a mechanism."[65]

---

62. Bavinck, *Christelijke wereldbeschouwing*, 79.
63. Bavinck, *Christelijke wereldbeschouwing*, 80.
64. Bavinck, *Philosophy of Revelation*, 100 and 101, respectively.
65. Bavinck, *Philosophy of Revelation*, 96.

It inadvertently reduces the richness of created life into a singular kind of uniformity, as if an explanation that works well in one sphere exhausts every other sphere.

Furthermore, the grand-narrative construal of history that neatly divided it up into categorized segments runs into another severe problem. Different historians divided history up into conflicting master narratives. Historians categorized phases of history into "Stone, Bronze and Iron Ages; between hunting, the pastoral life, agriculture, manufacture, and commerce . . . between savagery, barbarism, and civilization . . . between theological, metaphysical, and positivistic phases, etc."[66] Not only does this run against the theological and empirically verifiable unity of humanity, Bavinck thought; these narrative schemes also wrongly placed these predicates in "*succession* to one another" when "in reality" these had always occurred "*side by side.*"[67] Indeed, when the desire to explain all of history under "sharply defined periods" is relinquished, a more thorough investigation reveals that "high civilization existed even in antiquity; industry and technic, science and art, commerce and society had even then reached a high degree of development."[68] Human history does not form a neatly linear story of development that culminated in one nation or master philosophy but a rich and multifaceted maze of layered phenomena.

These observations guide Bavinck toward the conclusion that a unity that preserves this phenomena of irreducible diversity must be sought nowhere else but in a theological foundation. Preserving differentiation from a "false unity," in other words, requires that the "unity of all creation is not sought in the things themselves but transcendently . . . in a divine being, in his wisdom and power, in his will and counsel. . . . A person alone can be the root of unity in difference, of difference in unity. He alone can combine a multiplicity of ideas into unity, and he alone can realize them by his will *ad extra.*"[69] This is of great significance, especially as the historical discipline is dedicated to the study of *humanity in all of its stages and locations.* Bavinck argued that untethering the historical sciences from its Christian-theistic roots often leads to the denigration of one nation for another or the elevation of one phase of history over another, which often leads to supremacist undertones. The historian requires "revelation," precisely because in it God has revealed "a history of the world and a history

---

66. Bavinck, *Philosophy of Revelation*, 101.
67. Bavinck, *Philosophy of Revelation*, 101.
68. Bavinck, *Philosophy of Revelation*, 101.
69. Bavinck, *Philosophy of Revelation*, 111–12.

of humanity, in which all men, all peoples, nay, all creatures, are embraced, and are held together by one leading thought, by one counsel of God."[70] In short, "The unity of human nature and the human race is the presupposition of all of history, and this has been made known to us only by Christianity."[71]

Furthermore, humanity's unity and differentiation, identity and dignity, are all secured further not only by the personal counsel of God but also ultimately in their salvation procured by Christ—the "kernel" of history who himself revealed that history has a "plan, progress and aim" that evacuates the sinful tendency to exalt one's self as the historical ideal.[72] In other words, history's center, aim, progress, and end is not us but Christ—and this confession simultaneously preserves the unity-and-diversity of, and the meaningful norms within, human history. Bavinck's reasoning there leads us back to the conclusion of his *Christian Worldview*: that an "organic worldview alone answers the diversity and richness of the world"[73]—a worldview that says not only that history is governed by an archetypal divine will, but that same will itself "entered into it historically and as such lifts it up to the heights of its particular idea, to a work of God, to the genesis of the kingdom of heaven."[74]

Hence, if divine action has historically been deployed in relation to history in order to motivate supremacist imperialism, nationalist reductionism, or some form of colonialism, Bavinck deployed providence precisely to mitigate against them and to evacuate them of cogent reasons. The doctrine of divine providence points away from one's own time period and nation to the transcendent plans of God in Christ. This alone allows us to unite with other nations in solidarity and to place our hopes not in flesh and blood, or the will of man, but in God alone. It provides not merely the explanatory power that preserves unity-and-diversity but also the ethical virtue of humble patience, awaiting the Lord in faithful obedience.

CONCLUSION

In sum, when the natural or historical sciences are untethered from metaphysics and divine action, both lead to a kind of reductionism. On the one side in the natural sciences, materialism argues that what we *really* are

---

70. Bavinck, *Philosophy of Revelation*, 113.
71. Bavinck, *Philosophy of Revelation*, 113.
72. Bavinck, *Philosophy of Revelation*, 115–16.
73. Bavinck, *Christelijke wereldbeschouwing*, 97.
74. Bavinck, *Christelijke wereldbeschouwing*, 95.

or experience is just a collection of atoms—or, in today's more updated understanding, of subatomic particles, quarks, or so on. Others disregard the concrete phenomena with an appeal to some primal energy behind them. The historical sciences, likewise, ended up either propagating narratives of history that masked nationalist or imperialist agendas or reducing history into an inchoate mass of concrete particulars. That is, without the Christian doctrines of the divine counsel, which itself rests on the divine archetype's being as a unity-in-diversity, unity is often reduced into an unsatisfying and thin form of uniformity. The Christian doctrines of providence and the divine counsel preserve the richness of creation and provide a unity underneath the diversity that resists reductionisms.[75] As Bavinck argued in his treatise on Christian scholarship, the specialization and differentiation of the sciences ought to always remember that all of the scientific disciplines form a single organism: "If this unity never becomes forgotten, the splitting of science into a multitude of subjects is to be viewed as a healthy and normal phenomenon."[76]

Let me close with a few lessons from Bavinck here. The doctrine of providence and divine activity can become catch-all phrases to which Christians might flippantly appeal as an answer to the most beguiling questions. This temptation can be felt more acutely by those who hold to the classical doctrines of God's simplicity and transcendence. God does not compete with temporal acts but rather is their precondition, without whom creaturely acts are impossible.[77] So the classical theist might be tempted to respond rather flippantly: How do we know our thoughts correspond to reality? *God*. How do we know history is meaningful despite the presence of the most horrendous evils? *God*. How do we know that studying the physical processes by way of empirical investigation won't lead to the reductionist conclusion that we are nothing but matter? Well, *God*. At first glance, Bavinck's model echoes these answers and is curiously not novel. However, there are, I would suggest, features of his work that stand out

---

75. I explored Bavinck's application of divine revelation and providence to philosophy and the nature of perception in Nathaniel Gray Sutanto, "Herman Bavinck and Thomas Reid on Perception and Knowing God," *Harvard Theological Review* 111 (2018): 115–34.

76. Dutch original: "Mits deze eenheid nooit vergeten wordt, is echter splitsing der wetenschap in eene veelheid van vakken als een gezond, normaal verschijnsel te beschouwen." Bavinck, *Christelijke wetenschap*, 59.

77. Bavinck warns against reaching for a "god of the gaps": "The representation is therefore wrong that faith in the existence and providence of God finds its home exclusively in the chasms of our knowledge, so that as our investigation proceeds, we must be continually filled with anxiety and steadily lose the territory of our faith in proportion as more and more problems are solved. For the world is itself grounded in God; witness its law and order." *Philosophy of Revelation*, 72.

as worthy of emulation and are the reason that his account bears a sense of profundity missing in flippant appeals to divine action. Why is that so? I suggest that the model holds at least these four features.

First, Bavinck's method is distinctively *inductivist*. There is a sense in which he does not begin with divine providence as a way to dismiss the contemporary scholarship. Rather, readers get the sense that Christian theism is the inescapable conclusion of the successes and failures of that scholarship discovered after an inductive investigation. Secondly, then, his method was markedly *textual*. Readers receive the impression that Bavinck has covered the cutting-edge scholarship on the disciplines with which he engaged—he does not treat theology as the tyrant-queen that shouts at the other disciplines from above but rather demonstrates how she might serve them from below.[78] Third, Bavinck's method is *revelational*. There is a tone of measured confidence in the sources of divine revelation that permeates all of his writings—a confidence that God's revelation does indeed provide the fundamental resources from which and toward which all of the other disciplines are probing.[79] Finally, Bavinck's approach performs his own organic worldview. He practices what he preaches—that Christians ought to be holistic thinkers, taking all of the diverse phenomena into account while still at the same time rooting them in the triune God.

---

78. Cf. Wolter Huttinga, "'Marie Antoinette' or Mystical Depth?: Herman Bavinck on Theology as Queen of the Sciences," in *Neo-Calvinism and the French Revolution*, ed. James Eglinton and George Harinck (London: Bloomsbury, 2014), 143–54.

79. Recall Bavinck's oft-cited claim: "The world itself rests on revelation; revelation is the presupposition, the foundation, the secret, of all that exists in all its forms. The deeper science pushes its investigation, the more clearly will it discover that revelation underlies all created being." Bavinck, *Philosophy of Revelation*, 24. See also my "Neo-Calvinism on General Revelation: A Dogmatic Sketch," *International Journal of Systematic Theology* 20 (2018): 495–516.

CHAPTER 6

DIVINE AND CREATED AGENTS IN ASYMMETRIC *CONCURSUS*

A Barthian Option

W. ROSS HASTINGS

GIVEN HIS PERCEIVED EMPHASIS ON THE transcendence of God as a Reformed theologian, it may be surprising, on one account, to find Karl Barth in a study of providence that allows for the legitimacy of human freedom. His Catholic interlocutor, Hans Urs von Balthasar, famously suggested that Barth's christologically dominant anthropology reduced the rest of humanity to a mere epiphenomenon.[1] To the contrary, we hope to show that Barth's magisterial work on the doctrine of divine providence—its thoroughness, awareness of the tradition, and yet creativity—not only merits its place in this discussion but proves surprising with respect to the space it accords to both human and all created agents.[2] The focus of this paper will

---

1. Balthasar averred that "Barth ends up talking about Christ so much as the true human being that it makes it seem as if all other human beings are mere epiphenomena." Hans Urs Von Balthasar, *The Theology of Karl Barth*, E.T. Oakes, trans. (San Francisco: Ignatius Press, 1951, 1992), 243.

2. Karl Barth, Church Dogmatics III/3, §48–49, trans. G. W. Bromiley and T. F. Torrance (Peabody, MA: Hendrickson, 2010), 92. Barth's account is spoken of by David Fergusson in his recent work on providence as "one of the most sustained readings of providence" which "merits sustained attention." David Fergusson, *The Providence of God: A Polyphonic Approach* (Cambridge: Cambridge University Press, 2018), 271. See also his essay on providence in Paul Dafydd Jones and Paul T. Nimmo, eds., *The Oxford Handbook to Karl Barth* (Oxford: Oxford University Press, forthcoming). Fergusson points out the dependence of the doctrine of providence upon Barth's doctrine of the eternal election of human beings in Christ. This eternal decision of God before the foundation of the world means that his works, including providence, can only be known "on the basis of

be on the retrieval of the notion of *concursus* in Barth with a view towards a constructive consideration of this topic in the theology/science arena. Concursus refers to the freedom of God in his lordship and in his actions towards creation, a freedom which *includes* his divine "accompanying" of the creature such that the creature, too, is granted freedom of agency, with the qualification that this freedom is God's gift. God's own freedom will not only not be hampered by that of the creature but will actually prevail by it. In fact, the wider context of Barth's discussion of providence as well as the content of the passage where the *concursus* is most closely discussed make it clear that there can be no question of compromise with respect to the transcendence and sovereignty of God in this *concursus*. I suggest that Barth's doctrine may be named "asymmetric *concursus*"—"asymmetric" because God is seen to be lord in the divine *preserving, accompanying,* and *ruling* that constitute Barth's doctrine of providence;[3] "*concursus*" to connote that divine and human agency coexist or have autonomous actuality.[4] The notion of *concursus* communicates that God "does not play the part of the tyrant towards"[5] his creatures but rather "affirms and approves and recognizes and respects the autonomous actuality and therefore the autonomous activity of the creature as such."[6] We will first seek to understand and locate Barth's general theology of providence, speak briefly of its biblical underpinnings, consolidate its meaning, and then explore its traction for the theology/science interface and for various aspects of soteriology and the Christian life.

---

faith in Jesus Christ" (271) and therefore partially and tentatively at best (272). Fergusson notes that Barth follows the orthodox Reformed structure (this involves "two sets of tripartite distinctions," an initial three headings of divine preservation [*conservation*], accompanying [*concursus*] and ruling [*gubernation*], and then, within accompanying, the sequence of preceding [*praecursus*], concurring [*concursus*] and succeeding or overruling [*succursus*]) with respect to this doctrine (though in my opinion, he reimagines and revises it christologically). However, in the matter of the compatible nature of divine and creaturely freedom and the constant engagement of God with the life of the world (rather than occasional intervention, interspersed with kenotic withdrawal), Barth owes some debt to Schleiermacher (*The Christian Faith*, trans. H. R. Mackintosh and J. S Stewart [Edinburgh: T&T Clark, 1928], 723). Fergusson accurately reflects Barth when he states, "God and creatures must be considered active *subjects* (though quite unlike each other) and not objects" (274). Crucially, for Barth, "the *concursus divinus* must be filled with Christian content" (275), that is, fully Trinitarian content.

3. These are the three acts in providence that make up the three sections in paragraph 49 of the *Dogmatics*.

4. This phrase seems better than "asymmetric *compatibilism*" (which I used previously in *Echoes of Coinherence: Trinitarian Theology and Science Together* [Eugene, OR: Cascade, 2017]), even with the qualifier that this was a theological usage of compatibilism, not compatibilism as in philosophy, which means determinism.

5. Barth, *Church Dogmatics* III/3, 92.

6. Barth, *Church Dogmatics* III/3, 92.

THE NATURE AND LOCATION OF PROVIDENCE WITHIN BARTH'S THEOLOGY

THE DOCTRINE OF GOD: CREATION AND PROVIDENCE

Providence in Barth takes place against the background of his exposition of the doctrine of *creation*. Divine providence is the third item in his doctrine of creation, preceded by his discussion first of the doctrine of creation *per se* and second of the human as the creature of God. The section on providence concerns the comparison and contrast of the Creator and the creature. Creation for Barth is distinct yet inseparable from providence. *Creation* is that once-for-all act by which God called into existence something "other," ontologically distinct from himself. The act of creation was, for Barth, in accordance with the divine decree of God to be God, as Father, Son and Holy Spirit; to be God *for* his creation; and to fulfill his covenant with creation through the human, in particular through the one man, Jesus Christ. By contrast, the doctrine of *providence* describes the relationship between God and an *extant* creation. In accordance with post-Reformation dogmatics and over against medieval scholasticism, Barth chooses to locate providence within the doctrine of creation and *not* within the doctrine of God, since providence already assumes creation. To place it within the doctrine of God would be to make the being of God dependent on creation.

THE DOCTRINE OF GOD: PREDESTINATION AND PROVIDENCE

Providence, therefore, is *not* to be *equated* with predestination or election or the covenant of grace, though it flows out of these. Predestination, for Barth, is more than just one special example of providence. Providence has to do with care of a creation accomplished by the unique act of God in creating. As such it does not belong to the inner essence of the Godhead but rather is outside it and has to do with his relation to creation. There is a reason for Barth's distinction here. It arises out of his belief that predestination is "a matter primarily and properly of the eternal election of the Son of God to be the Head of his community and of all creatures."[7] The nature of the Word as eternally *incarnandus* (to be made incarnate) before he is incarnate brings correspondence to the act and being of God for Barth. Crucial to our theme of agency in God and then in creation, Barth suggests that God, described most tellingly as the One who loves in

---

7. Barth, *Church Dogmatics* III/3, 4.

freedom, eternally generated the Son in freedom to create and to become one with humanity. By creating in freedom and reconciling in freedom, he brings humanity and creation, by participation, into freedom.[8] This has to do fundamentally then with the eternal decree or election of God to be the triune God. This decree "does not therefore presuppose the act of creation and the existence of creatures, but is itself their presupposition."[9] Providence, by contrast, though it is grounded in the decree of predestination or election and covenant in Christ, presupposes the work of creation as done and the existence of the creature as given, whereas the electing decree of God to be God does not. Providence is "God's knowing, willing and acting in His relation as Creator to creature as such."[10] In sum, *providence* assumes an extant creation, which it will preserve and accompany and rule, whereas *predestination* is core to who God is as God and who he is in Jesus Christ with his covenant people as partner in the covenant of grace made by God in and with creation.[11] As such, predestination is the presupposition of history "and the basis and goal of its realization."[12] So, whereas Aquinas speaks of the election of grace as only a particular form of general providence, Barth is concerned to say that this election of God to be God is distinct from providence. The crucial consideration for Barth is that God would be no less God if the work of creation had never been done, for he is the self-existent God. Providence is the large category in Aquinas of which predestination is a part, whereas predestination or election is the large and inner category in Barth of which providence is a consequential or outer part in God. As Barth sums up the election of God, he states, "Like the doctrine of creation, and together with it, it rests on the doctrine of the *opus Dei internum*, which as such, while it is an *opus ad extra* as decree, belongs to the being of God and is identical with it, i.e. on the doctrine of God's eternal election of grace."[13]

PROVIDENCE AND CREATION: DISTINCTIONS IN RELATION

There is a profound connection and also irreducible distinction therefore between the providence of God and the act of creation. For Barth, the work

---

8. Barth, *Church Dogmatics* IV/3.1. See also *CD* IV/1, 42.
9. Barth, *Church Dogmatics* III/3, 5.
10. Barth, *Church Dogmatics* III/3, 5.
11. Barth, *Church Dogmatics* III/3, 4.
12. Barth, *Church Dogmatics* III/3, 4.
13. Barth, *Church Dogmatics* III/3, 6.

of *creation* is an unrepeatable, once-for-all act which results in a reality distinct from God, having been summoned forth from nothing; it begins in time and ends in it; the finished nature of this act of the creation of the creature means that its being includes all its "temporal developments, extensions and relationships . . . in all the individual forms of the creaturely world and in all the historical manifestations and modifications of its existence."[14] *Providence* is thus an act of God presupposed by the act of creation. Barth insists that providence "does not presuppose further acts of creation." Rather providence *guarantees* and *confirms* and *maintains* the creature and, as distinct from creation, "is God's knowledge, will and action in His relation to the creature already made by Him and not to be made again."[15] By providence God maintains the creature, but in contrast with Jonathan Edwards's occasionalism, Barth is clear that God does not continually create it afresh. The work of creation has been "done, and done perfectly, and therefore concluded,"[16] and this was clearly marked off by the sabbath in Genesis 2:1–3. Creation, as the unique act of God, is followed by the history of the *covenant,* which is "the meaning, basis and goal" of creation as the outworking of "the eternal decree of God's eternal election of grace."[17] The *telos* of this is of course a "new creation," but Barth insists this is not a repetition of the first creation, for it transcends the first creation in that it leads to a "radical alteration" and "transformation" in which its existence "is presupposed but not re-established."[18] If covenant follows creation, so does providence, "which accompanies, surrounds and sustains the history of the covenant," the fulfilment of divine predestination. However, providence is secondary to predestination and creation, as noted. It is required however, as a second history related to the first and determined by it. This is because the creaturely partner in the covenant of grace is "a mere creature needing creaturely life, and therefore its Creator, and therefore that the Creator should manifest Himself as such, as its Lord, Preserver and Governor." Barth's well-known statement is brought to bear on the matter of providence: "If the covenant is the internal basis of creation (Gen. 2), creation is the external basis of the covenant (Gen. 1)," and relevant to Genesis 1, there arises the "necessity of this second history accompanying, surrounding and sustaining the first, and therefore the

---

14. Barth, *Church Dogmatics* III/3, 6.
15. Barth, *Church Dogmatics* III/3, 6.
16. Barth, *Church Dogmatics* III/3, 6.
17. Barth, *Church Dogmatics* III/3, 6.
18. Barth, *Church Dogmatics* III/3, 6.

necessity and meaning of divine providence."[19] The covenant's history which follows from creation "needs an external basis," which is precisely "the sway of divine providence." It therefore "does not repeat or continue creation" but rather "corresponds to it in the continued life and history of the creature,"[20] proving the faithfulness of the Creator to his creation in maintaining it. This is a reality because the creature has as its head *the* human, the one man Jesus Christ; the creature is thus a partner in the covenant. But as such, the "creature continually needs Him as Creator and His action (in correspondence to the act of creation) as a confirmation of the external basis of the covenant."[21] And God is "resolved and able and ready to meet his need."[22]

In sum, for Barth, creation is what established an *incomparable beginning* of the relationship between Creator and creature, whereas providence concerns "its *continuation and history* in a series of different but comparable moments."[23] Creation stresses the *difference* between Creator and creature, whereas providence emphasizes their "*reciprocal relationship*, the address of the Creator to the existence of His creature on the one side, and the *participation* of the creature in the existence of its Creator on the other."[24] Creation takes place at a specific first time, whereas "the time of providence is the whole of the rest of time right up to its end."[25] Yet there is an undeniable relationship between them: both have to do with the relationship between Creator and creature; both reflect "the unconditional lordship of the will and Word of the Creator over the creature" in accordance with divine election.[26] The inseparable nature of the two is grounded in the faithfulness of the covenant God who could not possibly will and make the creation and then leave it to its own devices.

PROVIDENCE AND THE CREATURE

On the basis of the distinction between the Creator and creation and the "majestic freedom" of God who "confronts his creature with such transcendence,"[27] Barth rules out any concept of a demiurge as instrumental

---

19. Barth, *Church Dogmatics* III/3, 7.
20. Barth, *Church Dogmatics* III/3, 7.
21. Barth, *Church Dogmatics* III/3, 7.
22. Barth, *Church Dogmatics* III/3, 7.
23. Barth, *Church Dogmatics* III/3, 8, emphases added.
24. Barth, *Church Dogmatics* III/3, 8, emphases added.
25. Barth, *Church Dogmatics* III/3, 8.
26. Barth, *Church Dogmatics* III/3, 9.
27. Barth, *Church Dogmatics* III/3, 10.

in creation or in providence.[28] On the basis of the indissoluble relationship between creation and providence, grounded in the faithfulness of the Creator, he also therefore dismisses with strength the concept of *deism*, speaking of it as basically atheism in disguise. There can thus be no doubt about the sovereignty of God who confronts his creation with his transcendence in providence. Yet Barth draws upon Scripture (see the biblical section below) and his awareness of the nature of the triune God to affirm that "His lordship is not despotism" and that the ultimate evidence of this lies in the fact that God attained his goal in the economy of reconciliation "by God Himself becoming a creature in His Son, and in that way by His free act of obedience and suffering effecting the liberation of the creature."[29] Thus Barth confirms that God "no more wills to act alone than as the Creator He willed to be alone or as the Sustainer of the creature He affirms that He does not will to continue alone. . . . *Alongside Him there is a place for the creature.* Alongside His activity there is a place for that of the creature."[30] The "fatherly lordship" of God in providence over creation means that he "maintains its own actuality and gives it space and opportunity for its own work, for its own being in action, for its own autonomous activity."[31] In fact, Barth even dares to assert that God "*co-operates* with the creature, meaning that as He Himself works He allows the creature to work."[32] Since they are his creatures, Barth insists, "God Himself can guarantee this to His creature." It is clear here and in other places that this human and creaturely freedom is a derived one: "Just as He is active in His freedom, the creature can also be active in its freedom."[33]

Thus it is as the triune God and as the Lord of the covenant of grace that he is Lord in providence. "Grace would no longer be grace," notes Barth, "if its exercise consisted only in the elimination or suppression as an autonomous subject of the one to whom it was extended."[34] An extended quote is necessary to communicate Barth's intent at this point:

---

28. Barth, *Church Dogmatics* III/3, 10.
29. Barth, *Church Dogmatics* III/3, 93.
30. Barth, *Church Dogmatics* III/3, 92, emphasis added. Barth's notion of concursus at least leaves room for the proposal of triple agency in the matter of divine providence, that is, God, the human, and the demonic, as in Gustaf Aulén, even if the nothingness of evil and the nonbeing of the devil is prominent in Barth. Concursus, it seems to me, still allows for the dramatic dimension of providence.
31. Barth, *Church Dogmatics* III/3, 91.
32. Barth, *Church Dogmatics* III/3, 92, emphasis added.
33. Barth, *Church Dogmatics* III/3, 92.
34. Barth, *Church Dogmatics* III/3, 93.

The gracious God acts not only *towards* the creature but also—however we explain it in detail—*with* the creature. . . . If over against Him the act of the creature were autonomous only in appearance, the Lord of the covenant of grace would not be God the Creator, the true and living God. It is not in the might of an autocrat but in the *power of fatherly majesty* that God Himself, the living God, accompanies the creature, doing all things, and yet not doing them without the creature, but working with the creature.[35]

When it comes to speaking of the dynamics of the relationship of the providence of God to the creature, Barth speaks of it as one of *participation* in the existence or life of the Creator.[36] This is explained in terms of the coexistence of the creature with the Creator: "God the Creator has associated himself with His creature as such as the Lord of its history, and is faithful to it as such." He goes on to say that "God the Creator co-exists with His creature and so his creature exists under the presupposition, and its implied conditions, of the co-existence of its Creator."[37] Such is the closeness of the relationship between the creature and its coexistent Creator that "he causes the history of the creature to be the history of His own glory."[38] Thus, again, this is not at the expense of the freedom and sovereignty of God in his lordship over creation, for as Barth assures us, "The Lord is never absent, passive, non-responsible or impotent, but always present, active, responsible and omnipotent." He is "always holding the initiative," not intervening occasionally when needed.[39] And the coexistent creature, despite being coexistent, is always distinct from him. In sum, "The majestic freedom of the Creator in face of His creature" is that which guarantees his faithfulness and constancy with "which He is over and with it."[40] However, this works in the other direction too. The creature—and here I extrapolate Barth faithfully, I trust—the electron, the quark, the atom, and the paramecium all exist as such in dependence on their Creator, yet distinct from their Creator and in possession of their own real identity and agency.

But what is the biblical evidence for such a view? And how does Barth's asymmetric *concursus* view differ from other versions of the relation between

---

35. Barth, *Church Dogmatics* III/3, 93, emphasis added.
36. Barth, *Church Dogmatics* III/3, 8, emphases added.
37. Barth, *Church Dogmatics* III/3, 12.
38. Barth, *Church Dogmatics* III/3, 12.
39. Barth's is thus a noninterventionist account of the engagement of God with creation.
40. Barth, *Church Dogmatics* III/3, 13.

divine and creaturely agency in the tradition? What are the possible misconceptions of this proposal, and what are some applications that make it
useful in considering aspects of theology and the theology/science interface,
for example?

BIBLICAL UNDERPINNINGS

In this and most regards, Barth shows himself to be first and foremost a
biblical theologian. He is deeply immersed in the biblical text as the final
authority for his theology of providence and of *concursus* in particular. By
way of a foundation, for example, Barth goes back to Genesis 22. He asserts
that the term *providence* is actually derived from verse 14, where Abraham
calls the place God had prevented him from sacrificing his son and provided
a ram *Jehovah Jireh*, or *Deus providebit* in Latin—"the Lord will provide."
Clarity on the word *provide*, which is more like "to see about" rather than
just "to see," leads Barth to say that providence is more than just foreknowledge. He affirms that it "is an active and selective predetermining,
preparing and procuring of a lamb to be offered instead of Isaac. God 'sees
to' this burnt offering for Abraham." A unity of divine knowing, willing
and acting is in mind.[41] Providence is thus God's seeing ahead, providing
for, and so caring for his world, his humanity, and his church. Expressed
differently, "he sees to that which in their earthly lot is necessary and good
and therefore planned and designed for them, according to his wisdom
and resolve"[42] so that they fulfil his purpose for them and reveal his glory
through them.

On the agency of the Son in providence, Barth comments also on John
5:17, which equates the meaning and goal of the work of God the Father
in the work of God the Son. There Jesus says, "My Father is always at his
work to this very day, and I too am working"[43] (this is also the paradigm
for *concursus*). He speaks also of Colossians 1:17 ("in him all things hold
together"), which he thinks some of his Reformed predecessors paid insufficient attention to. He insists that "all things not only have their existence
(v.16) but their consistence, their order and continued existence . . . in the
Son."[44] Hebrews 1:3 is expounded in the same way. It expresses clearly that
the Son is "upholding all things by the word of his power" (KJV) and that

---

41. Barth, *Church Dogmatics* III/3, 3–4.
42. Barth, *Church Dogmatics* III/3, 4.
43. Barth, *Church Dogmatics* III/3, 34.
44. Barth, *Church Dogmatics* III/3, 34.

he is the same One who, when "he had by himself purged our sins, sat down on the right hand of the Majesty on high" (KJV). This means that "He sits at the place from which heaven and earth are ruled and all power has its origin and centre, not as a passive spectator, but as the epitome of the wisdom, will and power of the Father" and as the source of the Spirit of life "without which no creature can live and move."[45]

Barth also looks to a number of Scriptures in support of his view that providence, although it honors the lordship of God, particularly involves his fatherly "accompanying" through the agency of the Word and the Spirit, thus concomitantly preserving the freedom and integrity of the creature. For example, Barth affirms the interpretation of continental theologian P. van Mastricht's exegesis of the phrase in Romans 11:36, "*di' autou . . . ta panta*" ("through Him . . . are all things") when he expressed that "the *dia* did not define God as the *causa instrumentalis* but indicated the *ipsa operatio* (the very or actual working) of Father, Son and Holy Spirit as it takes place in the work of providence."[46] Philippians 2:12–13, "Continue to work out your salvation with fear and trembling, for it is God who works in you to will and to act in order to fulfill his good purpose," is a very important text for Barth also, as will become evident.[47]

BARTH'S *CONCURSUS* VIEW IN THE TRADITION

Surmising from his study of the relevant scriptures that he is "on the right track" in employing the concept of "accompanying," Barth nevertheless acknowledges the difficulty for the older Reformed theologians, and even himself, of presenting this relation "clearly in all the individuality in which it is revealed in Scripture."[48] He acknowledges his view might lead to many "misleading conceptions." In spelling out these various misconceptions, he shows awareness of the views of others in the tradition. The first is "an antithesis between an intrinsically unmoved and passive God, and an unmoved order of creation"; the second is an antithesis between a living, active, and working God and an order of creation which is moved by Him from without—and therefore passively and without any activity on its own

---

45. Barth, *Church Dogmatics* III/3, 34.

46. Barth, *Church Dogmatics* III/3, 95. The reference to P. van Mastricht is to *Theoretico-Practica Theologia*, 3 vols. (Gerardum Mutendam, 1698), 3:10.1.

47. The idea of asymmetric *concursus* is reflected in many other texts: Matt 10:29; Ps 127:1; Acts 17:27; Isa 26:12; Jer 10:23; Gen 45:8; various proverbs (Prov 16:1, 33; 19:21; 21:1); and Job 38–41.

48. Barth, *Church Dogmatics* III/3, 95.

account; third, the concept of "divine action which consists in invention, establishing and initiating of a *perpetuum mobile* which would have its own limit on the limit of creaturely action, which would make creaturely action possible, and then hand over the control to it, leaving it to run its course"; and last, one could conceive of "an identity between the divine and creaturely action, of the undifferentiated existence of a God-world, which in all its elements and movements might be interpreted equally well as divine or not divine, with a constant amphibole of concepts."[49] All of these possibilities have to be negated, Barth insists, as supported by Scripture and the "older theologians" (post-Reformation, including Turretini and van Mastricht).[50] Over against the opinion that *concursus* is present only in the Lutheran tradition, Barth shows it to be present within the theology of the Reformed dogmaticians, and that whereas the Lutheran form of *concursus* was more like *succursus* (being helped), the Reformed emphasized the absolute priority of divine over human activity, thus leading to the opposite error of *praecursus* (preceded). However, in general it may be said of the Reformed that whilst they laid emphasis on the *maior Dei gloria* in accordance with the Scriptures (e.g. Job 38–41), Barth notes that they did give full credence to the *minor gloria creaturae* as explicitly affirmed in the same Scriptures. Both traditions (Lutheran and Reformed) employed the *causal* concept arising from the philosophy of Aristotle and the theology of Aquinas. The Creator is the first cause (*causa prima*), the uncaused one (*causa sui*) who is "the basis and starting point of the whole causal series." On this account, "The creature is also *causa*, but as posited by God. God is *causa causans* whereas the creature *causa causata* in a two-fold sense—it is a cause by participation in the divine cause, and by its connection with other creatures. The divine causation takes place within the causation of the creature."[51] This Thomistic approach undergirded the dogmatics of both the Reformed and Lutheran theologians and Barth finds fault with it. Materially, as opposed to formally, "it missed completely the relationship between creation and covenant of grace. In its whole doctrine of providence it spoke abstractly not only of the general control of God over and with the creature, but of the control of a general and in some sense neutral and featureless God, an Absolute." It spoke also "abstractly of a neutral and featureless creature." It also "separated between world history

---

49. Barth, *Church Dogmatics* III/3, 95–96.
50. Barth, *Church Dogmatics* III/3, 96.
51. Barth, *Church Dogmatics* III/3, 99.

and salvation history." Stridently Barth remarks that the primary causation and secondary causation paradigm "lacked the Christian content without whose express indication that well-developed abstraction may well be informed by a dynamic and teleology which are nothing whatever to do with the exposition of the message of the Bible."[52]

Barth does, however, lay out some conditions on which the causation scheme can legitimately be applied to the doctrine of *concursus*. These are, briefly, as follows: (1) "cause" (*causa*) must not be regarded as if effective automatically, since this can only be applied to God and not to the creature or in science;[53] (2) in God and the creature we do not have two "things," or objects capable of being examined, recognized, analyzed, and defined, since neither God nor the creature is cause in this sense. Rather, in accordance with orthodoxy and theological realism, both God and creature must be "self-revealed."[54] (3) It must be understood that cause is not "a master-concept to which both God and the creature are subject, nor is it a common denominator to which they may both be reduced," as if *causa* is a genus and divine and creaturely *causa* can then be considered as "species."[55] Given that we are dealing with active subjects, the divine and creaturely subjects are "not merely not alike, but subjects which in their absolute antithesis cannot even be compared."[56] In fact, the work of God "takes the form of an absolute positing" which can never be true of the creature, who is always subject to "conditioning, determining and altering" of what is already there. There *is a correspondence* by way of analogy, which Barth calls *analogia operationis*, which parallels the concept of *analogia relationis*,[57] the idea that grace is always given rather than a given (as it is in the *analogia entis*) and that all correspondence is a consequence of the incarnation (point 5 below). Ultimately it is the absolute unlikeness of the divine *subject* and the creaturely *subject* that gives Barth concern about the use of primary and secondary causation within *concursus*. (4) Built on conditions (1)–(3), it must not be spoken of "with either the intention or the consequence that *theology* should be turned into *philosophy* . . . projecting a kind of total scheme of things." For, says Barth, when "theology is guilty of such a defection it is wilfully entangling its tenets in the contradictions and uncertainties of problems which are alien

---

52. Barth, *Church Dogmatics* III/3, 100.
53. Barth, *Church Dogmatics* III/3, 101.
54. Barth, *Church Dogmatics* III/3, 101–2.
55. Barth, *Church Dogmatics* III/3, 102.
56. Barth, *Church Dogmatics* III/3, 102.
57. Barth, *Church Dogmatics* III/3, 103.

to it," and so "it runs the risk of speaking about what are really two quite different quantities when it uses the titles God and the creature, and the encumbrance with another and alien task necessarily means that its own work suffers."[58] Barth expresses himself further along in this section with conviction in this regard: "And in all these things what is needed is a radical re-thinking of the whole matter. Firstly we have to drop the ordinary but harmful conception of cause, operation and effect. Then, when we know who God is and what He wills and how He works, we have to take it up again, but giving to it a new force and application in which we do not look back to what are at root godless notions of causality."[59] (5) There must be a clear connection between the first article of the creed and the second: "If the causal concept is to be applied legitimately, its content and interpretation must be determined by the fact that what it describes is the operation of the Father of Jesus Christ in relation to that of the creature"; in other words it is the reality that according to God's love and electing grace God "willed to become a creature . . . in order to be its Saviour." In other words, *the causal joint between divine causation and creaturely causation is in the incarnation of the Son.* He adds that "this same God accepts the creature even apart from the history of the covenant and its fulfilment . . . and He co-operates with it, preceding, accompanying and following all its being and activity, so that all the activity of the creature is primarily and simultaneously and subsequently His own activity, and therefore a part of the actualisation of His own will revealed and triumphant in Jesus Christ."[60] The *causa prima* thus *accompanies* the *causa secondae* in grace even before the incarnation and the new creation, for His grace precedes both, and the creation will be taken up into the new creation, which it already approximates.[61]

The upshot of this is that accompanying or *concursus* is not at the expense of the otherness and majesty of God and the power, which is to love in freedom: "It is because it is eternal love that the power of the divine operation is superior to all other powers, and the knowledge of it is not open to discussion."[62] In agreement with H. Heidegger and Heppe, Barth sums this up as follows: "Even as He gives Himself to this relationship to the creature, God is still its Lord."[63] Barth goes on to clarify what the *concursus*

58. Barth, *Church Dogmatics* III/3, 104–105.
59. Barth, *Church Dogmatics* III/3, 105.
60. Barth, *Church Dogmatics* III/3, 118.
61. Barth, *Church Dogmatics* III/3, 105.
62. Barth, *Church Dogmatics* III/3, 109.
63. Barth, *Church Dogmatics* III/3, 110.

divinus means. It must involve "God" as the triune God, the "will of God" as His "fatherly good-will," and "the work of God" as his "execution in history of the covenant of grace upon the basis of the decree of grace, with its fulfilment in the sacrifice of His Son and its confirmation in the work of the Holy Spirit awakening to faith and obedience: the work which as such is His work of power in the whole created sphere, above and in and before and with and after all creaturely activity; the work in virtue of which all creaturely activity is completely under his control and subject to Him."[64] It involves the activity of God which *precedes* the creature (*praecurrit*), or divine foreordination, and the activity of God which *accompanies* (*concurrit*) the creature (though this is one indivisible operation from God's perspective) so that "the *concursus divinus* is a *concursus simultaneous*."[65] Yet the "unconditional lordship of God" does not mean that the freedom of creaturely activity is "jeopardised or suppressed, but rather that it is confirmed in all its particularity and variety."[66] Rather God's action and the creature's are seen as a "single action,"[67] whilst at the same time it is "manifold, and therefore not uniform, monotonous and undifferentiated."[68] Even before the existence of the creature, Barth insists, it is more manifold due to the operation of "the Creator of all things, who knows not only the things themselves but all the potentialities intended for them, who is also free to give them new potentialities, i.e. those hitherto concealed both from the things themselves and from those who observe them." In other words, the power of the Creator is differentiated even as it is single in a manner that reflects the triune nature of God; God's simplicity is determined by his revealed richness "in his threefold being."[69]

But what of the actual "How?" question? What is the causal joint, exactly? How does this actually work? Barth acknowledges mystery and the difficulty of this question yet refuses to be an "ignoramus"[70] on it! Here is a summation of his solution:

> And now we can and must give the simple positive answer that the operation of God is his utterance to all creatures of the Word of God which

---

64. Barth, *Church Dogmatics* III/3, 117.
65. Barth, *Church Dogmatics* III/3, 132.
66. Barth, *Church Dogmatics* III/3, 146. The engagement of God *always* in his creation and yet its freedom to be seems to overcome interventionism and deism.
67. Barth, *Church Dogmatics* III/3, 132.
68. Barth, *Church Dogmatics* III/3, 137.
69. Barth, *Church Dogmatics* III/3, 138.
70. Barth, *Church Dogmatics* III/3, 139.

has all the force and wisdom and goodness of his Holy Spirit. Or, to put it another way, the operation of God is His moving of all creatures by the force and wisdom and goodness which are His Holy Spirit, the Spirit of his Word. The divine operation is, therefore, a fatherly operation.[71]

In other words, the furthest we can go is the answer given by divine revelation, which is that the *concursus* happens in a Trinitarian way, guided by the Father and enacted by the agency of the two hands of the Father—the Word which is given to the creature and the Spirit. The "mystery of His operation" that is acknowledged by Barth "is . . . safeguarded when we think of it as Word and Spirit."[72] "For," says Barth, "it is only in the divine inscrutability that it can be revealed to us how in His covenant of grace God calls, illumines, justifies and sanctifies man by His Word and Spirit, and it is in this inscrutability that we believe and recognize the whole activity of God as the activity of the Word and Spirit of God."[73] The omnipotence of the Word and the omniscience of His Holy Spirit lend character to the work of God in providence and *concursus* in particular, such that what is done is "unconditional and irresistible work."[74] The "flight into synergism" is thus averted. Yet the Word and the Spirit do their work in a manner that does "not prejudice the autonomy, the freedom, the responsibility, the individual being and life and activity of the creature, or the genuineness of its own activity, but confirms and indeed establishes them." In other words, "The One who rules by His Word and Spirit . . . takes His creature seriously."[75] Beyond these revealed Trinitarian assertions, Barth cannot go intellectually. In fact, he asserts that "the basic condition for a perception and understanding" is "spiritual" rather than intellectual.[76] In other words, it is the overcoming of the fear complex on behalf of the creature that assumes God is alien to and an enemy of the creature, or that assumes that he wishes to absorb or assimilate the creature, which leads the creature to assert "a sphere marked off from God" and to declare independence from God. Rather, Barth affirms, the creature is never more itself and never freer than when it lives in glad communion and *concursus* with the triune God who has made himself known to us.

---

71. Barth, *Church Dogmatics* III/3, 142.
72. Barth, *Church Dogmatics* III/3, 144.
73. Barth, *Church Dogmatics* III/3, 144.
74. Barth, *Church Dogmatics* III/3, 144.
75. Barth, *Church Dogmatics* III/3, 144.
76. Barth, *Church Dogmatics* III/3, 146.

MISCONCEPTIONS OF BARTH'S CONCURSUS VIEW

Beyond misconceptions that might arise in the tradition, two further mis-conceptions of *Barth's concursus* are as follows: (1) that it might be assumed that the human or created agent might be seen to be absolutely autonomous rather than having a derived autonomy. Barth is crystal clear, as already stated, that the sovereignty of the transcendent God is not compromised by his proposal. He states the clear priority of the "free God" who "is always a step in advance of the free creature," affirming that "the free creature does go of itself" but that "it can and does only go the same way as the free God" in the fulfilment of his covenant purposes. (2) It might be seen as some form of synergism. Barth insists in a number of places in this dis-course that the creature participates in the existence and life of God but that there is a clear ontological remove between God and created beings. It is a coexistence of *koinōnia*, not a Platonic version of substantial participation (often associated with *methexis*). And such participation is best described not by the category of synergism since Barth's proposal is that God acts and in his acting the creature acts, yet each has its own autonomy, albeit that of the human or created agent is a derived one.

APPLICATIONS OF BARTH'S CONCURSUS VIEW
CAUSATION
It seems to me that Barth has offered an alternative to deism; to its polar opposite, occasionalism (Jonathan Edwards), in which God is the primary cause of absolutely everything; and even to the "secondary causation" view of Aquinas. This is Barth's evangelical, biblical modification: one in which freedom is given to the creation, such that matter can actually participate in the life of God in Christ in a *concursus* way. I think that as such, Barth leaves room for the notion that it can also actually participate in its own development. That is, the Son and the Spirit are present and active in lovingly engaged ways yet not with any confusion of the divine and the elemental, and not in a manner that is coercive. On this view, that of asymmetric *concursus*, creation has a participatory freedom, but not one in which divine and created existence are blurred in neo-Platonic ways. Human persons and matter are never more themselves than when they exist in the freedom of participation in the life of God.

This also avoids causal determinism, which runs into the difficulty that it makes God the efficient cause of evil. It is a participational *concursus* in which there is affirmation of the providence of God and his ultimate sovereignty but also the allowance of space for human creatures, who have sufficient agency to be responsible for their actions, and for nonhuman creatures, which have a participational freedom also. The mechanisms by which this may be possible are approached by Barth, as we shall see, though not all mystery is resolved.[77] On the one hand, one is tempted to rest with a statement like that of seventeenth-century continental Reformed theologian Francis Turretini, who proposed that careful study of Scripture leads to two indisputable conclusions, both of which may be affirmed and held in tension:

> That God on the one hand by his providence not only decreed, but most certainly secures, the event of all things, whether free or contingent; on the other hand, however, man is always free in acting and many effects are contingent. Although I cannot understand how these can be mutually connected together, yet (on account of ignorance of the mode) the thing itself is (which is certain from another source, i.e., from the Word) not either to be called in question or wholly denied.[78]

On the other hand, Barth does in his corpus demonstrate the meaning of *concursus* in two key aspects of his theology, and he also speaks of a nonmechanistic mechanism by which this occurs. The first illustration is his Cyrilline view of the incarnation, and the second is his model for understanding divine-human action. He also avoids the pitfalls of open theism, which challenges the aseity and sovereignty of God, and process thought, which brings the further challenge of incipient monism.

The incarnate person of Jesus Christ in two natures existing and working together in a compatible way is a first window in Barth's theology of asymmetric *concursus*. In orthodox fashion, the two natures of Christ operated in a compatible way that was true to the fully divine and fully human natures of Christ. Barth insists that these were compatible even

---

77. Invoking "mystery" does not mean ceasing to seek knowledge reverently. It is mysterious in the sense that Scripture does not provide a mechanical solution as to how divine sovereignty and human freedom and that of created agents can be compatible. Views include theological determinism (called "compatibilism" in a philosophical sense); Molinism (see William Lane Craig, *The Only Wise God: The Compatibility of Divine Foreknowledge and Human Freedom* [Grand Rapids: Baker, 1987]—Craig's version of Molinism acknowledges the category of "middle knowledge," that is, his knowledge of the counterfactuals of creaturely freedom); and philosophical Arminianism. For a helpful presentation of the latter two views, see Jonathan Rutledge, "Philosophical Arminianism: Epistemic Conditionals of Creaturely Freedom," a paper presented at the Logos Institute, University of St. Andrews, Scotland, November 24, 2016.

78. Francis Turretini, *Institutes of Elenctic Theology*, ed. James T. Dennison, trans. George Musgrave Giger, 3 vols. (Phillipsburg: P&R, 1997), 1:512.

though the divine person and nature has a logical priority. He draws upon insights from Cyril of Alexandria that although the human nature of Jesus was fully human, there is a precedence to the divine person. Therefore the divine nature (and person) assumes the human nature, and not the other way around. The divine person in his divine nature is the giver and the human the receiver. The Son remains Lord as he assumes humanity. The role of the Holy Spirit as the mediator of the communion of the two natures also provides a model for how God by the Spirit accompanies creation. It has been well said, in sum, that "Jesus Christ is the ultimate revelation not only of the nature of God the Creator but also of *how* God the Creator relates to the created order."[79]

A second illustrative arena for *concursus* in Barth's theology has to do with the relationship between divine and human action, which actually mirrors his view of the hypostatic union of the divine and human natures of Christ. For Barth, "where God acts, there we are seen to act—precisely in receiving."[80] Barth is always careful to say that the lordship of God prevails in this *concursus*. For example, in his theological anthropology Barth insists that the best news of the Gospel is the election of the triune God to create and to be *for* humanity, to become one with humanity in Christ. The nature of humanity as defined first by this election, and *not merely evolutionary theory*, is what gives humanity the capacity to engage in scholarship and science and music as image bearers of the God of wisdom, knowledge, creativity, and beauty.

In keeping with this, there is again both an assertion of the compatibilism of divine and human action and a qualification. With respect to how human activity works within divine action in the Christian life, that is, the move from the indicative to the imperative, Barth stressed that this was "a perilous step."[81] Why so? Because when we raise the question of our own human activity, "we are only too readily inclined to turn things upside down . . . and to answer the question about the Christian life in a way that views the matter equilaterally: God has done something for us, now it is up to us to do something for him."[82] Barth's sketch of the Christian life is, in other words, shaped by a strong assertion that "the two sides in the

---

79. Andrew Torrance and Tom McCall, eds., *Christ and the Created Order: Perspectives from Theology, Philosophy, and Science* (Grand Rapids: Zondervan, 2018), back cover.

80. This is the description of Barth's thought in this regard by his disciple Eberhard Jüngel, "Gospel and Law: The Relationship of Dogmatics to Ethics," in *Karl Barth: A Theological Legacy*, trans. G. E. Paul (Philadelphia: Westminster), 105–26.

81. Karl Barth, *The Christian Life* (London: SCM, 1930), 16.

82. Barth, *Christian Life*, 26.

relationship are not on [sic] an equality."[83] *But alongside this there is another affirmation: our nonequality to God does not signify our obliteration.* In fact, we come to see that Barth's anthropology, linked as it is fundamentally to the one, true human—that is, his "the-anthropology"—rather than obliterating humanity is in fact a glorious anthropology. Humanity is more human, and the human self most truly itself in Christ. When understood correctly,[84] Barth will in fact be seen ironically to have a loftier view of the human than that of others in the Reformed heritage.

Similarly, we may assume, creation as the *trace* of God rather than his *image*—as in humans, who are in relation to God and distinct from God— has its own freedom and yet is not independent of God. Barth hints at this when he states that "freedom is given to man as every other creature is given its peculiar gift by God."[85] Every creature, from atom to animal, is imbued with divine freedom, and we may assume that it carries within it, by grace and in participation with Christ, its own identity and some creative power, derived and contingent though it may be. We may extrapolate Barth's view of providence to the question of the origin of the cosmos and humanity.

CREATION BY EVOLUTION?

Barth states that "we must not interpret providence as *continuata creatio*, but as *continuatio creationis*." That is, for Barth, whatever happens after the initial act of creation is providence, not continuation of creation or *creatio continua*. He grounds this in Genesis 2, where verses 1–3 "demand a break" between creation and providence whilst allowing for continuity. Barth means that providence is not "unceasing creation," but it is in "continuity with creation"—that is, it is a consequence of the creation act of the God who loves his creation and will see it through. It is clear elsewhere that Barth acknowledged that the theory of evolution was probably the means by which God created.[86] So how would he see the emergence of the cosmos from the Big Bang onward (if indeed what is operative in the

---

83. Barth, *Christian Life*, 26.

84. Misconceptions concerning Barth's anthropology have been corrected in the works of various Barth scholars, such as John Webster, Bruce McCormack, George Hunsinger, Nigel Biggar, Joseph L. Mangina, and W. Krötke.

85. Barth, *Church Dogmatics* III/2, 194.

86. In his letter to grandniece Christine, Barth wrote, "Has no one explained to you in your seminar that one can as little compare the biblical creation story with a scientific theory like that of evolution as one can compare, shall we say, an organ and a vacuum-cleaner—that there can be as little question of harmony between them as of contradiction? The creation story is a witness to the beginning or becoming of all reality distinct from God in the light of God's later acts and words relating to his people Israel—naturally in the form of a saga or poem. The theory of evolution is an attempt to explain the same reality in its inner nexus—naturally in the form of a scientific

Big Bang is in fact the first energetic particle created *ex nihilo*), and how does he view the process by which new life forms emerge throughout the evolutionary development of life on earth? Are they the product of creation or providence? Though he does contend that theology is a legitimate science,[87] Barth was not particularly interested in aligning his theology with science,[88] though his disciple T. F. Torrance showed much more interest in this, an interest which Barth did not censure.[89] Barth *might* say that all creation from the first atom onward was all a part of creation and that each planet and each species were all created gradually. He might also say that each thing and person in its final existence as a species was both the result of God's creation in a way that fulfilled creation's *telos* under the covenant of grace and then was the subject of his "accompanying" providence throughout the course of its existence. And importantly, this was

---

hypothesis." Karl Barth, *Letters: 1961–1968*, trans. Geoffrey Bromiley (Grand Rapids: Eerdmans, 1980), 184.

87. See H. Scholz, "Wie ist eine evangelische Theologie als Wissenschaft möglich?" *Zwischen den Zeiten* 9 (1931): 8–35, reprinted in G. Sauter, ed., *Theologie als Wissenschaft* (Münich: Chr. Kaiser, 1971), 221–64. Barth engaged with Scholz to insist that the foundation of what it means to be "science" involves one criterion only, that *of the adequacy of a discipline to its subject-matter*. This is expressed in the Greek term, *kata phusin*: according to the subject matter or object.

88. David Fergusson expresses the reality that "Barth has little interest in seeking a philosophy of divine action or a theory of the causal joint which attempts to show the compatibility of scientific and theological explanation . . . The *concursus* is based on confession rather than explanation—the confessing of Jesus Christ as the act of God as this reaches us through the Word and Spirit. Apart from this, the 'how?' of God's action is incomprehensible." Fergusson, *Providence of God*, 277. Yet Fergusson concludes that what is assumed in Barth's account is the Reformed notion that "every event" is "accompanied and ruled by God," and that this is the "fundamental problem of Barth's account" (277). He insists that "while the Christological determinism of his position offers a happier construction of God's intentions, the affirmation of a comprehensive set of divine volitions merely revives the anxieties that accompanied the older (Reformed) position." A view of *concursus* in which there is still on God's part a "meticulous causing of everything that happens," a "willing of each and every event," without allowance for the "general permission" (277) of God, prevents Barth's view from advancing the discussion. The expression of the freedom of the creature in Barth surely argues otherwise, as does the allowance for mystery in reconciling this with the divine freedom.

89. Torrance largely reflects Barth in his doctrine of providence. Torrance does not see providence as exercised from afar in a dualistic separation from the world, but in Jesus Christ, and by the Spirit, God is "personally and directly present and active in creation, even in its fallenness." Elmer M. Colyer, *How to Read T. F. Torrance* (Eugene, OR: Wipf & Stock, 2007), 166, reflecting T. F. Torrance, *The Christian Doctrine of God* (London: T&T Clark, 2016), 221–22. Because of this God is not deistically abandoning it but bearing its suffering, and "ruling over all things without detracting from their reality or impairing their contingent nature, freedom or order, yet in such a way that in his absolute freedom he makes everything to serve his ultimate purpose of love and fellowship with himself" (Torrance, *Christian Doctrine of God*, 224). Torrance is in fact convinced that "providential power and activity cannot be construed in logical-causal or deterministic categories, but only in terms of the inexplicable power and activity of the immediate personal presence and operation of God" (Colyer, *How to Read T. F. Torrance*, 166). It is the virgin birth and resurrection of Christ that must form our categories for understanding the working of God in creation. How this works out *exactly* is "incomprehensible mystery," just as creation *ex nihilo* is mystery, comprehensible only as far as the revelation of the activity of God in Jesus Christ (Torrance, *Christian Doctrine of God*, 223). This resonates with the asymmetric *concursus* viewpoint.

divine governance over against the Stoic idea of fate and over against the Epicurean doctrine of chance.[90]

If Barth's differentiation of creation and providence possibly poses a challenge for an evolutionary view of creation, his understanding of the *mode* of providence does serve the process of Big Bang theory and evolution quite well. That is, his view of providence as asymmetric *concursus*, including the "accompanying" of creation by the triune God through the Spirit, gives creaturely agents—from quarks to atoms to amoebas to elephants—their own real existence and "thisness," their own real agency. Indeed it gives them their own real fecundity, or capacity for complexity, yet under a telos guided by the unconditional and irresistible lordship of God. Scientist theologians have applied this *concursus* view without using the term. John Polkinghorne, for example, has referenced the development of the theory of evolution as an arena in which awareness of the freedom and agency of creation became apparent.[91] The impulse to preserve the particularity and variety and relative freedom of the creature in Barth's view of "accompanying" echoes the early Franciscan notion of *haeccitas*, which was then developed by Duns Scotus. This awareness of the irreducible uniqueness and particularity of things, that is, the "thisness" (*haeccitas*) of things,[92] was important to the development of science. And for Barth, the lordship of God enacted by the gracious work of the Word and the Spirit meant "there is no reason whatever why the activity of the creature should be destroyed or suppressed by His omnipotent operation."[93] The bondage of the creature to the Word and the Spirit was precisely its "true freedom."

PASTORAL AND DOCTRINAL APPLICATIONS

Though space prevents a full treatment of this, the way in which Barth works out his doctrine of providence for the life and practices of the Christian are edifying and pastorally fruitful. He finds no room for anxiety "in face of the omnipotence of the Word and the omnipotence of the

---

90. Barth, *Church Dogmatics* III/3, 162. See Barth's discussion of the Lutheran opposition to chance and the Calvinist opposition to fate.

91. Space does not permit a fuller description of Polkinghorne's thought on causation and his move from a "top-down information" model to the invocation of kenosis in the giving by God of space to creation. For more on this see Hastings, *Echoes of Coinherence: Trinitarian Theology and Science Together* (Eugene, OR: Cascade, 2017).

92. John Duns Scotus, *Ordinatio* 2.3.1.2n48.

93. Barth, *Church Dogmatics* III/3, 150.

Spirit."[94] The Spirit's role in this is particularly emphatic. Suffice it to say that the freedom of the creature in covenant and within the divine *concursus* is not only guaranteed in the action of the Word, Jesus Christ, but through the mystery of the Spirit's mediation. The Spirit is the particular person in the Trinity who originates and effects all events in history by *accompanying* them.[95] The implications of the trinitarian nature of providence for prayer in Barth's work has been ably expounded by both James Torrance[96] and more recently by C. C. Green[97] in his *Doxological Theology*. Prayer on this account becomes *gift* before it is *task*, a participation in the Spirit's communion on our behalf—a participation in the high priestly intercession of the Son from and to the Father. Green draws attention to the *pneumatic* nature of providence; the Spirit and the covenantal (human) partner mysteriously "condition" each other. It is the Spirit who makes this "conditioning" possible on each side, and the irreducible mystery of providential causality is thus grounded in the life of the triune God. He is the *free* Holy Spirit, and therefore his work is sovereign and mysterious from a human perspective.[98] Yet this pneumatic reality in *concursus* allows Barth to speak of a causality that is not "mechanical."[99] The Spirit is both the effect of the action of Christ in providence and at the same time the conditioning of his partner, the creature. Christ's providential action is "causal" because it is a "conditioning" of the creature, but this is not "mechanical" but rather a *covenantal* conditioning. Barth's soteriology qualifies his account of the appropriate use of causal terminology, and yet *divine and human agents do have a real impact on each other* precisely due to this soteriological context (Phil 2:12–13). God may even be said to be "determined" by the creature in the act of prayer. This happens, furthermore, because God allows this exchange to occur mysteriously in the Spirit. The Holy Spirit is the "Lord of our hearing" in such a way that "no method" can approach him on the side of the creature.[100]

---

94. Barth, *Church Dogmatics* III/3, 150.

95. Barth writes a whole section on the implications of this providence for the Christian in the Christian life, which is beyond our scope here. See Barth, *Church Dogmatics* III/3, 239–88.

96. James B. Torrance, *Worship, Community and the Triune God of Grace* (Downers Grove, IL: InterVarsity Press, 1996).

97. C. C. Green, *Doxological Theology: Karl Barth on Divine Providence, Evil, and the Angels* (London: T&T Clark, 2011), 88, referring to Barth, *Church Dogmatics* III/3, 102.

98. Barth, *Church Dogmatics* III/3, 88.

99. Green, *Doxological Theology*, 89, reflecting on Barth, *Church Dogmatics* III/3, 101–2. See also G. Hunsinger, *How to Read Karl Barth* (Oxford: Oxford University Press, 1993), 111–12.

100. Green, *Doxological Theology*, 89, reflecting on Barth, *Church Dogmatics* III/3, 101–2.

CHAPTER 7

DIVINE PROVIDENCE
A Distorted Theology of History?

BRENDA DEEN SCHILDGEN

THIS ESSAY TAKES A LONG LOOK at the concept of providence, a long-used but slippery term at best, particularly when adopted by political and historical theory. Examining its uses in what I will call, for the sake of convenience, the Catholic or Roman tradition, we will start with the Bible and early Christianity from Lactantius (240–320 CE) and Eusebius (263–339 CE) to Augustine (354–430 CE) and Orosius (c.375–c.418 CE) through to Thomas Aquinas's discussion of providence. In the final section, I will touch on some modern versions of the concept of providential history in what I would label a distorted theology of history.

Many texts in the Hebrew Bible attribute Israel's successful claiming of lands to the patronage of the God of the Hebrews. Redacted into its canonical form in exile, the Hebrew Bible, that is the Septuagint or the Masoretic Bible,[1] tells the history of a people from the position of exile and even political abjection. The visionary mode of the prophets, who seek to understand loss of homeland (Ezekiel especially), creates a critical distance from political and religious assumptions that in turn questions a divinely sanctioned ideology of the saeculum. A similar observation can be made about Augustine, who, probing the rise of the Roman Empire and its pending end, in the *City of God* systematically opposes humility before

---

1. Brevard S. Childs, *Old Testament Theology in a Canonical Context* (Philadelphia: Fortress, 1985). I adopt Childs's approach of reading the Hebrew Bible from the hermeneutical position of its canonical formation, whether third century BCE for the Septuagint or 90 CE for the Masoretic text.

the ineffable divinity of Psalms to secular realms and their divine destinies to insist that humans cannot determine divine purposes.[2] When Orosius in his *History against the Pagans*[3] created the first Western Latin version of universal history, fusing *saeculum* and *evangelium* in an unholy union that has persisted as an ideology even to today, he argued that the God of the Christians was guiding history, as demonstrated by the fact that the *pax Romana* of Augustus Caesar coincided with the birth of the prince of peace. This idea, that God is guiding certain histories, though vigorously contested by Augustine, was bequeathed to the West and remains a working theory even to this day. Let us trace its origins.

The fourth-century Christian apologists for Emperor Constantine and the empire, Lactantius and Eusebius,[4] together created a strand of Christian providential political theory that Orosius's *History* would develop further at the moment when Rome faced a major threat to its survival as city and empire in the early fifth century.[5] In the fourth century, despite the fact that by most scholarly assessments Christians were a minority population of the Roman Empire,[6] Constantine took the world by surprise. According to Eusebius, he attributed his victory against Maxentius in the battle for Milvian Bridge outside Rome on October 24, 312, to the vision of the cross in the sky he had witnessed before the battle: "He said he saw with his own eyes, up in the sky and resting over the sun, a cross-shaped trophy formed from light, and a text attached to it, which said, 'By this

---

2. Augustine, *De Civitate Dei Contra Paganos. Libri I–X*, ed. Bernard Dombart and Alphonse Kalb, CCSL 47 (Turnhout: Brepols, 1955); Augustine, *De Civitate Dei Contra Paganos. Libri XI–XXII*, ed. Bernard Dombart and Alphonse Kalb, CCSL 48 (Turnhout: Brepols, 1955).

3. Orosius, *Le Storie Contro I Pagani*, 2 vols., ed. Adolf Lippold, trans. Aldo Bartalucci (Verona: Arnoldo Mondadori, 1998).

4. Besides *Histoire Écclesiastique*, trans. Gustave Bardy, *Sources Chrétiennes*, vols. 31, 41, 55, and 73 (Paris: Éditions du Cerf, 1952–1960), see also Eusebius, *Vita Constantini*, *Patrologia Graeca* 20 (Paris: Migne, 1856). Translations are from *Eusebius: Life of Constantine*, trans. Averil Cameron and Stuart G. Hall (Oxford: Clarendon, 1999).

5. For a thorough study of the relationship between Orosius and Eusebius and Lactantius, see Antonio Polichetti, *Le "Historiae" di Orosio e la "Storiografia Ecclesiastica" occidentale (311–417 D.C.)* (Naples: Edizioni Scientifiche Italiane, 2000). Eusebius came to Orosius through the translation of Rufinus. Also, see Eugenio Corsini, *Introduzione alle "Storie" di Orosio* (Turin: G. Giappichelli, 1968), 97–98. Hervé Inglebert, *Les Romains Chrétiens face à l'histoire de Rome: Histoire, christianisme et romanités en occident dans l'Antiquité tardive (IIIe-Ve siècles)* (Paris: Institut d'Études Augustiniennes, 1996) also treats the indebtedness of Orosius's *History* to Eusebius, which he calls the renewal of Latin "eusebianism" (505–89).

6. Robin Lane Fox, *Pagans and Christians* (New York: Alfred A. Knopf, 1987), 269–73. See also Timothy D. Barnes, *Constantine and Eusebius* (Cambridge, MA: Harvard University Press, 1981), who argues that Christianity was a "respectable institution" at the time of Constantine's conversion (21, 49–54, 144–45). H. A. Drake, *Constantine and the Bishops: The Politics of Intolerance* (Baltimore: Johns Hopkins University Press, 2000) estimates the population of Christians at six million, about 10 percent of the entire population of the empire (73, 109–10).

conquer.'"[7] Constantine's victory, which Eusebius interpreted in terms of divine providence, led to the end of persecutions of Christians (313 CE),[8] to Constantine's conversion, and to the eventual Christianization of the Roman Empire.

The theology of providential destiny as Eusebius and Lactantius developed it argues for God's interest, guidance, and intervention into the events of human history, as opposed to history as arbitrary, cyclical, discontinuous, or even chaotic. While the victories Constantine won on the field gave him absolute power in the empire, he was also the political beneficiary of the cultural legacy of the Virgilian imperium and the biblical narratives when the fourth-century Christian theologians combined *imperium* and *evangelium* to support their version of providential history.

Lactantius rekindled Virgil and Livy's idea that Rome was destined to rule the world. Made public between 305 CE and 310 CE, Lactantius's *Divine Institutions*, it has been persuasively argued, was a "manifesto for political and religious reform."[9] The work is steeped in classical poetry, mythology, and philosophy that Lactantius puts at the service of Christianity. In fact, a trained rhetorician, Lactantius pays greater heed to classical culture without pitting it against Christian tradition than any other Christian writer of the period.[10] Intellectually struggling to restore the empire in the form of Augustus's reign, Lactantius turns to Virgil to recall the first century's golden age: "It is therefore clear that it is on the earth that he was king; this is affirmed more clearly elsewhere: 'He instituted a golden age, he who in his turn, will possess the lands of Latium, the ancient realm of Saturn.'"[11]

The first to interpret Virgil's *Fourth Eclogue* allegorically as Christian prophecy, Lactantius links the Sibylline Oracle with Isaiah's prophecy: "The Lord of His own accord will give you a sign; it is this: A young woman is with child, and she will give birth to a son and call him Immanuel"

---

7. Eusebius, *Vita Constantini* 1.28., col. 943–44; *Eusebius: Life of Constantine*, 81.

8. This occurred through the signing of the so-called "Edict of Milan," based on Lactantius, *De Mortibus persecutorum*, Sources Chrétiennes 39, 2 vols., ed. J. Moreau (Paris: Éditions du Cerf, 1954), 48.1; and Eusebius, *Histoire Écclesiastique* 10.5.4, which refers to the meeting of emperors at Milan to rescind the persecution of Christians. But, in fact, numerous measures had already been taken to end the persecutions prior to the date of this supposed Edict (313 CE). See Barnes, *Constantine and Eusebius*, 318, and Norman H. Baynes, *Constantine the Great and the Christian Church* (London: Proceedings of the British Academy, Humphrey Milford, 1929), 351–57; also see Elizabeth DePalma Digeser, *The Making of a Christian Empire: Lactantius and Rome* (Ithaca, NY: Cornell University Press, 2000), 122–23.

9. DePalma Digeser, *Making of a Christian Empire*, 13.

10. DePalma Digeser, *Making of a Christian Empire*, 89.

11. "Unde apparet illum regem fuisse terrenum: quod alibi apertius declarat: 'aurea condet / Saecula qui rursus Latio regnata per arva / Saturno quondam.'" *Institutions Divines*, Sources Chrétiennes 326, ed. Pierre Monat (Paris: Éditions du Cerf, 1986), 1.13.13, quoting from *Aeneid* 6.792–94.

(Isa 7:14), which Christians were already interpreting as having prophesied the coming redeemer.[12] Lactantius reads the eclogue as a prophecy of a thousand years of happiness that would procure the return of the terrestrial reign of Christ.[13] Lactantius's chiliastic interpretation of the *Eclogue* that predicts the birth of a child, who will herald a new age,[14] identifies the infant of the *Eclogue* with the infant Jesus. Appropriating the authority of Virgil, Lactantius's interpretation of the *Fourth Eclogue* makes Virgil a Christian prophet and simultaneously ties Hebrew messianic expectation to Christian eschatological hope and Roman political ambition. This marriage of Virgilian oracle to Isaiah's prophecy endured for centuries, and although Orosius ignores it, even Augustine hesitantly finds Christian resonances in Virgil's words.[15]

Eusebius, on the other hand, combines biblical notions of God's providential guidance of the Hebrew people with the goals of the empire to remake the founding myth of the Romans. Eusebius uses the first census of the Roman world that links Luke's narrative of Jesus's birth to Roman politics (Luke 2:1) to wed Christianity to the empire. This connection between the incarnation and the reign of Augustus provides Eusebius the means to establish Jesus's birth date and place in Palestine and under Roman rule.[16] Eusebius, like Lactantius, adopts the idea that God orchestrated Augustus's reign to prepare the world for Jesus's teaching. He also makes Christian universalist teaching that stripped away the differences between Greek and non-Greek and simultaneously conquered polytheism parallel the political achievement of the Roman Empire. He proposed that the power of Christ overcame polyarchy and polytheism to install one kingdom of God over Greeks, barbarians, and all humans everywhere, with the Roman Empire abolishing the need for multiple governments and merging all humans into one unified government.[17] Writing a historical narrative with convenient chronological coincidences, by inserting divine providence, Eusebius constructs a parallelism between Christ's soteriological role and Constantine's

---

12. Pierre Courcelle, "Les Exégèses Chrétiennes de la Quatrième Églogue," *Revue des Études Anciennes* 59:3–4 (1957): 294–319.

13. *Institutions Divines* 7.24.7, quoting Virgil, *Eclogue* 4.38–41, 28–30, 42–45.

14. Virgil, *Eclogues, Georgics, Aeneid 1–6, Eclogue* 4.8–17 (Virgil, *Eclogues, Georgics, Aeneid 1–6* [Cambridge, MA: Harvard University Press, 1999]). Also, Isaiah 9:6–7 and 11:1–5 elaborated further on this messianic expectation.

15. *City of God* 10.27.

16. Eusebius, *Histoire Écclesiastique* 1.5.2.

17. Eusebius, *Laudibus Constantini* 11–18 (col. 1375–1440); see also Johannes Van Oort, *Jerusalem and Babylon: A Study of Augustine's City of God and the Sources of His Doctrine of the Two Cities* (Leiden: E. J. Brill, 1991), 154–57.

political rise to power. As H. A. Drake writes, "By yoking the mission of Rome to subdue barbarians on earth with Christ's divine mission to fight demons in the spiritual world, Eusebius fused what had been a simple chronological correlation into a powerful, cosmic model of causation, a 'political theology' that equated polytheism with polyarchy and division, monotheism with monarchy and unity."[18] As inventor of ecclesiastical history, Eusebius created the idea of the Christian nation. Here Christ and Christians were the good and true, and their enemies were the devil, heresy, and the persecution of Christians.[19]

Constantine's attribution of his victory at the Milvian Bridge to the Christian God contrasts with the common reaction when a century later Alaric sacked Rome. While on both occasions, victories and defeats were attributed to gods, in the fifth century, Rome's weakness before the barbarian threat was blamed on Christians and the Christian Empire. Pagan Roman beliefs resurfaced as means to understand Rome's vulnerability, while fear of conquest before the barbarian onslaught prompted Romans to view Alaric's crushing success a result of Roman abandonment of the pagan divinities in favor of Christianity. In part, these allegations prompted Augustine to write the *City of God* and Orosius his history against the pagans, both works that seek to come to terms theologically with the relationship between Christian experience and Christian sacred texts and the temporal political order in the form of the Roman Empire. Thus, in the fifth century after Alaric's attack, the idea of the providential Christianization of the Roman Empire was directly confronted and at the same time, at least Augustine and Orosius, probed the divine interest in the Roman imperium.

Several fundamental ideas inform Orosius's historical theory: (1) God is one; (2) God is the creator of the world and of mankind; (3) God is providence and is occupied with his creation; (4) the providence of God operates in history with a slow and almost incomprehensible economy, but it infallibly functions. Two moments clarify this disclosure: the incarnation of Christ, and after the incarnation, the Christian revelation.[20] Because the incarnation occurred at the pivotal time when Augustus Caesar, the first Roman emperor, took a census of Roman citizens, Orosius makes the Roman *imperium* and

---

18. Drake, *Constantine and the Bishops*, 363–64.
19. Arnaldo Momigliano, "Pagan and Christian Historiography in the Fourth Century A.D.," in *The Conflict between Paganism and Christianity in the Fourth Century*, ed. Arnaldo Momigliano (Oxford: Clarendon, 1963), 79–99.
20. Eugenio Corsini, *Introduzione alle "Storie" di Orosio* (Turin: G. Giappichelli, 1968), 89.

the Christ event intrinsic to the divine plan. Orosius could look back to Livy and Virgil for the *imperium* argument and to Lactantius and Eusebius to tie *imperium* with *evangelium*. Following Eusebius,[21] for Orosius, the birth of Christ, the "Christianorum caput" (head of the Christians),[22] who had been born to save the good and punish the bad, confirmed the primacy of Rome's destiny. This particular version of incarnational history circumscribes the theology of the incarnation to a temporal event, and among other lapses fails to understand its potential meaning beyond particular historical circumstances. But for Orosius, it signaled an epochal change that coincided with Roman imperial victory and produced what would become the dominant Latin Western theory of Christian providential history, in which a new time begins with the birth of Christ and the Roman *regnum* under Augustus Caesar.[23] To further cement this coincidence and to link Hebrew, Christian, and Roman histories, Orosius organizes his work on Daniel's interpretation of Nebuchadnezzar's dream of a giant statue of a man (Dan. 2:31–45). But he collapses the four empires (Babylonian, Median, Persian, and Macedonian) into two, making Rome rise as Babylon falls,[24] thus successfully on a theoretical level joining Jerusalem and Rome.

The link between *imperium* and *evangelium* that Eusebius and Lactantius articulated had appeared as early as the second century in Melito of Sardis,[25] and it would continue both as a theme and as a concrete politics to the high

---

21. Eusebius, *Histoire Écclesiastique* 1.5.2.

22. Orosius, *Hist.* 7.3.2, 4.

23. For this theory of history, see Paul Ricoeur, *History and Truth*, trans. Charles A. Kelbley (Evanston, IL: Northwestern University Press, 1965), 81–97; Hayden White, "Getting out of History: Jameson's Redemption of Narrative" and "The Metaphysics of Narrativity: Time and Symbol in Ricoeur's Philosophy of History," in *The Content of the Form: Narrative Discourse and Historical Representation* (Baltimore: Johns Hopkins University Press, 1987), 142–68, 169–84.

24. Jerome's commentary on Daniel had not made the fourth kingdom Rome in contrast to Hippolytus (170–236 CE), bishop of Rome, who, in his commentary on Daniel, had identified Daniel's fourth beast with the Romans (*Dan.* 7.7), predicting the imminent end of time with Roman hegemony. Clearly Orosius does not share Hippolytus's scorn for Rome, and he introduces a radical innovation because he brackets the African and Macedonian realms, which for him were of brief duration (*Hist.* 2.1.6), and argues that the first and last of the kingdoms, Babylon and Rome, are the most important. Like an old father to a son still small, Babylon in a perfect temporal symmetry, he writes, gave way to Rome, which had already begun to rise as the first fell (*Hist.* 2.1.6). Inserting God as the director of these risings and fallings (*Hist.* 2.2.4), he makes the Macedonian and Carthaginian Empires transitional and Rome unique because it had opened itself to Christianity. Thus he synchronizes the history of the world's civilizations with both Jewish and Christian history (*Hist.* 1.1.14). See "Commento: Libro Secondo," in Orosio, *Le Storie Contro I Pagani* 1, 393; Jerome, *Commentarium in Danielem, Corpus Christianorum Series Latina* 75A (Turnhout: Brepols, 1964); Hippolytus of Rome, *Commentarium in Danielem*, ed. and trans. Maurice Lefèvre (Paris: Éditions du Cerf, 1947).

25. See Hervé Inglebert, *Les Romains Chrétiens face à l'histoire de Rome: Histoire, christianisme et romanités en occident dans l'Antiquité tardive (IIIe-Ve siècles)* (Paris: Institut d'Études Augustiniennes, 1996), 57–58.

Middle Ages and the early modern period.[26] It became a crucial element of the ideology of many early modern European monarchies where ruler and God were aligned in processes of nation building, geographical expansion, religious evangelizing, or colonial conquests. In fact, one could propose that it was Napoleon who finally overturned this as a working theory in Europe while making himself temporal ruler of his own imperial domain without divine patronage.

Orosius follows the providential theory developed by Eusebius and Lactantius, and therefore he disagrees with Augustine, even though he claims he has followed Augustine's prompts. Augustine's insistence on the biblical idea that "the Earth is the Lord's and everything in it" (Ps 94:4–5 [95:4–5]) or Jesus's remark that "my kingdom does not belong to this world" (John 18:36), raised human individual conscience above the political order, making it possible to challenge the goals and purposes of the state. Augustine argued that the providential intervention into human history of the Christ-event and God's soteriological plan for humans had changed the conditions whereby humans act in and understand their place and time on earth. In meditating on a divine order that transcended human constructs, Augustine had separated God from particular histories, dismantled the idea of the providential history of nations, and challenged the Roman Empire in terms that question the ethical foundation of all imperial ventures. But for Augustine, the repudiation of empire did not deny the claims of the saeculum. Just the reverse, to achieve the city of God, Christians were enjoined to love one another and provide for those in need. Augustine, like Thomas Aquinas, whose book 3 of the Summa Contra Gentiles[27] offers an extended exploration of the nature of divine providence, repudiates pleasures of the flesh, worldly honors and glory, worldly power, and wealth to reveal how human felicity, the divine gift of a providential incarnation, ultimately consists in the pleasure of contemplating God.

In fact, the differences between Orosius's and Augustine's views have led some to suggest that despite the fact that Orosius claims Augustine asked him to write the book, he either did not understand Augustine or deliberately opposed him.[28] Augustine's City of God specifically confronts

---

26. See chapters 2 and 3 in Antony Black, *Political Thought in Europe 1250–1450* (Cambridge: Cambridge University Press, 1992), 42–84; 85–116; Prue Shaw, introduction to Dante Alighieri, *Monarchia*, ed. and trans. Prue Shaw (Cambridge: Cambridge University Press, 1995).

27. Thomas Aquinas, "Providence," in *On the Truth of the Catholic Faith: Summa Contra Gentiles*, trans. Vernon J. Bourke (New York: Doubleday, 1956), 1.3.

28. See Lippold, introduction to Orosio, *Le Storie Contro I Pagani*, 41–42.

questions about who one should blame for historical tragedy or historical triumph, what the relationship between gods and the temporal domain is, and for Christians, what constitutes the relationship between sacred and temporal history. These issues emerged as critical during the unstable political and military situation when Rome was sacked. Augustine began to write the *City of God* after the 410 sack of Rome, working on it almost to the end of his life (412–427), dedicating fifteen years to the work and struggling to make it true to Christian doctrinal foundations and at the same time unambiguous. [29] He must have been aware that the old pagan world in which he had been born and educated was about to change; his work would become a theological encyclopedia for the future. Augustine presents history and geography from a metaphysical view of time and space because, for Augustine, neither citizenship nor the geography of the Roman Empire determined one's spiritual status. Just as for Paul, citizenship, geographical location, ethnic identity, or any worldly convention that determined human status did not create community. In Augustine, community was membership in the city of God—for him the church,[30] which itself was a "reading" group that shared the same hermeneutic, ethical practice, and teleology—that was the ultimate purpose of life.[31] He differed in this regard from other thinkers of the ancient world, like Virgil, Livy, and even Cicero, as well as the Christians Lactantius, Eusebius, and Orosius, for whom civic action, citizenship, and nobility of soul were inevitably aligned.[32]

Writing of God's city, the heavenly country, Augustine uses Virgil's promise of an empire to the Romans ("[Jove] Fixes no bounds for you of space and time / But will bestow an empire without end [*nec metas rerum nec tempora ponit, Imperium sine fine dabit*]")[33] to exhort the Romans to reject both their empire and their gods for the one true God, who provides a heavenly empire without end, thus redefining empire from an eternal perspective. Christianity, he claims, was blamed for the great catastrophe of Rome's demise on the grounds that the Romans had deserted their gods in

---

29. See Gustave Bardy, introduction to *La Cité de Dieu*, in *Oeuvres de Saint Augustin*, vols. 33–37 in Bibliothèque Augustiniennes (Paris: Desclée de Brouwer, 1959–1960); *La Cité de Dieu*, vol. 33, 9–22; also John M. Rist, *Augustine: Ancient Thought Baptized* (Cambridge: Cambridge University Press, 1994), 19.

30. Augustine, *City of God* 20.9.

31. The principal idea of Brian Stock, *Augustine the Reader* (Cambridge, MA: Harvard University Press, 1996).

32. See Ernest L. Fortin, "The Political Implications of St. Augustine's Theory of Conscience," *Augustinian Studies* 1 (1970): 133–52 for how Augustine attempts to finesse Roman ideas of civic virtue as the rule for living in temporal societies.

33. *Aeneid* 1.278–79.

favor of the Christian God. Calling this explanation for the attack against Roman power blasphemous and wrong, Augustine described his decision to undertake the project in his *Retractations*: "Burning with the zeal of the house of God, I began to write against these great errors and blasphemies in the books of the *City of God*."[34] Addressing his friend Marcellinus in the first paragraph of the *City of God* and playing on the "founding of the city" tradition of Livy and Orosius, he writes, "I have taken upon myself the task of defending [the glorious City of God] against those who prefer their own gods to the Founder of that City" (*debito defendere adversus eos qui conditori eius deos suos praeferunt*).[35]

Although it is misguided to try to elaborate an Augustinian systematic political or historical theory because his positions differ depending on the time and the circumstances he addresses in his various works,[36] nonetheless we can see that he rethinks many ideas about history circulating in the ancient period.[37] He undertakes to unravel the Virgilian historical legacy and to separate Christianity from the temporal domain in which Lactantius and Eusebius had entangled it. His sources for the concept of the two cities, a *terrena civitas* and a *civitas Dei*, although showing similarities with neo-Platonist, Manichaean, and Tyconian notions, most likely stem from Christian, Jewish, and Jewish-Christian north African traditions.[38]

In the six hundred years from the definitive collapse of the Roman Empire to the times of the crusades, ideas of Christian providential history were in decline, but in the period of the crusades, the idea resurfaced when both Christians and Muslims claimed divine support for their ambitions in the "land called holy." What was the obsession with the "holy land," pretentions to which invariably implicate divine plans and providence? In ancient

---

34. "Ego exardescens zelo domus dei adversus eorum blasphemias vel errores libros de civitate Dei scribere institui." Augustine, *Retractionum Libri II*, ed. Almut Mutzenbecher, in *Corpus Christianorum Series Latina* 57 (Turnhout: Brepols, 1984), 2.43.

35. *City of God* 1.pref.

36. See, for example, François Paschoud, "Saint Augustin," *Roma Aeterna: Études sur le patriotisme romain dans l'occident latin à l'époque des grandes invasions* (Rome: Institut Suisse de Rome, 1967); *Augustine: Political Writings*, ed. E. M. Atkins and R. J. Dodaro (Cambridge: Cambridge University Press, 2001); R. W. Dyson, *The Pilgrim City: Social and Political Ideas in the Writings of St. Augustine of Hippo* (Woodbridge, Suffolk: Boydell and Brewer, 2001); John von Heyking, *Augustine and Politics as Longing in the World* (Columbia, MO: University of Missouri Press, 2001).

37. See Paschoud, *Roma Aeterna*; Peter Busch, "On the Use and Disadvantage of History for the Afterlife," in *Augustine and History*, ed. Christopher T. Daly, John Doody, and Kim Paffenroth (Lanham, MD: Lexington, 2008), 3–30; Andrew R. Murphy, "Augustine and the Rhetoric of Roman Decline," in *Augustine and History*, 53–74; Brian Harding, *Augustine and Roman Virtue* (New York: Continuum, 2008).

38. For a full discussion of the theories of the origins of the ideas and their persuasiveness, see Johannes Van Oort, *Jerusalem and Babylon: A Study of Augustine's City of God and the Sources of His Doctrine of the Two Cities* (Leiden: E. J. Brill, 1991), 199–359.

Hebrew history, Jerusalem only emerged as a political and religious center with the rise of the Davidic dynasty, but the Hebrew Scriptures' sagas of its history of sackings and forced exile of the people for whom it was a holy city became a prevailing tragedy, for which the "elect" people invariably blame themselves. The New Testament repudiates Jerusalem's importance as a religious center and makes it the site of corruption and unjust execution as the disciples in the post-parousia era fan out as far as Antioch, Rome, and even India. Moving away from the idea of Jerusalem as a sacred city—since, according to Orosius, it had been destroyed by an act of divine rage—Rome emerged as the divinely elected site, the *caput mundi* of the Roman Empire. For Augustine, in stark contrast to Orosius's providential view, neither historic Rome nor historic Jerusalem were divinely elected, even though sacred events had occurred in both places. Augustine makes Jerusalem a symbolic city, and Rome, founded in slow, accumulative warfare, was the daughter of Babylon, a second Babylon.[39] Rome is just like a Western Babylon.[40]

As the longest discussion of Thomas Aquinas's *Summa Contra Gentiles* (*SCG* hereafter), showing how important he considered the subject, book 3 is dedicated to providence. But his position, like Augustine's, differs markedly from the attempts to align *imperium* and *evangelium* that occurred in the patristic era. Living at a time when a dangerous theory of divine kingship was emerging, Thomas Aquinas goes so far as to argue that the evil efforts of those who seize power over temporal rule contravene divine order or providence. His concept of natural law, an element of divine order, poses a challenge to installed social practice and to the thirteenth-century emerging authoritarian kingships of Frederick II of Sicily and Louis IX of France.[41]

In his discussion of providence, Thomas begins with the premise that the "unmoved mover" that is God, the end of all things, "governs, or rules, the whole of things by His providence."[42] Further expanding this premise, he writes, "God, to whom all goodness primarily belongs, as something substantially possessed and known and loved, must be the governor of all things."[43] But this goodness that is God who orders all things, does not result in "material necessity," the consequence of which would be that "all

---

39. "*Civitas Roma velut altera Babylon et velut prioris filia Babylonis.*" *City of God* 18.22.1–2; "*ubi et ipsa Roma quasi secuda Babylonia est.*" *City of God* 18.2.65–66.

40. "*Veluti alteram in occidente Babyloniam.*" *City of God* 16.17.33–34; 18.27.28–29.

41. Alasdair McIntyre, "Natural Law as Subversive: The Case of Aquinas," *Journal of Medieval and Early Modern Studies* 26, no. 1 (1991): 67–68 (61–83); Thomas Aquinas, *Summae Theologiae*, in *Opera Omnia* (Rome: Polyglotta, 1903), Ia–IIae 96.2.

42. *SCG* 1.3.64.

43. *SCG* 1.3.64.

things happen by chance and not from the order of providence."[44] Still, his position on providence appears to pose some problems for Christian foundations, for example, the origin of evil, the human dispensation of free choice, and the issue of contingency in human affairs. Thomas's arguments are subtle, as he takes the position that providence does not exclude evil[45] and neither does it exclude contingency.[46] On human freedom, Thomas posits that it results because "man is made in God's image . . . it remains to consider man as the source of his own actions, having free choice and power over his acts."[47] Providence, he argues, is not incompatible with freedom of choice.[48] That providence does not exclude contingency and free choice and does preclude determinism are necessary premises for Aquinas to address the issue of "order among men," also occurring in this book on providence in the *SCG*. After discussing the order of angels, which he links with the spectrum of human activities, he explores the "order among men." Just as angels have an order, so "divine providence," he writes, "imposes order on all things." Following Aristotle (*Politics* 1.4), Aquinas emphasizes that humans have a natural order: those with understanding are naturally suited to governance while those with strong bodies are naturally fitted for service. But disorder occurs, he explains, in human government "as a result of a man getting control, not because of the eminence of his understanding, but because either he usurps dominion for himself by bodily strength or because someone is set up as a ruler on the basis of sensual affection."[49] Aquinas's main point is that divine providence, with the angels as agents, imposes order, but humans, through the exercise of their free choice, force this order awry. Thomas here recognizes the role of social and political mores (human systems) in contravening nature (a divine order), thus setting up a contrast and possibly a conflict between what is natural and what is social or political. Aquinas proposes that natural law is not coercive, in other words, and does not force individuals into particular roles; in fact, natural law might oppose socially and politically condoned behavior as being practiced by the potentates of his time. In the *ST* (Suppl. 41.2), in fact, he argued that natural human diversity generating diverse talents was necessary

---

44. *SCG* 1.3.64.
45. *SCG* 1.3.71.
46. *SCG* 1.3.72.
47. *Summae Theologiae* I–IIae.1.prol.: "*Quia . . . homo factus est ad imaginem Dei dicitur, secundum quod per imaginem significatur intellectuale et arbitrium liberum . . . restat ut consideremus de homine secundum quod ipse est suorum operum principium, quasi liberum arrbitrium habens, et suorum operum potestatem.*"
48. *SCG* 1.3.73.
49. *SCG* 1.3.81.

to create a society: one might choose to be a nun, a farmer, a builder, and so on.[50] Thus, for Aquinas, providence is God's divine order, but human willfulness invariably challenges it to install its own order.

Emanating from the ancient world when kings and emperors claimed divine privileges, the ideas of divine election, providential movements West or outward to "unchristian" or "empty" lands, and claims on the "holy land" with their notions of the inevitable victory of a "chosen people," echo throughout Western history. Still alive today, the idea of providential history follows a trajectory that includes such notions as the divine right of kings; manifest destiny; "the Great Trek"; secular versions of an inevitable march of history as developed in the *Communist Manifesto*; or social Darwinism and nineteenth-century capitalism, with its persistent view of American exceptionalism. How many times have nations and leaders invoked the divinity to claim themselves as agents of God or to justify their wars as rightful claiming of lands?

In the Nobel Prize–winning author's novelistic autobiographical memories of his youth after he had left South Africa, J. M. Coetzee remembers himself among a busload of children hauled to wave flags at the floats carrying the heroes of South Africa's Boer past, the founding fathers of South Africa's Dutch colonial rule. School children, indoctrinated to believe that the Lord, through the divine agency of the Boer South Africans, had brought Christianity to the "tip of Africa," gaze at a shadow of this past glory. The narrator, remembering the twelve-year-old before this parade, recalls that neither he nor his classmates, more eager for a Coke and a sandwich, took pleasure in this display of an exalted past. Rather, ironically adopting the language and claims of the propaganda, he sees "history being unmade" as the Lord withdraws his "protective hand."[51] South Africa's apartheid regime, of course, is not unique in its claims to divine providence at work.

The idea of American exceptionalism and the chosen, providential destiny for its Anglo-Saxon descendent population was perhaps most clearly articulated by John L. O'Sullivan's "Manifest Destiny," an essay published in 1845 in *Democratic Review*, where he wrote of the boundless and divinely chosen future for "America":

---

50. Brian Tierney, *Liberty and Law: The Idea of Permissive Natural Law, 1100–1800* (Washington, DC: Catholic University of America Press, 2014), 81–86.

51. J. M. Coetzee, *Youth* (London: Penguin, 2003), 39.

The far-reaching, the boundless future will be the era of American greatness. In its magnificent domain of space and time, the nation of many nations is destined to manifest to mankind the excellence of divine principles; to establish on earth the noblest temple ever dedicated to the worship of the Most High—the Sacred and the True. Its floor shall be a hemisphere—its roof the firmament of the star-studded heavens, and its congregation an Union of many Republics, comprising hundreds of happy millions, calling, owning no man master, but governed by God's natural and moral law of equality, the law of brotherhood—of "peace and good will amongst men."

O'Sullivan had founded *Democratic Review*, where he published the major literary figures of the first half of the nineteenth century, including Emerson, Thoreau, Whitman, and Hawthorne. Although early in his career O'Sullivan had advocated for the rights of women and working people, opposed the death penalty, and promoted educational reform, he was pro-slavery and supported the Confederacy during the Civil War. Thus we can see that his endorsement of "freedom" in the "Manifest Destiny" essay was strictly limited to the white European immigrants who were to inherit this equal brotherhood. The essay continues to spell out the future of this "exceptional" nation:

Yes, we are the nation of progress, of individual freedom, of universal enfranchisement. . . . We must onward to the fulfillment of our mission—to the entire development of the principle of our organization— freedom of conscience, freedom of person, freedom of trade and business pursuits, universality of freedom and equality. This is our high destiny, and in nature's eternal, inevitable decree of cause and effect we must accomplish it. All this will be our future history, to establish on earth the moral dignity and salvation of man—the immutable truth and beneficence of God. For this blessed mission to the nations of the world, which are shut out from the life-giving light of truth, has America been chosen; and her high example shall smite unto death the tyranny of kings, hierarchs, and oligarchs, and carry the glad tidings of peace and good will where myriads now endure an existence scarcely more enviable than that of beasts of the field. Who, then, can doubt that our country is destined to be the great nation of futurity?[52]

---

52. *The United States Democratic Review* 6, no. 23 (Nov 1839): 426–30.

In South Africa on December 16, 1838, the Boers, the same group who would establish the Afrikaner National Party and eventually establish apartheid, took a dramatic vow in what they perceived as a life-and-death struggle against the Zulus. Produced just a year after the original manifest destiny statement, the vow offers an unnerving parallel to its claims. Before the Battle of Blood River, the fight that crushed the Zulus and established the Republic of Natal, they promised the following:

> At this moment we stand before the Holy God of heaven and earth, to make a promise if He will be with us and protect us, and deliver the enemy into our hands so that we may triumph over him, that we shall observe the day and the date as an anniversary in each year, and a day of thanksgiving like the Sabbath in His honour; and that we shall enjoin our children that they must take part with us in this for a remembrance even for posterity.[53]

This vow was repeated every December 16, which became a quasi-religious day of nationalist unity from 1838 until 1994, when the apartheid regime finally fell. It established the grounds for the fundamental belief in racial separation and social and religious priority of the separatist policies. Adopting a strict binary view that divides black from white, Europe from Africa, and Christianity from heathens, when he won the all-white general election based on the apartheid platform in 1948, Dr. Daniel Malan, the first (Afrikaner) National Party Prime Minister, explained the unholy matrimony of apartheid and Christianity:

> The Church believes that God in His wisdom so disposed it that the first White men and women who settled at the foot of the Black Continent were profoundly religious people, imbued with a very real zeal to bring the light of the gospel to the heathen nations of Africa. These first South Africans lit a torch which was carried to the farthest corners of the subcontinent in the course of the last three centuries and whose light now shines upon the greater part of all non-White peoples south of the Equator.[54]

A dangerous and one might even say pernicious version of the idea of divinely destined history has emerged in the United States in the last four decades. It goes back to earlier Puritan notions of the United States'

---

53. As quoted in Jennifer Nelson, "The Role the Dutch Reformed Church Played in the Rise and Fall of Apartheid," *The Journal of Hate Studies* 2, no. 1 (2003): 65.

54. Nelson, "Role of the Dutch Reformed Church," 66.

destiny as a "City upon a Hill" (1630), a term used first by John Winthrop (1588–1649), governor of Massachusetts Bay Colony, to describe the new settlement. In a sermon titled "A Model of Christian Charity," the hoped-for new land is called the city on a hill. Quoting Matthew 5:14, when Jesus says, "You are the light of the world. A town that stands on a hill cannot be hidden," Winthrop wrote, "Wee shall finde that the God of Israell is among us, when tenn of us shall be able to resist a thousand of our enemies, when hee shall make us a prayse and glory, that men shall say of succeeding plantacions: the lord make it like that of New England: for wee must Consider that wee shall be as a Citty upon a Hill, the eies of all people are uppon us."[55] Winthrop's providentialism was typical of Reformation England, where, it has been recently argued, it became "central to the political, medical, and philosophical thought and the literary and historical discourse of the period."[56] This perfect republic of Winthrop's, however, included repression of religious differences, even if the Puritans had fled religious persecution in England. His suppression of Anne Hutchinson (1590–1643) for suspected heretical beliefs, like other acts of religious repression, eventually reinforced the argument for separation of church and state in the constitution that was still 150 years in the future. The American Constitution in essence rejected Winthrop's idea of a city on the hill. Still, American exceptionalism as presently articulated by the religious right holds that the United States *possesses* a divine role in history.

What happened in the early modern period, partially due to the Reformation and the counter-Reformation, was what Charles Taylor in *A Secular Age* accurately observes as a collapse of the two spheres, the "spiritual" or "sacred" and the "saeculum," into one. With the king, as in England, now the head of the church, the king divinely elected, as in France, or the colonization of the Americas both as an evangelizing and "civilizing" project, the saeculum assumed the erstwhile roles of the church, resulting in what Taylor describes as "the Christian life becomes living in the world."[57] He expands on this to observe,

> But to the extent that churches, and later states with churches, set themselves the goal of mobilizing and organizing and actively bringing about these higher levels of conformity to (what was seen as) the Christian life,

---

55. John Winthrop, "We shall be a City upon a Hill" (1630), in *Speeches that Changed the World*, ed. Owen Collins (Louisville: John Knox, 1998), 63–65.

56. See Alexandra Walsham, *Providence in Early Modern England* (Oxford: Oxford University Press, 1999), 3.

57. Charles Taylor, *A Secular Age* (Cambridge, MA: Harvard University Press, 2007), 266.

this latter came to be codified, laid out in a set of norms. Reform comes to be seen as a serious business, brooking no alternatives. There is no more separate sphere of the "spiritual" where one may go to pursue a life of prayer outside the saeculum; and nor is there the other alternation, between order and anti-order, which Carnival represented. There is just this one relentless order of right thought and action, which must occupy all social and personal space.[58]

This overlapping of religion and the state that emerged so forcefully in the early modern period has a much longer history, as discussed in the beginning of this essay. But beginning with the forced conversions of the Carolingian period, followed by the Crusades and the missionary journeys, themselves followed by the rise of the Inquisition, we see an increasing connection between institutional religion and political ambitions, together representing national consolidation and imperial ventures rather than the practice of charity that the New Testament sponsors. However, although the idea of a descending order of power (from God to royal divinely chosen leader to the people) existed in the Middle Ages, the idea of a "divine right for the sovereign" in the West emerged victoriously in the early modern period. This theory is usually attributed to Jean Bodin (1529/30–1596), who today is considered one of the major political theorists of the period.

Writing from his own experience that was formed in France in the context of the religious wars, in *On Sovereignty: Six Books of the Commonwealth*, in his chapter on "The True Attributes of Sovereignty," Bodin states that "because there are none on earth, after God, greater than sovereign princes, whom God establishes as His lieutenants to command the rest of mankind, we must enquire carefully into their estate, that we may respect and revere their majesty in all due obedience, speak and think of them with all due honour. He who contemns his sovereign prince, contemns God whose image he is."[59] Bringing back the ancient Roman imperial idea of the divine ruler, Bodin thus argues that the monarch is equivalent to God on earth. Making an analogy between the prince on earth and God in heaven, he elaborates on this premise to show that the attributes of the sovereign are unique to that person and states that "just as Almighty God cannot create another God equal with Himself, since He is infinite and two infinities cannot co-exist, so the sovereign prince, who is the image of God, cannot

58. Taylor, *Secular Age*, 266.
59. Jean Bodin, *Bodin on Sovereignty: Six Books of the Commonwealth*, trans. M. J. Tooley (Oxford: Basil Blackwell, 1955), 80.

make a subject equal with himself without self-destruction."[60] Because of this foundational premise, Bodin rejects the idea that subjects could rebel against the sovereign, and as a consequence citizens were obliged to be obedient, even if the ruler was a tyrant, because he represented God on earth.[61] This is a long way from Augustine's idea of the prudent discernment of the conscience, the internal voice that separates the person from the state.

Bodin's theory, which in actuality described the emerging political situation at least in England, France, and Spain, was more recently explored by Carl Schmitt (1888–1985), the leading jurist during the Weimar Republic and author of many books, including *Political Theology*, written in the 1920s in Germany. Today considered a central political thinker of the last century, he joined the Nazi party in 1933 and held his position at the University of Berlin as a professor of law from 1933 to 1945, when he was detained by the Allies, although he was not charged with any crimes.[62] The tract is about "the nature, and thus about the prerogatives, of sovereign political authority as it develops in the West, about its relation to Western Christianity."[63] He begins the tract with the line that made him famous: "Sovereign is he who decides on the exceptional case."[64] For Schmitt, "sovereign power precludes it from being subject to law all the time, even in exceptional times."[65] Schmitt recognized Bodin as the critical voice in the concept of sovereignty in the early modern period, who stands at the forefront of the "modern theory of the state." [66] What Schmitt argued, and I would suggest accurately, was that "all significant concepts of the modern theory of the state are secularized theological concepts not only because of their historical development—in which they are transferred from theology to the theory of the state, whereby for example, the omnipotent God became omnipotent lawgiver—but also because of their systematic structure, the recognition of which is necessary for a sociological consideration of these concepts."[67] Seeing the beginning of this secularized theology of the state emanating from the seventeenth century, when the monarch was identified with God and possessed "a position analogous to that attributed to God in

---

60. Bodin, *Bodin on Sovereignty*, 81.
61. Introduction to *Bodin on Sovereignty*, 26.
62. For Schmitt's importance to modern political theory and the virtual ignorance of his work in English until recent times, see George Schwab, introduction to Carl Schmitt, *Political Theology*, trans. George Schwab (Chicago: University of Chicago Press, 2005), xxxvii–lii.
63. Tracy B. Strong, foreword to Schmitt, *Political Theology*, vii.
64. Schmitt, *Political Theology*, 5.
65. Schwab, introduction to Schmitt, *Political Theology*, xliv.
66. Schmitt, *Political Theology*, 8.
67. Schmitt, *Political Theology*, 36.

the Cartesian system of the world," Schmitt sees this fact as the foundation for the king's right to establish the laws, just as God determines the laws of nature.[68]

What these kinds of assertions lead to is a complete unraveling of the Augustinian separation of the *saeculum* from the city of God, not to mention of the dispensation and ontological freedom opened to mankind by the incarnation, as explored in Augustine. In fact, in order for the modern state to succeed with presuppositions of divine rights of kings and divine duties for people, the Christian way of life had to be made attainable in this world, that is, realizable in history. The distinction between the secular and religious had to be erased, with the one appropriating the other.[69] This is a move that essentially sacralizes the state and sidelines New Testament notions of a loving divinity who asks us to love one another. Rather, we are asked to put our faith, hope, and love in the nation. Still, some of the consequences of the dismantling of the distinction between the spheres of the state and of the moral conscience have produced ideals that contribute to the common good. This is precisely Jürgen Habermas's point that he articulates in *Religion and Rationality*: "Universalistic egalitarianism, from which sprang the ideals of freedom and a collective life in solidarity, the autonomous conduct of life and emancipation, the individual morality of conscience, human rights and democracy, is the direct legacy of the Judaic ethic of justice and the Christian ethic of love."[70] As Terry Eagleton, who is more famous as a Marxist critic than as a defender of Christianity, writes, "The Christian church has tortured and disemboweled in the name of Jesus, gagging dissent and burning its critics alive . . . It supports murderous dictatorships in the name of God, views both criticism and pessimism as unpatriotic, and imagines that being a Christian means maintaining a glazed grin, a substantial bank balance, and a mouthful of pious platitudes."[71] But Eagleton correctly labels this brand of religion ideological belief and not scriptural faith.[72]

Charles Taylor attributes the narrowing of the gap between the city of God and the earthly saeculum that grew and developed in the eighteenth and nineteenth centuries in Western societies to the increasing

---

68. Schmitt, *Political Theology*, 46–47.
69. Taylor, *Secular Age*, 735.
70. Jürgen Habermas, *Religion and Rationality: Essays on Reason, God, and Modernity*, ed. Eduardo Menedieta (Cambridge, MA: MIT Press, 2002), 149.
71. Terry Eagleton, *Reason, Faith, and Revolution: Reflections on the God Debate* (New Haven: Yale University Press, 2009), 56–57.
72. Eagleton, *Reason, Faith, and Revolution*, 57.

interconnection of ideas of progress, order, and prosperity, themselves ideologically driven, with the Christian ethos. He argues that what led to the sense of civilizational superiority, which grew with Western colonial power, became interwoven with a sense of Christendom as the bearer of this civilization. Missionaries brought Christianity to the non-Western world, often with the sense that they were bringing the bases of future prosperity, progress, order and (sometimes also) democracy and freedom. It became hard for many to answer the question, What is Christian faith about? The salvation of humankind, or the progress wrought by capitalism, technology, and democracy? The two tended to blend into one. Even harder did it become to distinguish between salvation and the establishment of good moral order.[73]

The examples cited here, whether the claims of manifest destiny or of the Boer vow, demonstrate this profound breakdown of the gap between the claims of the state and those of religion or religious conscience. In the United States, a cynical hijacking of religion that appropriates the rhetoric of divine providence to lend support to political and economic goals contributes to an overall negative attitude toward religion in general and particularly toward Christianity among many educated citizens. This political appropriation of Christianity makes it difficult for educated people to grapple with what religion can offer to ameliorate our social and political ills, a position that Eagleton cogently argues in *Reason, Faith, and Revolution*.[74] This has significantly undermined the potential of Christianity as a conscientious force of moral resistance to political and economic policy that can be seen as contradicting or disregarding religious values, particularly those that recommend charity toward the poor, counsel justice for all, chastise the rich and powerful for abuse of privilege, and recall the dominant theology of love of the New Testament, which opposes violence and force, typified in Jesus's statement in the gospel of Matthew: "Put up your sword. All who take up the sword die by the sword" (Matt 26:52).[75]

Like Emperor Constantine's role as Jesus and Moses redivivus, the United States, as understood by millions, is proposed as chosen by God to promulgate its way of life to the world. But this hegemony rose when the "secularism" and "political realism" that Augustine had proposed in *The City of God* declined as foundations for a conscience of political resistance.

---

73. Taylor, *Secular Age*, 736.
74. Eagleton, *Reason, Faith, and Revolution*, 140–69.
75. For other New Testament statements against violence, see 2 Cor 13:11; Rom 15:33; 12:17, 19, 21.

In the Augustinian tradition, religious convictions, that is, one's relationship to the divinity, as separate from one's national, racial, gender, social, or familial identity was the conscience that distanced and protected the individual from the state and served as a corrective to the claims of the state, the family, or any other social or political unit—outside, of course, the divine mandate to be charitable to those in need. Augustine had argued, as Charles Taylor puts it, that "a Christian state could help the Church repress heretics and false cults, but it couldn't improve its citizens; only the City of God, represented by the Church, could aspire to that."[76] Indeed Augustine had a profound sense of the gap between the claims of the earthly city, even if it pretended to bring God to earth, and the claims of the heavenly city. As he wrote in the *City of God*, "God, therefore, the author and giver of happiness (*felicitatis*), because he is the only true God, himself gives earthly kingdoms to the good and the bad. This is not done rashly or at random, for he is God, not Fortuna, the goddess of luck. . . . But as for happiness (*felicitatem*), he gives it only to the good."[77] Both servants and rulers may gain or lose ultimate happiness in contrast to earthly kingdoms, which God grants both to the good and to the evil. The idea of a providential theory of heaven on earth would have struck Augustine as perilous ground on which to stake one's temporal or eternal felicity.[78]

---

76. Taylor, *Secular Age*, 122.

77. "*Deus igitur ille felicictatis auctor et dator, quia sous est verus Deus, ipse dat regna terrena et bonis et malis, neque hoc temere et quasi fortuito, quia Deus est, non fortuna . . . feliciattem vero non dat nisi bonis.*" *City of God* 4.33.

78. Taylor, *Secular Age*, 243.

CHAPTER 8

OLD AND NEW ACTIONS OF GOD

Reimagining Divine Agency after the Apocalyptic Turn

R. DAVID NELSON

> *Beginning with Moses and all the prophets, he interpreted*
> *to them the things about himself in all the scriptures. As they came*
> *near the village to which they were going, he walked ahead as if he*
> *were going on. But they urged him strongly, saying, "Stay with us,*
> *because it is almost evening and the day is now nearly over." So he*
> *went in to stay with them. When he was at the table with them, he*
> *took bread, blessed and broke it, and gave it to them. Then their*
> *eyes were opened, and they recognized him; and he vanished*
> *from their sight. They said to each other, "Were not our*
> *hearts burning within us while he was talking to us on*
> *the road, while he was opening the scriptures to us?"*
> —LUKE 24:27–32

WHEN WE STUMBLE UPON OUR TWO travelers on the road to Emmaus in this familiar passage from Luke's Gospel, we find them in the throes of confusion and despair. The events surrounding Jesus's condemnation and crucifixion were fresh on their minds. "We had hoped that he was the one to redeem Israel," Cleopas exclaims to Jesus, not recognizing him at this point in the narrative. But, he laments, "it is now the third day since these things took place" (v. 21). Jesus's reaction to the travelers' despondency is astonishing. Instead of unveiling to them his true identity, he continues to mask himself. He rebukes them: "Oh, how foolish you are, and how slow of heart to believe all that the prophets have declared!" (v. 25). But then he tarries with them, joining them on their journey for a little while, filling the time of their passage to Emmaus by leading them back to the Scriptures; to the stories and songs and prophecies which they knew well, showing them how these very Scriptures speak, in fact, of him.

"The Christ becomes a teacher" on the Emmaus road, as Jean-Luc Marion puts it in his interpretation of the Lukan pericope.[1] We note that Jesus does not merely select a handful of passages from the Scriptures, arguing that this or that text points beyond its original circumstances to the Messiah, perhaps by way of prophecy and fulfillment, or type and antitype. Rather, according to the grammar of Luke's tale, Jesus teaches them how *all* of the Scriptures together find their meaning in the Christ's coming. And this insight forces Cleopas and the other traveler to reimagine how they understood the identity of the Messiah and, what is more, everything which had occurred in God's dealings with the world and with Israel prior to the Messiah's arrival. To be sure, our travelers thought they knew the very Scriptures Jesus taught them afresh on the way to Emmaus. And they thought, too, that they had pegged Jesus as the militant Messiah who would not suffer, and whose coming the Scriptures foretold. But the new light Jesus shines upon the old texts disrupts the travelers' certainty of and confidence in their long-held assumptions about how God is at work in the world.

In a striking way, Luke's pericope of the Emmaus encounter leads us directly to the theme of divine action. On the way to Emmaus, Jesus teaches Cleopas and the other traveler that the gracious actions of God toward and on behalf of God's creatures find their unity and meaning in the advent of the Messiah. The notion that the Scriptures convey such an unfolding plan would not have been alien to Jesus's original followers. We catch a glimpse of this fact in the text itself when Cleopas declares that they "had hoped that Jesus would redeem Israel." Jesus's admonition to Cleopas indicates that this messianic hope originated in the promises of the prophets, and that his travelers had proven slow to learn all they had heard

---

1. Jean-Luc Marion, "The Recognized Him; and He Became Invisible to Them," trans. Stephen E. Lewis, *Modern Theology* 18, no. 2 (2002): 145–52.

about the Scriptures from Jesus during his itinerant ministry. We might dare put it this way: from Jesus's public teaching the disciples had come to hold something like a doctrine of providence, according to which the ancient stories of creation and Israel's election and redemption convey the unfolding of a plan ordained and enacted by God, and reaching its climax in the Christ. And yet, without the new light of Easter, they are unable to understand how this plan hangs together, and precisely the sense in which it anticipates and is accomplished in the Messiah's arrival on the scene.

Among other things, what is at stake in this passage is, as it were, the relationship between *old* and *new*. Other passages of Scripture juxtapose old and new more directly and contrastively, of course, as in Isaiah's well-known oracle: "Do not remember the former things, or consider the things of old. I am about to do a *new thing*; now it springs forth, do you not perceive it?" (Isa 43:18–19). What makes the Lukan passage remarkable is how the evangelist draws together old and new while keeping them in tension. Jesus leads his disciples back to the old actions of God to explain the new divine actions they are just now witnessing in the events surrounding Jesus's ministry, trial, and execution. And yet, crucially, it is only a bit later when Jesus unveils himself to them, in the "Aha!" moment when "their eyes were opened," that they are fully and finally able to see the old in a new light.

My modest goal in this chapter is to inspect this relationship between the old and new actions of God. I do not wish to resolve or escape from Luke's tension between old and new but to remain there, in these comments uncovering a few significant aspects of old and new for Christian theology.[2]

Now, the question of how the new relates to the old has become a matter of some urgency with the recent rise of theology "after the apocalyptic turn."[3] In 1960, Ernst Käsemann famously declared that "apocalyptic

---

2. As will become clear, I especially am interested in this chapter in testing theology's *categorical* employment of old and new. Throughout the sections that follow, I use the adjectives old and new to draw distinctions between particular pairs of opposites: e.g., between Old and New Testaments, between the old actions of God in Israel and the new actions of God in Jesus Christ, between the old and new "ages," and so on. What I hope to show is that theology must take pains to sort out how the new arises and yet is distinct from the old. While I am largely persuaded by many of the claims of the new apocalyptic theology, I am made uneasy by the dualistic, oppositional distinction some of its adherents draw between old and new. The Lukan pericope and others like it beg for a more delicate approach.

3. Philip G. Ziegler offers a programmatic introduction to apocalyptic theology in the book *Militant Grace: The Apocalyptic Turn and the Future of Christian Theology* (Grand Rapids: Baker Academic, 2018). I am indebted to Ziegler for my own understanding of the "apocalyptic turn" and its importance for systematic theology. On the concerns, tasks, and ends of apocalyptic theology,

was the mother of all Christian theology"[4] but that, since the period of incipient Christianity, theology has wandered far from its apocalyptic origins. The new apocalyptic theology seeks to recover for today's theological work the significance of the apocalyptic imagination supposedly found at the wellspring of the New Testament and the early Christian witness. Capitalizing upon apocalyptic interrogations of some key New Testament texts—chiefly, but not exclusively, Pauline[5]—today's apocalyptic theologians are advancing a brand of theological discourse which stresses the radical newness, unearthliness, mysteriousness, and disruptiveness of Good Friday and Easter Sunday. Moreover, the rediscovery of these emphases at the heart of the early Christian gospel has engendered new ways of understanding subsequent Christianity's (and Christian theology's) entanglements with structures of power. By underscoring the Pauline notion that the gospel of Jesus Christ cuts against the "rulers . . . authorities . . . and cosmic powers of this present darkness" (Eph 6:12), apocalyptic theology is inspiring new and creative ways for addressing issues such as racism, colonialism, misogyny, xenophobia, disenfranchisement, poverty, and so on as genuine theological problems. Indeed, it is demonstrable that some of the most provocative and profitable work being done at the intersection of theology and areas of inquiry such as politics, economics, and sociology is drawing its inspiration from contemporary theology's engagement with apocalyptic themes.[6]

---

see also Joshua B. Davis and Douglas Harink, eds., *Apocalyptic and the Future of Theology: With and Beyond J. Louis Martyn* (Eugene, OR: Cascade, 2012); Cyril O'Regan, *Theology and the Spaces of Apocalyptic* (Milwaukee: Marquette University Press, 2009); and the essays anthologized in the special issue of *Theology Today* on apocalyptic theology, edited by Nancy J. Duff and Philip G. Ziegler: *Theology Today* 75 no. 1 (2018).

4. Ernst Käsemann, "The Beginnings of Christian Theology," in *New Testament Questions of Today* (Philadelphia: Fortress, 1969), 102. On Käsemann's significance for contemporary apocalyptic theology, see Ry O. Siggelkow, "Ernst Käsemann and the Specter of Apocalyptic," in *Theology Today* 75, no. 1 (2018): 37–50.

5. Research emerging at the intersection of apocalyptic theology and New Testament exegesis and interpretation is an ever-expanding field. For reasons which take us well beyond the scope of this chapter, but which are well worth exploring, contemporary apocalyptic theology has depended mainly upon engagements with Paul's letters. On the apocalyptic reading of Paul, see the essays collected in Ben C. Blackwell, John K. Goodrich, and Jason Matson, eds., *Paul and the Apocalyptic Imagination* (Minneapolis: Fortress, 2016). J. P. Davies provides a comprehensive, well-researched, and highly critical assessment of the apocalyptic school of Pauline scholarship in *Paul among the Apocalypses? An Evaluation of the "Apocalyptic Paul" in the Context of Jewish and Christian Apocalyptic Literature*, ed. Chris Keith (London: Bloomsbury, 2016).

6. To mention a handful of key texts which exhibit the application of apocalyptic discourse to the discipline and concerns of practical theology: Nancy J. Duff, "Pauline Apocalyptic and Theological Ethics," in *Apocalyptic and the New Testament: Essays in Honor of J. Louis Martyn*, ed. Joel Marcus and Marion L. Soards (Sheffield: Sheffield Academic, 1989), 279–96; Nathan R. Kerr, *Christ, History and Apocalyptic: The Politics of Christian Mission* (Eugene, OR: Cascade, 2009); Travis Kroeker, *Messianic Political Theology and Diaspora Ethics: Essays in Exile* (Eugene, OR: Cascade,

The new apocalyptic theology stresses the sheer novelty of divine agency. In an era of theological discourse in which discussions of this theme by and large are dominated by analytic accounts of the logic of divine action in a world putatively governed, as a closed system, by natural processes, apocalyptic theology advises us to consider the revelatory, disruptive character of God's outer works. When God acts, that is, God does something *new* in the world. God *intervenes*, breaking into the course of the world, which otherwise is ensnared by evil, dominated by the powers and principalities, and, as it were, passing away. As Fleming Rutledge puts it, summarizing J. Louis Martyn, a seminal figure in theology after the apocalyptic turn[7] and to whose work we will return momentarily, God's creatively redemptive actions mark "a genuine *novum*, a first-order reversal of all previous arrangements, an altogether new creation *ex nihilo*, out of nothing."[8] Philip G. Ziegler likewise proposes that the apocalyptic expressions found in the early Christian witness "are not images of mere repair, development, or incremental improvement within a broadly stable situation" but rather suggest "a radical break with what has gone before, its overturning, its revolution, its displacement."[9]

I wish neither to dispute nor to disparage the thesis that God has done something utterly and disruptively new in Jesus Christ. But what are the theological consequences of describing that new divine action as "an altogether new creation *ex nihilo*" (Rutledge) or "a radical break with what has gone before" (Ziegler)? After all, in our opening passage from Luke's Gospel, Jesus teaches his disciples about, as it were, the *continuity* between Easter Sunday and everything they knew of God's work in the world from of old. To put it better, in appearing to the disciples, teaching them, blessing and breaking bread with them, and revealing to them that he had defeated death and now lives, Jesus pries open their eyes to see the old things of God anew. The new apocalyptic theology urges us to consider the radical discontinuity between old and new. But our passage and others like it compel us to take seriously the continuity between old and new as well.

2017); and Paul L. Lehmann, *Ethics in a Christian Context* (New York: Harper & Row, 1963). See also the essays composing the third unit (titled "Part 3: Living Faithfully at the Turn of the Ages") in Ziegler, *Militant Grace*, 113–200.

7. The key contributions are J. Louis Martyn, *Galatians*, Anchor Bible 33A (New York: Doubleday, 1997); *History and Theology in the Fourth Gospel*, 3rd ed. (Louisville: Westminster John Knox, 2003); and *Theological Issues in the Letters of Paul* (Nashville: Abingdon, 1997).

8. Fleming Rutledge, *The Crucifixion: Understanding the Death of Jesus Christ* (Grand Rapids: Eerdmans, 2015), 355.

9. Ziegler, *Militant Grace*, 28.

To further illustrate the problem here, let us briefly appraise an important passage from one of the new apocalyptic theology's signature texts—J. Louis Martyn's oft-cited essay "Epistemology at the Turn of the Ages."[10] The piece is an exercise in Pauline exegesis, and, as the title suggests, Martyn is concerned to test Paul's understanding of how we *know* God in light of the apostolic message concerning Jesus. In the essay he argues that, for Paul, "there are two ways of knowing, and . . . what separates the two is the turn of the ages, the apocalyptic event of Christ's death/resurrection. There is a way of knowing which is characteristic of the old age . . . there must be a new way of knowing that is proper either to the new age or to that point at which the ages meet."[11] For Martyn's Paul, that is, the crucifixion and resurrection of Jesus signify the invasion of the new age into the fabric of the old, and this intervention ushers in a new mode of epistemology. Furthermore, in Martyn's reading, for Paul the "two ways of knowing" which diverge at the fulcrum of the gospel correspond to "two kinds of knowers."[12] The knowledge proper to the old age is knowledge *kata sarka*, knowledge according to the flesh. Apart from the gospel, presses Martyn, every one of us knows according to the flesh, and knowledge *of God* according to the flesh avails us nothing, for God is known only according to the Spirit. The one who knows and thinks *kata sarka* is, for Paul, "the *psychikos anthrōpos* ('the unspiritual person')."[13] Unanimated by the Spirit, the unspiritual person is incapable of knowing that the new age has arrived in the crucified Christ. Hence, "it is

---

10. J. Louis Martyn, "Epistemology at the Turn of the Ages," in *Theological Issues in the Letters of Paul*, 89–110. As we shall see, in the essay Martyn focuses on the distinctions between the old and new *ages*, and between the old and new *ways of knowing* which correspond to the two ages. I concede that these distinctions indeed might do a bit of work soteriologically and exegetically, as Paul does appear to use the two-age structure to describe the event of salvation and the epistemological change occurring in conversion. However, and as will become apparent, I am less inclined than Martyn to draw the distinction between the old age/way of knowing and new age/way of knowing as one of sheer opposition and antagonism.

11. Martyn, "Epistemology at the Turn of the Ages," 95. It is worth noting that Martyn here does not map out the old and new ages *chronologically*. The sense of the essay, rather, is that the new age is the apocalyptic revelation of the crucified Christ, the old age *everything* that is not (yet) governed by Christ's lordship. As much as I am persuaded by the radical novelty marking Martyn's understanding of Paul's two-age eschatology, I am yet troubled that the chronological dimensions of this approach are left unexplored. Are the old things of God recounted in the narrative of Israel among the "everything" upended by the cross? Or does Israel somehow participate in the revelation of the new? Martyn does not devote attention to such questions, as they are tangential to his concerns in the essay. But a comprehensive apocalyptic theology taking its cues from Martyn will need to do the work of sorting out how the two-age structure of Paul's eschatology relates to the chronologically old and new.

12. Martyn, "Epistemology at the Turn of the Ages," 99.

13. Martyn, "Epistemology at the Turn of the Ages," 99.

clear that the implied opposite of knowing by the norm of the flesh is not knowing by the norm of the Spirit, but rather knowing *kata stauron* ('by the cross')."[14] In Martyn's reading, then, Paul understood the cross as "the absolute epistemological watershed," a dividing line between knowledge *kata sarka* and knowledge *kata stauron*. In the present epoch stretching from the crucifixion to the parousia, the foolishness of the cross is set alongside the wisdom of the world—that is, knowledge is *either* according to the flesh *or* according to "the Spirit of the crucified Christ."[15]

On one hand, Martyn's understanding of Paul's epistemology appears to shed at least a bit of light on the question of the *knowledge* of old and new which emerges in our Emmaus road pericope from Luke. Consider Cleopas. We encounter him at the very meeting point of the ages: on Easter Sunday, just after the others had discovered the empty tomb. Cleopas almost assuredly had been a follower of Jesus during the years of itinerant public ministry. As such, in addition to what he would have learned of the law and the prophets in synagogue, he would have heard the Scriptures as Jesus had taught them. For precisely this reason, Jesus appears exasperated that Cleopas cannot make sense of the immediate news on the basis of everything he already had heard. Cleopas, we might say, possesses knowledge but lacks understanding. But even Jesus's overview of "Moses and all the prophets" does not suffice to turn the light on. While the travelers' hearts were burning within them while Jesus recounted the Scriptures to them, it was only when Jesus fully unveiled himself, and they knew for certain the reality of the resurrection, that Cleopas and his companion understood. Martyn's Pauline epistemology, once again, seems helpful here. The appearance of the resurrected Jesus before the travelers signifies the incursion of a new reality that shatters the course of their world. A "new way of knowing" intrudes upon Cleopas and his companion once the reality of the resurrection of the crucified Christ is revealed. In his essay, Martyn draws the starkest possible contrast between the new knowledge marking the age which dawns upon the world on Easter Sunday and the old knowledge which dominates the world otherwise. Accordingly, one way of reading Cleopas's sudden conversion from knowledge to understanding might be to perceive him as, at first in the passage, being stuck in the "old way of knowing," but then, at the end of the passage, knowing things ever anew in light of the resurrected Christ's full self-disclosure.[16]

---

14. Martyn, "Epistemology at the Turn of the Ages," 108.
15. Martyn, "Epistemology at the Turn of the Ages," 108.
16. The passage nicely illustrates the question I posed above concerning the relation between Paul's two-age epistemology and the chronologically old and new. At the end of the Lukan narrative,

While we might be able to imagine some connections between Martyn's interpretation of Paul's epistemology and our Lukan passage, I continue to worry that Martyn stresses the discontinuity between old knowledge and new knowledge, and between the two ages, too sharply and categorically. Even if we are to grant that Martyn's "epistemological watershed" is illustrated in the travelers' sudden arrival at new insight, there remains the matter of the journey through Moses and the prophets that unfolds as Jesus, Cleopas, and the third companion head toward Emmaus. If the new age and the knowledge corresponding to it indeed are *sheerly new*, why would Luke's Jesus spend the miles leading to Emmaus retelling old news?

Let me take us to one additional passage from Martyn which sheds further light on the problem here. While the stark discontinuity between old age and new age is prominent throughout the essay on Paul's epistemology, elsewhere Martyn gives us something of a summary statement on the matter. In a piece in which he places Paul and Flannery O'Connor in a dialogue across the centuries, he summarizes the sheer contrast between the old age and the "new creation," a Pauline locution recurring throughout Martyn's writings which functions as a near equivalent to the idea of the "new age." Martyn draws out the differences this way:

In Paul's apocalyptic, as in war, there are two opposing sides, the Old Age and the new creation.

Old Age	New Creation
orb of evil and sin	orb of grace
sphere under the power of Satan, the ruler of this age	sphere under the power of God, the Spirit of Christ
slavery	freedom
death	life
the oppressive status quo	the genuinely new

---

we witness Cleopas's eyes being opened by his encounter with the risen Lord. He *converts*, that is, from the old way of knowing to the new knowledge revealed in the resurrection. And yet, Jesus's summary of Israel's story is the prominent feature of the first half of the passage. Jesus's report of old news somehow anticipates Cleopas's conversion—"Were not our hearts burning within us . . . ?" But the decisive moment comes with the blessing and breaking of the bread, and this instant sheds light on everything. We might say that Cleopas arrives at the continuity between old and new—the insight that all of God's actions toward creatures find their unity in Christ—*retrospectively* and only in view of Easter. In any case, the passage ties together old and new rather than sheerly drawing them apart.

Here the imagery of apocalyptic war presupposes a *provisional eschatological dualism.* As in war, so in apocalypse, two sides are dynamically interrelated.[17]

In this passage, Martyn describes the distinction between new and old as a *war* between two opposing sides engaged in a fierce skirmish with each other.[18] The new creation violently interrupts and invades the old, exposing it for what it is; namely, a downward slide toward the abyss of death and nothingness. But the old is a sturdy foe of the new creation, resisting at all costs the light shed abroad in the gospel against the world's darkness.[19]

With Martyn and the new apocalyptic theologians he has inspired, we must appreciate the unexpectedness and radical newness of the apocalypse of Good Friday and Easter Sunday. But if we draw the distinction between that apocalypse and everything else too stringently, such that all of God's old actions in the world become just that—old—we risk neutralizing the full scope of Scripture's witness to God's gracious and providential agency. These passages from Martyn, whose insights I take to be representative of the new apocalyptic theology, vividly illustrate the concern. For here we discover a *dualistic* arrangement of old and new, an *antinomy*—one of Martyn's favorite terms[20]—between the old age and the new age, between God's actions from of old and the new thing of God at work in the world in Jesus's crucifixion and resurrection.[21]

On the way toward what I hope is a better way to conceive the relationship between old and new, let us spend a few moments with an extended citation

---

17. Martyn, "From Paul to Flannery O'Connor with the Power of Grace," in *Theological Issues in the Letters of Paul,* 281–82. Emphasis added.

18. Further to the usage of warfare imagery in early Christian apocalyptic, see Martyn's comments in *Galatians,* 100–102 and 530–34.

19. Eberhard Jüngel, to which I will return in a moment, is especially insightful on this point. See Eberhard Jüngel, "The Emergence of the New," trans. Arnold Neufeldt-Fast, in *Theological Essays II,* ed. John B. Webster (Edinburgh: T&T Clark, 1995), 35–58; "New–Old–New: Theological Aphorisms," *Theological Theology: Essays in Honour of John Webster,* ed. R. David Nelson, Darren Sarisky, and Justin Stratis, trans. R. David Nelson (London: Bloomsbury, 2015), 131–35.

20. See, for instance, the essay "Apocalyptic Antinomies," in Martyn, *Theological Issues in the Letters of Paul,* 111–23; and *Galatians.*

21. We may well fully agree with Martyn, of course, if the oppositional arrangement he posits between the two ages is meant to be understood in a soteriologically restricted sense. Just here emerges the proper *distinction* between old and new. "The old" is the world held sway by sin, death, and the devil; "the new" is God's militant action against the hegemony of evil. However, it remains unclear how, for the new apocalyptic theologians, the old things *of God*—particularly the election and redemption of Israel—fit within the Pauline two-age eschatology. As I have suggested here, more work needs to be done to account for what we might call the *chronologically* old and new in light of the *apocalyptically* old and new.

from Eberhard Jüngel. While Jüngel is a bit too early to be considered among the new apocalyptic theologians, his work certainly touches upon a number of apocalyptic themes. In his splendid essay "The Emergence of the New," Jüngel addresses two aspects of "newness" in Christian theology. He first explores whether theological insights or movements or modes of discourse can be said to be authentically new and then considers the significance for Christian dogmatics of Scripture's witness to the renewal of all things that takes place in Jesus Christ. Up until the very end of the essay, Jüngel says nary a thing about "the old" or "oldness." Tacitly, the old functions as the opposite of "the new" he is laboring to describe in the piece's three major sections. In the final paragraph, however, Jüngel gives a nod to the old. His comments here, while hasty and incomplete, reveal some provocative intuitions. He writes,

> I do not want to conclude this discussion of the new without expressly giving something like a formal theological apology for the old. As a precautionary after-thought it needs to be said that it would be appropriate to reflect once more on the category of the old with equal thoroughness and detail from the perspective of the new. . . . In this essay I have spoken of the old almost without exception as an *antithetical concept* to the new. . . . But the old has another side to it. . . . The old is not necessarily hopeless, for it also belongs to the *good order of creation* in which each day has its evening, each human life may and should become old. Old age has its proper dignity. For God himself . . . in the person of the heavenly Father is also the essence of the old . . . the one from whom not only the eternal Son of God whom we have come to know in the person of Jesus Christ has his origin, but from whom also *everything* originates, and to whom not only the creative, renewing power of the Holy Spirit returns, but to whom also *everything* returns, so that through participation in the mystery of the trinitarian God everything is as it was of old, *with this ancient God* without whom everything simply is and remains utterly new.[22]

Three things of note stand out in this fascinating passage. First, Jüngel is not expressing an interest in the old for its own sake but calls for a theological appraisal of the old "*from the perspective of the new.*" Jüngel is clear in the earlier sections of the essay that Christian theology must prioritize the category of the new over the category of the old. But on the basis of its understanding of the new, theology can and should reflect upon the old.

---

22. Jüngel, "Emergence of the New," 58.

To put this less abstractly, and to return for a moment to our passage from Luke, I take the sense of the pericope to be that Jesus's rehearsal of the old news of Moses and the prophets availed Cleopas and his companion nothing *as such*, for Jesus remained veiled to them at that point in the narrative. The old, as it were, *became new* to them only when Jesus revealed to them his identity, an event which signified the dawn of the new age of Easter. The new thing revealed in Jesus Christ, we might say, freshly illuminates God's work in creation and in the election, preservation, and restoration of Israel. Second, I want to earmark for now Jüngel's assertion that the old "*belongs to the good order of creation.*" To be sure, and as Martyn underlines, certain New Testament passages urge us that a new creation springs forth in the world as dawn breaks on Easter Sunday. But Scripture also says much about *original* or *first* creation and about God's work of sustaining and governing creation and the creatures God has made. Jüngel's comments suggest that theology must coordinate these two dimensions of the doctrine of creation; namely, the first and new events of creation. Third, we observe that Jüngel sketches the *Trinitarian coordinates* of the distinction between old and new. Those familiar with Jüngel's theological work will not find such a move surprising, for he is well known for his explorations of the significance of the doctrine of the Trinity for a host of topics. The long final sentence with which he concludes "The Emergence of the New" is highly evocative. For Jüngel, the Christian confession of God as Father, Son, and Spirit requires us to give due acknowledgment to old *and* new, for insofar as we participate in the triune life of God, we live and move and have our being (Acts 17:28) in One who is *ever ancient* in the person of the Father and *ever new* in the persons of the Son and the Spirit. In our eternal presence before the triune God, the "total and perfect possession at one time of unlimited life," as Boethius famously puts it,[23] old and new will become one.

Jüngel never returned to expand upon these comments. He published one other piece on the theological problem of the new after the appearance of the essay we have considered here,[24] and the later piece lacks a "formal theological apology for the old." The apologetic paragraph from "The Emergence of the New," then, stands as a signpost of a theological path not taken. But the inchoate remarks yet offer some clues for how we might

---

23. Boethius, *The Consolation of Philosophy* 5.6, trans. Scott Goins and Barbara H. Wyman, ed. Joseph Pearce (San Francisco: Ignatius, 2012), 167.
24. Jüngel, "New–Old–New."

do justice to the old while appreciating the sheer novelty of the new thing emerging in the world in the resurrection of the crucified one.

Working out a comprehensive theological account of the old in light of the new is a task which transcends the boundaries of the present chapter. In lieu of such an account, let me here briefly attend to two significant aspects of the tension between the old actions of God in the world and the new thing which interrupts the world in Jesus Christ. To my mind, a serious theological treatment of old and new would need to address these two issues at length. We may begin with a question: What are some of the "old things of God," as we might put it, which are seen anew in the light of Easter?

First, and as we encountered in our exposition of the Lukan pericope, the advent of the new in Jesus Christ illuminates the old actions of God recounted in "Moses and all the prophets" (Luke 24:27). Jesus takes Cleopas and his companion back to the Jewish Scriptures to teach them all that had been said from of old about the events they were just now experiencing. Luke's Emmaus road passage is by no means the only text from the New Testament to suggest that, as Richard Hays puts it, "the whole story of Israel builds to its narrative climax in Jesus."[25] Peter, for instance, begins his sermon at Pentecost by leading his listeners back to the prophets and the Psalter (Acts 2). Stephen, likewise, defends his newfound faith before the high priest by epitomizing the history of the patriarchs and the exodus, arguing at his own peril that these old narratives receive new meaning when measured against "the coming of the Righteous One" (Acts 7:52). Paul's epistles, too, are replete with citations from and paraphrases and interpretations of the Scriptures of Israel. To be sure, Paul endeavors in his letters to displace a certain construal of those Scriptures, according to which "the boundary between light and darkness has been set at the border between the holy people and the idolatrous realm of the Gentiles."[26] Paul's new construal, however, "purports to be grounded in Scripture itself" rather than in a concept or worldview alien to it.[27] Paul, we might dare say, rereads the Jewish Scriptures in light of his encounter with the resurrected Christ and

---

25. Richard B. Hays, "Can the Gospels Teach Us How to Read the Old Testament?" *Pro Ecclesia* 11 (2002): 416.

26. Francis Watson, *Paul and the Hermeneutics of Faith* (London: T&T Clark, 2004), 168.

27. Watson, *Paul and the Hermeneutics of Faith*, 167. On this tension between Paul's "hermeneutic" of faith and the "construal" against which Paul is writing, see 167–69.

rebuilds the continuity between old and new on the basis of that disruptive experience. To point to one additional example: the exordium of Hebrews begins with the assertion that "long ago, in many and various ways, God spoke to our ancestors through the prophets" (Heb 1:1). Hebrews presupposes that God indeed was speaking *back then*. "In these *last days*," however, "he has spoken to us by a Son" (2:2). As Craig R. Koester comments, the switch to the indicative mood in the second verse signifies that, for the author, "the Son is God's *definitive* mode of communication."[28] From this beginning, Hebrews unfolds for us a literary Emmaus road experience, showing us how the word definitively spoken in the Son obliges us to reimagine the entire sweep of God's agency toward Israel.

This is not the place to try out a solution to the thorny problem of supersessionism, into the brambles of which my comments here might be seen to lead. A comprehensive theological treatment of old and new would need to address supersessionism and also test the various models theology has proposed for the relationships between Israel and the church and the Old and New Testaments. Above all, theology's urgent task in regard to these matters is to clarify how the astonishingly and disruptively new thing of Easter morning yet stands—somehow—in continuity with God's actions from of old. Sheerly contrastive or dualistic categorical accounts of old and new do not work, for they invariably marginalize, neutralize, or even obliterate the old for the sake of the new. What is needed, then, and to put it abstractly in hopes of perhaps pointing to one plausible solution, is a model of old and new in which the continuity conjoining them must be seen in light of the even greater distinction between them.[29]

Second, and as Jüngel urges us in the passage cited at length above, in light of the new we must give due attention to the oldness of first creation, to the old—and *good*—actions of God in creating, sustaining, and governing the world and all creatures. Demonstrably so, Christian theology always has reserved a special significance both for the doctrine of first creation

---

28. Craig R. Koester, *Hebrews*, Anchor Bible 36 (New York: Doubleday, 2001), 177. Emphasis added.

29. The nod here is to the structure of *analogy*, and my language deliberately invokes the classic expression of the *analogia entis* from Lateran IV: "For between creator and creature there can be noted no similarity so great that a greater dissimilarity cannot be seen between them." See Lateran IV, constitution 2, in *Decrees of the Ecumenical Councils*, ed. Norman P. Tanner, SJ (London: Sheed and Ward, 1990), 1:232. I am open to the possibility that the *structure* of analogy, and not the *analogia entis* itself, may be of use in clarifying the sense in which old and new are continuous and discontinuous at the same time—precisely the impression one gets when reading passages from the New Testament such as those cited above. I certainly prefer an analogical account to the dualisms funding the new apocalyptic theology. In any case, the task of refining such an account exceeds the limits of the present chapter.

and for the doctrine of God as Creator. The new apocalyptic theology, however, is challenging theology's longstanding investment in the theme of *first* creation, underscoring instead the *new* creation emerging in the world on Easter Sunday. We discover here once again that the dualistic categorization of old and new appears to lead inevitably to the annihilation of the old. Illustrating this concern, in his Galatians commentary, Martyn makes the startling claim that Paul's depiction of creation in the epistle is "not altogether dissimilar to the one later proposed by Marcion and the second-century gnostics." Martyn wonders aloud whether Paul in fact "denies the divine origin . . . of creation." He proposes, however, that a proper understanding of the dualistic apocalyptic structure of God's creative agency in the world helps to resolve these tensions. According to Martyn, "What is fundamentally wrong with . . . creation . . . is that (it has) fallen into the company of anti–God powers . . . *God's* creation has fallen prey to anti–God powers that have turned it into 'the present evil age,' and that is the reason for God's having to act in Christ to terminate the elemental pairs of opposites that are anything but his servants."[30] For just this reason—that is, because God's creation has been usurped and is no longer sustained or governed by God, hence God has to intervene anew to rescue creation—we must, for Martyn, conceive the first creation and new creation as relating to one another in oppositional fashion. Something is "fundamentally wrong" with first creation; we hardly can say that first creation is *good*. At best, the doctrine and confession of first creation simply is of little or no use to us theologically, since it draws our attention to what may or may not have occurred prior to the invasion of the world by "anti–God powers." Data from prelapsarian times is not available to us; all we know, rather, is the present evil age from which God has delivered us on the cross.

To his great credit, Martyn urges us to take with dead seriousness the Pauline claim that our world presently is besieged by evil powers and principalities. Both Scripture and the classical tradition of theological discourse support him on this point. Theology, however, ordinarily looks for ways to distinguish between, on one hand, the evil which ever threatens us and, on the other, the inherent goodness of the world God has made. To cite but one example, in his "Treatise on Creation," Thomas refuses to concede the goodness of creation to the evil which ever wages war against the good. Toward this end, and idiosyncratically, he draws a distinction between goods which are wholly corrupted by evil, goods which are neither wholly

---

30. Martyn, *Galatians*, 417.

destroyed nor diminished by evil, and the essential aptitudes of a subject, which likewise cannot be utterly ruined by evil.[31] Thomas's distinction allows him to acknowledge the pervasiveness and corrupting potency of evil while maintaining that the goodness of creation is not altogether overwhelmed by sin, death, and the devil.

My point here, simply, is that theology must take care to nuance the complicated relationship between first creation and new creation. We are obliged, I contend, to seek ways to describe the great continuity between God's original creative actions and the new thing intruding upon the world in Jesus Christ, just as we stress the even greater discontinuity between them.

I have spent most of this chapter arguing that Christian theology must take pains to properly sort out the relationship between old and new, between God's ancient actions and the newness of Easter's dawn. I would be remiss if I failed to at least briefly touch upon how we experience the tension between the old and the new in the course of the Christian life. Let me conclude my remarks, then, with a brief proposal: In the Christian life, we encounter the convergence of old and new primarily whenever we hear the Word of God proclaimed and receive the mysteries of the faith in the sacraments. The proclamation of the ever-living Word of the Gospel—which is always new, and never gets old—occurs with the opening of *ancient* texts. Especially for those of us who have grown up hearing them, the stories of the Bible, the narratives of Israel and of Jesus and of the apostles, are intimately familiar. And yet, when we hear the preaching of those same old texts, we are confronted with, to borrow the words of Barth, the *new world* in the Bible.[32] Scripture, when recited and proclaimed, marks for us a nexus of old and new, taking us back to the things long past, even while renewing us.

The sacraments, too, I propose, are events of the Christian life in which we encounter the sublime intersection of old and new. For baptism and

---

31. *ST* I.48.1. As Gilson points out, the basis of Thomas's distinctions is a theodicy according to which the good is acknowledged as the material cause of evil. See Gilson's discussion in *The Philosophy of St. Thomas Aquinas*, ed. G. A. Elrington, trans. Edward Bullough (New York: Dorset, 1987), 159–62; also the entirety of Thomas's argument in question 48. I am less interested here in Thomas's differentiated causality than I am with his principle that evil cannot fully overwhelm the good.

32. From Barth's well-known essay, "Die neue Welt in der Bibel," which was first rendered in English under the adjusted title, "The Strange New World in the Bible." See Karl Barth, *The Word of God and the Word of Man*, trans. Douglas Horton (Cleveland: Pilgrim, 1928), 28–50.

the Lord's Supper pivot on the postures of memory and anticipation. In Christian baptism, we *remember*, and in our liturgical actions *re-present*, the death, burial, and resurrection of Jesus Christ. But Scripture declares that "we have been buried with him by baptism into death, so that, just as Christ was raised from the dead by the glory of the Father, so we too might walk in newness of life" (Rom 6:4). As such, just as baptism draws us back to the finished events of Jesus Christ, by the promise it bears it awakens in us *anticipation* of the resurrected life, the newness of which we may experience now in the power of the Spirit. Likewise, when we gather to celebrate the Lord's Supper, we recall the last meal that Jesus shared with his disciples on the very night in which one of them betrayed him. We *remember* that night, and in our liturgical actions we *re-present* the very words of promise Jesus shared with his first disciples, recognizing those words as promises made to us as well. And when the bread is broken and the wine is poured, we *remember* and *re-present* the breaking of Christ's body and the scattering of his blood. In all of this we also *anticipate* the great eschatological banquet awaiting us, the benefits of which are ours even now by virtue of the tokens of Christ's promises. Baptism and the Lord's Supper lead us directly to the crossroads of old and new.

It is fitting, in light of these immediate comments, to end where we began. On the road to Emmaus, the Christ becomes a *preacher*. Jesus proclaimed to Cleopas and his companion the ancient stories, showing them how what was known from of old points to the new of the Messiah's advent. And yet the moment of true insight for the disciples comes later, when Jesus sits for a moment among them, and blesses and breaks the bread. Old and new collide on Easter Sunday, first along a dusty road a few miles from Jerusalem, and later around a quiet table and as the risen Jesus unveils himself to his friends.

CHAPTER 9

THE DEVIL'S WORK
Divine Providence and its Antithesis

PHILIP G. ZIEGLER

> *But the Lord is faithful; he will strengthen*
> *you and guard you from the evil one.*
> —2 THESSALONIANS 3:3

INTRODUCTION: THE DEVIL AND THE PROVIDENCE OF GOD

In the course of her landmark study *Evil in Modern Thought*, Susan Neiman observes that it was characteristic of some of the most honest and searching philosophical critics of the modern age to "reject every reference to Providence as a sign of cowardice."[1] Confrontation with evil marked by intellectual and moral courage demanded that pious and rationalising appeals to divine causality and sovereignty be jettisoned for the sake of both honesty and the active amelioration of suffering. These kinds of challenges, issued by Bayle, Hume, and their like, have long conspired with the corrosive effects of scientific naturalism upon the necessity and intelligibility of explanatory invocation of God in relation to the nature both of things and of human affairs. The result has been to fund a cultural situation in which Christian talk of providence "comes to be considered as at best redundant

---

1. Susan Neiman, *Evil in Modern Thought: An Alternative History of Philosophy* (Princeton: Princeton University Press, 2002), 115. She has Bayle and Hume foremost in mind in this remark.

and at worst destructive."[2] It is no surprise then, that, as Langdon Gilkey famously put it years ago, the doctrine of providence under the conditions of modernity became "the forgotten stepchild of contemporary theology."[3]

It seems perverse to imagine that this situation could in any way be improved in the early twenty-first century by a fresh and a vigorous recollection of the inalienable place and importance of the devil within the normative sources of Christian faith, life, and thought. But the suggestion is perhaps so counterintuitive that we should be allowed to pursue it, if only because so little might be expected from it. In fact, I am not ambitious to argue that attending to the "works of the devil" offers a comprehensive curative to all that ails the doctrine of providence. Rather, in what follows I would like to offer some modest reflections on the way in which our grasp of the grammar and function of the doctrine of providence might be altered in light of some explicit thinking about the problem of the devil in relation to the sustaining and governing sovereignty of God.

As recent scholarship continues to establish and detail, the discourse about the reality, presence, and agency of evil powers essentially inimical to both God and humanity is a widespread and inalienable feature of the biblical witness. While the specific discourse of "satan" or "the devil" is more narrowly attested, when the full semantic field of synonymous, analogous, synecdochical, and related discourse is taken into consideration, there is really quite a bit of "diabolical data" in the details of the scriptural record.[4] And not only incidentally so. Joseph Ratzinger comments upon

---

2. John Webster, "Providence," in *Mapping Modern Theology: A Thematic and Historical Introduction*, ed. K. M. Kapic and B. L. McCormack (Grand Rapids: Baker Academic, 2012), 209.

3. Langdon Gilkey, "The Concept of Providence in Contemporary Theology," *The Journal of Religion* 43, no. 3 (1963): 174 (171–92). More recently see also Wilhelm Hüffmeier, "Deus providebit? Eine Zwischenbilanz zur Kritik der Lehre von Gottes Vorsehung," in *Denkwürdiges Geheimnis: Beiträge zur Gotteslehre—Festschrift für Eberhard Jüngel zum 70. Geburtstag*, ed. I. Dalferth (Tübingen: Mohr Siebeck, 2004), 237–58. The appearance of new constructive dogmatic discussions of the doctrine are notable; see for example the programmatic essays of Kate Sonderegger ("The Doctrine of Providence") and John Webster ("On the Theology of Providence") in *The Providence of God*, ed. F. A. Murphy and P. G. Ziegler (London: T&T Clark, 2009), 144–57 and 158–75, as well as David Fergusson, *The Providence of God: A Polyphonic Approach* (Cambridge: Cambridge University Press, 2018). Mark Elliot, *Providence Perceived: Divine Action from a Human Point of View* (Berlin: De Gruyter, 2015) offers a wide-ranging historical presentation of the vicissitudes of the doctrine from the early church to the present day.

4. See *Evil and the Devil*, ed. I. Fröhlich and E Koskenniemi (London: T&T Clark, 2013); Thomas J. Farrar and Guy J. Williams, "Diabolical Data: A Critical Inventory of New Testament Satanology" and "Talk of the Devil: Unpacking the Language of New Testament Satanology," *Journal for the Study of the New Testament* 39, no. 1 (2016): 40–71 and 72–96; as well as Sydney H. T. Page, "Satan: God's Servant," *Journal of the Evangelical Theological Society* 50, no. 3 (2007): 449–65; and Derek R. Brown, "The Devil in the Details: A Survey of Research on Satan in Biblical Studies," *Currents in Biblical Research* 9, no. 2 (2011): 200–227. Peggy L. Day's study, *An Adversary in Heaven: Satan in the Hebrew Bible* (Atlanta: Scholars Press, 1988), remains a touchstone study of the

the "movement of expansion" that marks the biblical witness on this theme in this way:

> The notion of demonic powers enters only hesitantly into the Old Testament, whereas in the life of Jesus it acquires unprecedented weight, which is undiminished in Paul's letters, and continues into the latest New Testament writings. . . . This process of amplification from the Old Testament to the New, along with the extreme crystallization of the demonic precisely in contact with the figure of Jesus and the persistence of the theme throughout the New Testament witness, is telling.[5]

One of the things of which this amplification, crystallization, and persistence tells is that the drama of salvation rendered by the apostolic witnesses is in fact a "three-agent drama" of divine redemption wherein human beings are delivered by God from captivity to the anti-God powers of sin, death, and the devil.[6] When salvation comes it finds us not only morally malfeasant, impious, and disobedient but also and most fundamentally subjugated by inimical forces beyond our ken, the "cosmic powers of this present darkness" (Eph 6:2). These forces are ruthless to diminish our humanity, to secure our collusion, and so to recruit us to—and make us complicit in—the work of unwinding the good creation and resisting the reign of God. The New Testament is bold to cast these legion powers as the devices and implements of an enemy it various names as the "god of this age" (2 Cor 4:4), the "prince of this world" (John 8:23; 14:30; Rom 12:2; 1 Cor 3:19), the "ruler" of "this present and passing evil age" (1 Cor 2:6; 7:31), and indeed, the devil or Satan.

Any Christian theology keyed to the evangelical centrality of the eschatological conflict between God and these inimical powers becomes responsible for taking seriously this integral concentration upon "the demonic nature of the evil from which the world has to be redeemed" and

---

Old Testament occurrences of the term. The somewhat older study by Jeffrey Burton Russell, *The Devil: Perceptions of Evil from Antiquity to Primitive Christianity* (Ithaca, NY: Cornell University Press, 1977), continues to afford good concise access to relevant history of religions material.

5. Joseph Ratzinger, "Farewell to the Devil?," in *Dogma and Preaching: Applying Christian Doctrine to Daily Life*, ed. M. J. Miller, trans. M. J. Miller and M. J. O'Connell (San Francisco: Ignatius, 2005), 200.

6. On this concept see J. Louis Martyn, "The Gospel Invades Philosophy," in *Paul, Philosophy, and the Theopolitical Vision*, ed. D. Harink (Eugene, OR: Cascade, 2010), 26–33; and "God's Way of Making Things Right," in *Theological Issues in the Letters of Paul* (Edinburgh: T&T Clark, 1997), 152–56 (where he actually speaks of the four agents of the drama in Galatians: "human beings, Christ, God, and the *anti-God powers*" (152). Cf. Philip G. Ziegler, *Militant Grace: The Apocalyptic Turn and the Future of Theology* (Grand Rapids: Baker Academic, 2018), 28–29.

its implications across the range of doctrinal *loci*.[7] In this chapter I want to reflect briefly upon what might be involved in exercising such responsibility in relation to the doctrine of providence. I ask: In what directions is this doctrine driven when the "God who provides" is specifically identified from the revelatory advent of the Son of God who "appeared for the very purpose of undoing the devil's work" (1 John 3:8), and when the nature and course of divine governance is thus reconceived with specific reference to the virulent, deceitful, and murderous opposition of the "ruler of this age" to both God and his good creatures? The twentieth-century Swedish Lutheran theologian Gustaf Aulén will afford us a "worked example" of a treatment of providence framed by reference to the three-agent drama of salvation in which "the old enemy" plays a notably prominent role. Aided by reflection on Aulén's work, I will advance the thesis that, when tethered firmly to the gospel of God's redeeming grace, the doctrine of providence acquires a decidedly dramatic-pragmatic form. Rightly subject to a soteriological concentration, the doctrine can be republished as a doctrine of faith able to help fund what we might call the "practice of providence" in the form of patient and defiant discipleship in a world still distressed by devilish redoubts. God's governed creation is the theatre of faith's proper, hopeful struggle to witness in word and deed to the lordship of Christ in light of the promise that "the God of peace will soon crush Satan under your feet" (Rom 16:20).

Within the limited scope of this essay I restrict myself to extended interaction with Aulén as my primary interlocutor. In a wider effort it would be desirable to interact with other related theological proposals, not least Karl Barth's much debated revisioning of the doctrine of providence.[8] In that account, a strong soteriological focus together with specific attention to the nature and role of the inimical power of evil—for the Swiss theologian, a christological reinterpretation of election and an arresting account of evil as *das Nichtige*, respectively—also combine to notable effect to "licence a practical and *prayerful* discourse about the way God identifies himself as almighty in providence" of the kind pursued in miniature here.[9] We must leave that wider discussion, however, for another occasion.

7. For a concise and vigorous statement of this, see James S. Stewart, "On a Neglected Emphasis in New Testament Theology," *Scottish Journal of Theology* 4, no. 3 (1951): 294 (292–300). This remains an extraordinary and extraordinarily prescient essay.

8. Karl Barth, *Church Dogmatics* III/3, trans. T. F. Torrance and G. W. Bromiley (Edinburgh: T&T Clark, 1960).

9. Christopher Green, *Doxological Theology: Karl Barth on Divine Providence, Evil, and the Angels* (London: T&T Clark, 2011), 11.

"A Certain Dualism": Providence and the Agonism of Faith and Discipleship

No Christian dogmatics can entertain a strict, cosmic, or metaphysical dualism, for whatever it is that faith acknowledges when it acknowledges the devil it is *not* a principle of evil directly proportional to the good God is.[10] Yet even after Manicheism is ruled out, the specific contours of Christian soteriology continue to put particular "dualistic" pressure on elements of the doctrine of providence. This is visible within the history of the doctrine in its recurrent concern to forefend the threat of divine authorship of sin and in the unending labour of theodicy more broadly.[11] Such pressures are only heightened when our thinking about salvation concentrates afresh upon the "three-agent drama" and thus also upon the strict opposition of divine saving grace to the vicious enmity of "sin, death and devil."[12] And so a Christian faith whose hope is funded principally by trust in Christ's victory over the adversary for us necessarily entails *a certain kind* of dualism. But of just what kind, and to what effect?

One of the more direct and elegant efforts to confront the question of the meaning of providence within such a scheme is set out in Gustaf Aulén's *The Faith of the Christian Church*.[13] As is well known, Aulén's account of the Christian faith is centred upon his recovery of the primacy of what he styled the "classic view" of atonement under the rubric of *Christus Victor*.[14] On this view, salvation is won by way of the *mirabile duellum*—the wondrous and dreadful struggle of God against the enslaving power of evil.[15] At the

---

10. For a fascinating and detailed account of the history of ancient dualistic religions and their effect upon European Christianity, see Yuri Stoyanov, *The Other God: Dualist Religions from Antiquity to the Cathar Heresy* (New Haven: Yale University Press, 2000).

11. For discussion of these historic contours of the doctrine see, Charles M. Wood, "Providence," in *The Oxford Handbook of Systematic Theology*, ed. J. Webster, K. Tanner, and I. Torrance (Oxford: Oxford University Press, 2007), 91–104; G. C. Berkouwer, *The Providence of God*, trans. L. B. Smedes (Grand Rapids: Eerdmans, 1952).

12. Herbert Haag observes that Roman Catholic dogmatics is committed "in principle" to just such a kind of dualism for these reasons and observes that Protestant theology at key junctures secured this same affirmation by way of a *"massiven Teufelsglaube"* that almost amounted to an article of faith; see his *Teufelsglaube* (Tübingen: Katzmann Verlag, 1974), 48–51.

13. Gustaf Aulén, *The Faith of the Christian Church*, trans. E. H. Wahlstrom (Philadelphia: Fortress, 1960).

14. His widely read and debated 1931 study of the atonement takes this phrase as its title, of course: Gustaf Aulén, *Christus Victor: An Historical Study of the Three Main Types of the Idea of the Atonement*, trans. A. G. Herbert (London: SPCK, 1980).

15. For discussion see Gerhard O. Forde, "The Work of Christ," in *Christian Dogmatics*, ed. R. Jenson and C. Braaten (Philadelphia: Fortress, 1984), 2:36–41. Forde notes the coalescence of the rediscovery of Luther's theology of the cross and Aulén's interpretation of Luther as a "deepening" of the so-called "classic view" of atonement with interest. Cf. Gustaf Aulén, "Chaos and Cosmos: The Drama of the Atonement," *Interpretation* 4, no. 2 (1950): 157 (156–67).

climax of this contest, God himself invades the world beset by sin and death, becoming in the incarnate Son the effective agent of redemption.

The defeat of the devil and others is accomplished and placarded on the cross (Gal 3:1), where the apparent victory of the powers hostile to the purpose of God in Christ proves no victory at all as "divine love is victorious in self-giving and sacrifice."[16] The idiom here is dramatic rather than legal; and the scope is universal and cosmic rather than merely personal, for the triumph of God's grace needs to and does extend "as far as the sphere of these [evil] forces extend."[17] As Aulén stresses, if we but breathe "the gospel's own atmosphere" we find ourselves before a fundamental and ultimate antagonism, not between God and humanity, or between eternity and time, but between "God and the inimical domination" of sin, darkness, death, and the devil *"just as a whole."*[18]

All of this proves decisive for Aulén's direct discussion of providence in two paragraphs titled "God and the World" and "The Legitimacy and Limitation of Dualism."[19] In line with the broad tradition, from the outset Aulén rules out what he calls absolute dualism, which is to say any account of evil that "encroach[es] upon the sovereignty of the divine will in relation to existence" (175). Neither does evil represent a "metaphysical antithesis" to God, but it is rather specified as a hostile contradiction of the divine will, "defined as love" (177). This is the proper theological "limitation" of dualism.[20] But Aulén is less concerned with suppressing dualism as such than he is with specifying the nature of that dualism which befits the gospel. But he is anxious to refuse any *metaphysical* characterisation of the matter as a whole, whether as a contrast between being and nonbeing, or between the infinite and the finite. For such contrasts, however radical, simply do not map the one contrast that matters: namely, that between divine love and all that essentially—if vainly—contradicts it.

The larger part of Aulén's discussion of dualism is accordingly given over to explicating the nature and legitimacy of precisely *this* contrast— the "conflict motif" as he styles it (176)—as a feature of Christian faith.

---

16. Aulén, *Faith of the Christian Church*, 201.

17. Aulén, *Christus Victor*, 35.

18. Aulén, "Chaos and Cosmos," 160, emphasis in original.

19. Aulén, *Faith of the Christian Church*, 167–79. In what follows, citations from this section are noted in parentheses in the main text.

20. Aulén points to Marcion's position as one in which the evangelical dualism properly primitive to Christian faith wrongly "receives a metaphysical character foreign to it." *Faith of the Christian Church*, 176.

Christian faith must oppose any and all efforts to "blunt," "minimize," "obscure," or "eliminate" full and frank acknowledgement both of the existence of evil in its pure hostility to God's will and purposes and of God's implacable antagonism toward it (175). Aulén is particularly suspicious of the encroachment into theology of monistic logics which suppress this antagonism, effacing it by incorporating evil in this or that manner as a necessity within a comprehensive causal or moral system. Said differently, from the fact that our world contains features which are "foreign to the divine will and in conflict with it," faith rightly discerns that "existence as such is not an adequate expression of [the] divine will" to love, and concludes that the will of God is *not* reflected in everything that takes place. It is because God is love that "all compromises with evil on God's part are completely excluded," for faith knows and trusts the "God whose only purpose is to vanquish evil and thus realize the dominion of his love" (175). This tension between the revealed love of God and the actual "course of this world" crossed by the power of an active evil that is "in radical antithesis to the will of God" (167) is an ingredient in the posture of faith. It cannot and must not be relaxed.

Aulén sets out this aspect of his position programmatically in this way: "Christian faith does not conceive of everything that happens as a direct expression of the divine will. If this is done, it obscures the reality of evil and destroys the character of the Christian conception of God. Since existence also contains elements that are hostile to the divine will, a certain 'dualism' is inseparably connected with the viewpoint of faith" (167).

What imperils right thinking about the doctrine of providence, Aulén contends, is our desire to pass beyond the perspective of faith and to eliminate this dualism by way of "rational adjustments" ambitious to deliver what divine omnipotence abstractly seems to demand: a monistic view in which all world-historical occurrence is somehow evidently a reflection of the divine will (169). Aulén suggests that the history of dogma is piled high with the wreckage of such "sleight of hand"—seen for example, in toothless accounts of sin reduced to creaturely limitation or merely miscalibrated desire, and resigned discourses of divine "sufferance" or "permission" of evil that fatalistically dissolve the distinct identity of the *deus revelatus* back into the indefinable and inscrutable *deus absconditus*. Against this, he offers the axiomatic claim that faith "cannot attribute to the divine will that which is contrary to the revelation and action of this will in the work of Christ," or, said more sharply yet, "faith refuses to attribute to God that which the

Gospel attributes to Satan" (170). Monism must be refused, on this view, for the sake of the "purity of the Christian conception of God" (171).[21]

When consideration of the course of human affairs is controlled by these axioms, Aulén suggests that faith is led to see all of existence as "a *dramatic struggle*" the meaning of which only emerges where the loving divine will "stands in conflict with hostile forces" and reveals itself to be "victorious" (170). Every occurrence has divine meaning because, as Aulén explains in a memorable turn of phrase, "God does not will everything that happens, but with everything that happens he does will something" (171). What God wills is the realisation of the divine sovereign love even and especially in relation to all that opposes it. God's sovereignty, we might say then, is found not in the course of events *per se* but in the divine decision concerning them. This is reflected in Aulén's claim that "divine love always appears to the eye of faith as the irresistible power sovereign *in grace and in judgment*" (171, emphasis original).[22] The doctrine of providence cannot—indeed must not—deliver conceptual resolution of the agonistic tension between God and the course of events in the present; yet it can and does fund hope in a dramatic *dénouement* of the present struggle in which the ends of God's "condemning and redeeming love" will be the only ends "ultimately realised," while the anti-God powers are brought to naught (172–73).

And this is precisely the posture of providential faith that Aulén proposes. Amidst the jarring contradictions between divine love and the actual course of our existence, faith "flees to God" and finds in Christ's defeat of the hateful and inimical powers of sin, death, and the devil on the cross a soteriological ground for confidence in God's providential care. Trusting that God is "*able to overcome* evil," faith affirms not that events are "mapped out beforehand by God" but that "God is living and active in what happens" and that "the sovereignty of his care is revealed in his ability to turn evil into good" as the drama unfolds (173–74). Such faith is a "conquering conviction" that wagers everything on the fact that it is

---

21. "Either God discloses himself in Christ in that spiritual life which he dominates, in which event he is divine love but his will is not reflected in every occurrence; or everything that happens is actually an expression of the divine will, in which event the characteristic feature of love in the Christian idea of God is enveloped in obscurity, and nothing remains except mysterious impenetrable Fate." Aulén, *Faith of the Christian Church*, 171. This essential point might be thought to chime with the concerns motivating Christine Helmer's explorations of the ideological captivity of the doctrine of the providence in the modern age, and Brenda Deen Schildgen's account of the providential conflation of *evangelium* and *imperium* in late antiquity, both found elsewhere in this volume: in both instances, the distinctiveness of the God of the Christian gospel is, finally, at issue.

22. Some pages later, Aulén writes again that as regards evil, the God of the gospel is "unconditionally sovereign whether this sovereignty reveals itself *in grace or in judgment*." Aulén, *Faith of the Christian Church*, 176.

the God of the gospel of redemption who *"cares for all things*, [and] that his love wills something in everything that happens" (174).

Providence here offers no resources for rational theodicy. For the interest of evangelical faith in the problem of evil runs no further than the practical existential problem of God's conquering of it (178). What Walter Sundberg says of Martin Luther's theodicy holds here as well: "That God governs the world and brings salvation, justice, and peace is the good news; but it can only be understood eschatologically. . . . That God is *gubernator mundi*; that he is doing all things for the good, will only be known in the last days."[23] For this reason, trust in the goodness of divine providence is simply an echo and reiteration of faith's original trust in the victory of the Savior over the inimical power of sin, death, and devil in Christ.[24] To trust in providence has no further, distinctive object or content; it is, rather, to wager one's existence upon the ultimate sovereign victory of God's love over evil. It is, in the midst of a world contested by evil, *nevertheless* to live under the lordship of the victorious crucified Christ in patient and defiant hope.

To summarise: focused interest in God's saving confrontation with evil conceived as a "third agent" hostile to the divine will and so also to human welfare brings particular pressures to bear upon the doctrine of providence, as is clear from this brief exposition of Aulén's systematic account. In terms of the classical threefold division of the doctrine, we might say that the question of concurrence becomes particularly neuralgic as reflected in Aulén's polemics against monism and its "rational accommodations" of evil. The notion of divine accompaniment proves too elastic, too abstractly capacious, to be helpful for faith; instead a sharp distinction between alignment and antagonism, and a keenness to see and to hold God in unmitigated contradiction to the activity of the inimical forces of sin, death, and devil, is on display. The God of love does *not* concur with, indirectly cause, or otherwise align with the business of the devil: that business is absolutely *antithetical* to the divine will, and never otherwise. Clarity on this point is of primary importance for Aulén, for as he sees it, the very identity of the God of the gospel—"that which is to faith Alpha and Omega" (178)—is at issue here.

---

23. Walter Sundberg, "Satan the Enemy," *Word and World* 28, no. 1 (2008): 34. Sundberg draws on insights into Luther's influential thinking about the devil concisely set out in Heiko O. Oberman, *The Reformation: Roots and Ramifications*, trans. A. C. Gow (Edinburgh: T&T Clark, 1994), especially in its third chapter, 53–76.

24. Christian faith "regards sin as an objective power standing behind men, and the Atonement as the triumph of God over sin, death, and the devil . . . it is over this objective power of evil that God's victory is won." Aulén, *Christus Victor*, 147.

As concerns divine *conservation* and *governance*, here the eschatological drama of salvation is, as it were, extended or expanded to embrace the whole of creaturely life and fills out the meaning of these concepts for faith. As he writes elsewhere, "The safeguard of the continuity of God's operation is the dualistic outlook, the Divine warfare against the evil that holds [hu] mankind in bondage, and the triumph of Christ."[25] Divine "care" and "sovereignty" are correspondingly specifically predicates of saving divine love, that is, they are concepts tethered to and filled out with exclusive reference to the soteriological career of the incarnate Son of God come low to rescue, redeem, and deliver creatures from their diabolical captivity. Aulén's account is marked by an extraordinary concentration at this juncture, drawing faith's attention back to that point where it is rightly concerned with the character of divine action: namely, the eschatological event at the heart of the drama of salvation that illumines all else. On this score, providence aims only to secure that which is sufficient—*satis est!*—to fund faith's hopeful participation in the unfolding of the next acts in that same drama and so to testify to that "light in the darkness" (179) by which we can, in fact, travel onward.[26]

SOME REFLECTIONS AND CONCLUDING REMARKS

In light of this exposition of Aulén's treatment, what wider lessons concerning the doctrine of providence might be drawn at this point?

At the outset of this chapter I ventured two claims. The first was to suggest that when firmly coupled to the gospel of God's redeeming grace in which the devil figures prominently, the doctrine of providence will acquire a decidedly dramatic-pragmatic form. This is certainly on display in Aulén's treatment. Providence is a doctrine to which those who are working out their salvation in fear and trembling (Phil 2:12) teach and trust. Just as claims about the devil are never and can never be merely "theoretical" but are always "stationed within the experience of faith," having their place within the "authentic living out of the faith," as Ratzinger puts it, so too with the doctrine of providence entangled with them.[27] Providence is, in short, a doctrine of living faith articulated from within the drama of salvation and

---

25. Aulén, *Christus Victor*, 146.

26. The deflationary notion of *sufficiency* here seems very apt to express the properly gauged ambitions of the discourse of providence on this account.

27. Ratzinger, "Farewell to the Devil?" 201.

not otherwise. More than that, the very act of articulating faith in providence is itself a move in the drama, something integral to the performed life of faith *coram deo* in the midst of the troubled and troubling world. We might say that even when theology performs third-person assertive speech acts concerning the doctrine of providence, these arise from within the determinative field of directive, commissive, and expressive speech acts in such a way that they are in fact fully part of the self-involving discourse of faith.[28] Faced with the terrible realities of the devil's work, faith's testimony to the God who provides is never, "Let me explain . . ." but rather and always, "Fear not, for you stand redeemed" (Isa 43:1).

The dramatic and pragmatic form of the doctrine is, however, not merely a function of the subjectivity of faith. As the Reformed theologian Otto Weber explains in a slightly different idiom, it is primarily because "the rejection of evil by the Creator takes place as an *event* and is never presented as a given" that we are unable to approach "the problem of evil and its relationship to God's good and omnipotent will merely in an intellectual paradox, but must also see it "dynamically."[29] This also tracks closely with what Jon Levenson has argued is the cumulative witness of the Hebrew Scriptures, namely, that divine omnipotence is an event Israel has behind it in joyful memory and *ahead of it* in hopeful prayer as redemption unfolds.[30] For the church's faith, Jesus Christ is the sum and substance of this eventful divine repudiation and defeat of evil, the One in and by whom the sheer *enmity* of the evil one is disclosed and mastered. In as much as we are caught up in this event and its entailments, it is far too late for speculative theodicy under the guise of providence. Instead, when providence is rendered properly remote from philosophical determinism, what remains is simply the free human vocation to "repeat" the divine "No" to evil in "the fearless and alert 'No' of faith."[31]

The second claim I ventured in my introduction was that in confrontation with the reality of the "three-agent drama" of salvation, providence ought to undergo a soteriological concentration which would allow the

---

28. For a highly suggestive discussion of the matter of variant perspectives and the semantics of providence, see Niels Henrik Gregersen, "Trial and Temptation: An Essay in the Multiple Logics of Faith," *Theology Today* 57, no. 3 (2000): 325–43.

29. Otto Weber, *Foundations of Dogmatics*, trans. D. L. Guder (Grand Rapids: Eerdmans, 1981), 1:524.

30. Jon D. Levenson, *Creation and the Persistence of Evil: The Jewish Drama of Divine Omnipotence* (Princeton: Princeton University Press, 1988).

31. Weber, *Foundations of Dogmatics*, 1:492–93. Weber cites 1 Peter 5:8 and Ephesians 6:1 in connection with this last assertion.

doctrine to be republished as a doctrine of faith able to help fund what we might call the "practice of providence" in the form of patient discipleship. And this was certainly also evident in Aulén's treatment, in which divine provision and providential sovereignty are known as they take shape solely *in grace and in judgment*. Indeed, we might do well to speak here of a "soteriological reduction" of providence, by which the latter is brought back (*reducere*) into decisive contact with the original redemptive core of Christian faith upon which providence itself fully depends for its evangelical intelligibility. This suggests that talk of divine governance should quickly and rightly be able to become talk of the kingdom of God. For the providential rule of God is the "powerful arrangement of all events toward one event in the midst of history," namely, the event of Jesus Christ in which God is merciful to human beings in redeeming them from captivity to the evil one; God does this precisely in order that they may live in faith and humility, taking their properly human place "in the event which applies to [themselves] most of all," that is, the advent of the reign of God.[32]

Perhaps this is why the discourse of providence in this mode draws away from the structural articulation of a metaphysics of creation and moves instead toward the dramatic announcement of the vivifying force of eschatological—even apocalyptic—hope. Present contradictions of the kingdom can only be discerned, acknowledged, and resisted in faith when they are set against the eschatological horizon of that dramatic *dénouement* that will prove "the final and decisive revelation of the power and purpose of God vis-à-vis what has been dark, doubtful and seeming to contradict what faith asserts of God," which is to say, in love's overthrow of "the forces of Chaos in all their forms which militate against the Reign of God, and His good government."[33] When the doctrine of providence assumes this form—when it articulates the full breadth of faith's "nevertheless" uttered in the teeth of the ambivalence of natural and historical world occurrence—it becomes a fighting doctrine able to fund proclamation and *paraenesis* sufficient to sustain faith's defiant life by recalling to mind just how full and ambitious Christian hope is.

The great providential text on such a view is and can only be Romans 8:31–39. Here Paul offers to those who were once enslaved by sin, ruled by death, and captive and colluding with the diabolical god of this age, this astonished confession:

---

32. Weber, *Foundations of Dogmatics*, 1:522.
33. John Gray, *The Biblical Doctrine of the Reign of God* (Edinburgh: T&T Clark, 1979), 272.

What then are we to say about these things? If God is for us, who is against us? He who did not withhold his own Son, but gave him up for all of us, will he not with him also give us everything else? Who will bring any charge against God's elect? It is God who justifies. Who is to condemn? It is Christ Jesus, who died, yes, who was raised, who is at the right hand of God, who indeed intercedes for us. Who will separate us from the love of Christ? Will hardship, or distress, or persecution, or famine, or nakedness, or peril, or sword? As it is written, "For your sake we are being killed all day long; we are accounted as sheep to be slaughtered." No, in all these things we are more than conquerors through him who loved us. For I am convinced that neither death, nor life, nor angels, nor rulers, nor things present, nor things to come, nor powers, nor height, nor depth, nor anything else in all creation, will be able to separate us from the love of God in Christ Jesus our Lord.

The movement of this passage exemplifies the *ratio* of providence set forth here: Calling to mind the specific saving work of God in Christ ("these things") in the face of the pressing threat of the accuser ambitious to separate us from God, and with an unflinching acknowledgment of the reality of evil, suffering, and death, Paul provides no divine explanation of the course of events but instead offers up a faithful confession of eschatological hope in the sovereign love of the God of the gospel. Without mitigating the reality of the evil and suffering that stand in open contradiction of the loving divine will, faith dares to extend its radical trust in the God who saves out across the full scope of world-historical occurrence, testifying thereby to the finality of providential divine love, *notwithstanding* the all-too-real and painful experience of evil's enmity.[34] Precisely in this way faith "gives no room to the devil" (Eph 4:27).

In an essay on Satan written in 1989, Robert Jenson comments that the struggle to discern and resist the works of the devil in the midst of the God's working "goes on, and is called theology. For what theology attempts to do is to identify God, to say who God is, and just so, to unmask Satan."[35] This chapter has reflected on the fate of the doctrine of providence in relation to this specific task of Christian theology. It has suggested that the more intensely we identify the God of providence with the Father who

---

34. See my essay "A Sovereign Love: The Royal Office of Christ the Redeemer," in *Militant Grace: The Apocalyptic Turn and the Future of Theology* (Grand Rapids: Baker Academic, 2018), 35–51 for additional comment on the theological significance of this passage from Romans.

35. Robert Jenson, "Evil as Person (1989)," in *Theology as Revisionary Metaphysics* (Eugene, OR: Wipf & Stock, 2014), 143 (135–44).

sent the Son to "destroy the works of the devil" in the power of the Spirit, the more sufficient and serviceable our doctrine of providence might be to those struggling to live from the evangelical promise of redemption in the time that remains. If Jenson is right, then we would do well to recognize that theological labour along these lines has a modest yet serviceable place within the ongoing dramatic unfolding of our salvation. The effort to recast providence in light of the gospel of our redemption from "the god of this age" might well be part of the invaluable equipment of our Christian existence in the church militant. For, as Calvin has taught us, "If we are animated with proper zeal to maintain the kingdom of Christ, we must wage irreconcilable war with [the devil] who conspires its ruin."[36]

36. John Calvin, *Institutes of the Christian Religion*, ed. J. T. McNeill, trans. Ford Lewis Battles (Philadelphia: Westminster, 1960), 174 (1.14.15). Cf. J. Louis Martyn, "From Paul to Flannery O'Connor with the Power of Grace," in *Theological Issues in the Letters of Paul*, 297: "Where are *we* in the truly real world, that is to say in this apocalyptic, cosmic conflict? . . . And the answer is as clear as the question: Look! God has placed us in his struggle for redemption, the ultimate outcome of which is not in question."

CHAPTER 10

SHOULD A CHRISTIAN BE AN OCCASIONALIST?

Jonathan Hill

OCCASIONALISM IS THE THEORY THAT GOD—and God alone—causes everything that happens. If the white billiard ball strikes the black one, then the motion of the black ball is caused not by the white ball but by God, who moves it directly. The motion of the white ball is merely the "occasion" for God's moving the black one. Historically, occasionalism has been a minority view among theists,[1] being popular mainly among Muslim theologians of the early Middle Ages and Cartesian philosophers of the late-seventeenth century.

But in a recent paper, Alvin Plantinga has offered an analysis and tentative defense of the doctrine. Plantinga distinguishes between three ways in which causation could function. The first possibility is *secondary causalism*, according to which God creates things "with a certain nature or certain powers,"[2] such that they act in certain ways, including acting upon each other. So in this case, laws of nature describe how created things behave, and the fact that they behave in this way is because God gave them the ability to do so. This, as Plantinga observes, is "the common-sense way of thinking of the matter."[3]

The second possibility is what Plantinga calls *strong occasionalism*.[4] On

---

1. Its main rivals are *conservationism*, the view that created things have genuine causal powers, and God merely keeps them in existence to allow them to exercise those powers; and *concurrentism*, the view that events are directly caused by both creatures *and* God. Historically, concurrentism has been the majority view among theists.
2. Alvin Plantinga, "Law, Cause, and Occasionalism," in *Reason and Faith: Themes From Richard Swinburne*, ed. Michael Bergmann and Jeffrey Brower (Oxford: Oxford University Press, 2016), 133.
3. Plantinga, "Law, Cause, and Occasionalism," 134.
4. Before distinguishing between strong and weak occasionalism, Plantinga also makes another

this view, everything that happens in the created realm is directly caused by God. This includes both physical events and mental ones. So the revolution of the moon around the earth, for example, is caused by God directly moving it. The movement of my fingers as I type is caused by God directly moving them. And even my intention to move my fingers in that way is caused by God causing that intention in my mind.

The third possibility is *weak occasionalism*. On this view, God still directly causes all physical events, but not mental ones. God directly causes the moon to revolve around the earth and my fingers to move on the keyboard, but God does not cause me to have the intention to move my fingers—that is entirely my own. My forming of that intention is, in the classical terminology, the "occasion" for God's intervention to cause my fingers to move, so the two events are not wholly unconnected, but their relation is not causative.

Plantinga's argument is that strong occasionalism is incompatible with Christianity, but while both secondary causalism and weak occasionalism are compatible with Christianity, weak occasionalism is philosophically superior.

I want to challenge all of these claims. I will begin by considering strong occasionalism and argue that, contra Plantinga, it is compatible with the Christian belief that people are responsible for their actions. I will then go on to consider Plantinga's distinction between strong and weak occasionalism and argue that the distinction is not viable: either weak occasionalism collapses into strong occasionalism, or it is not a plausible theory in itself. So the Christian should either be a strong occasionalist or not be an occasionalist at all. I will end by considering the main reasons—including Plantinga's—for favoring occasionalism over its alternatives. I conclude that any theist who holds perdurantism has a good reason to hold occasionalism as well, but otherwise there are no compelling reasons to prefer it to secondary causalism.

IS STRONG OCCASIONALISM INCOMPATIBLE WITH CHRISTIANITY?

Plantinga argues that if God is the direct cause of all mental phenomena as well as physical phenomena, then we do not really *do* anything at all.

---

distinction between different kinds of occasionalism—one between *decretalism* and the theory of *counterfactuals of divine freedom*. This is really only a distinction between different ways of characterizing the laws of nature, given occasionalism, and as it is not important for our purposes in this paper, I will ignore it.

We make no decisions—God makes them *through* us. Plantinga sees this as incompatible with the Christian affirmation of creaturely responsibility and moral significance:

> If God causes me to do whatever I do, then, when, for example, I make a wrong decision, deciding to act in a self-aggrandizing way, it is not I who am responsible for or who causes that decision; it is God who does so. Indeed, I do not really do anything that could sensibly be called "making" that decision: it is rather that God just causes a particular mental state to occur at that time.[5]

It is important to recognize what Plantinga's complaint is here. He is not simply arguing that if our decisions are divinely caused, we have no free will. That is, this is not a version of the traditional worries about determinism, predestination, and the like. Rather, he is saying that if strong occasionalism were true, we would never make any decisions *at all*, not even unfree ones. The argument, then, is something like this:

1. If my decisions are directly caused by something other than me, then I do not make them.
2. If strong occasionalism is true, then my decisions are directly caused by something other than me.
3. Therefore, if strong occasionalism is true, I do not make my decisions.

But Plantinga offers no argument to support premise (1). And why should we assume that that premise is true? If strong occasionalism is true, then divine action *is how* we make choices. That is, in assuming this premise, Plantinga is effectively assuming the falsity of strong occasionalism to start with.

Now one might argue, as philosophers often do, that a person who makes a choice under the strong compulsion of someone else is not really making a choice at all. If I am hypnotized or brainwashed into behaving in a certain way, then I cannot be held responsible for that behavior because it is not really mine. But thought experiments of this kind derive their intuitive force from the fact that they portray unusual cases. That is, most of the time our actions are not the result of hypnotism or brainwashing, so we have a standard of "normal" responsible action with which we can compare the unusual case. But if strong occasionalism is true, then this is

---

5. Plantinga, "Law, Cause, and Occasionalism," 139.

not the case. If strong occasionalism is true, then *all* creaturely decisions are caused by God. That's simply part of what it is to be a creature.

Here is a comparison. Theists commonly think that God sustains the universe from moment to moment, and that nothing can have any independent existence without God's actively sustaining it. Does this mean all theists who believe this are committed to monism, the denial that there are any substances other than God? After all, a substance is supposed to be something that exists in its own right, without depending on anything else. No, most of them do not think this. They would say that the notion of something that is so independent it does not even require God's existence to continue existing in its own right is incoherent. A substance, then, is something that doesn't depend on anything else *other than* God. In other words, in a theistic context, the word *substance* means something slightly different from what it would mean in an atheistic context.

Similarly, if strong occasionalism is true, the term *creaturely decision* means something different from what it would mean if strong occasionalism were false. God's causing of a decision in my mind is simply what it is for me to make a decision.

But on this view, how can we distinguish between decisions that are mine and those that are other people's? One obvious way is to say that *my* decisions are those that occur in *my* mind.[6] But that would include decisions that occur there as a result of hypnotic suggestion or something similar, which we want to say are not really mine. We might get around this by saying that my decisions are those that are caused in my mind *by God* rather than by other external agents. But isn't this special pleading? Aren't we just saying that God doesn't count as a defeater of my decisions simply because we want to say I make decisions?

The strong occasionalist has ways around this. Consider Donald Davidson's influential analysis of the role of reasons in explaining action: "Whenever someone does something for a reason . . . he can be characterized as (*a*) having some sort of pro attitude toward actions of a certain kind, and (*b*) believing (or knowing, perceiving, noticing, remembering) that his action is of that kind."[7]

---

6. This assumes that, on strong occasionalism, we have some way of distinguishing between different created minds. Quite what that way would be may be unclear, given that it cannot have anything to do with causal powers of those minds. I'm grateful to Joanna Leidenhag for pointing out this issue.

7. Donald Davidson, "Actions, Reasons, and Causes," *The Journal of Philosophy* 60, no. 2 (November 1963): 685.

So an action comes about as a result of a *desire* and a *belief* (using these terms broadly) on the part of the agent. Since Davidson's articulation of this view, it has become so common that for some, such as Jennifer Hornsby, it can be regarded as "the standard story of action."[8] Davidson's main aim in his article was to defend the view that the desire and belief that constitute the primary reason for an action are the *cause* of that reason. A strong occasionalist cannot agree with that. But a strong occasionalist could still adapt an account of this kind. Suppose I decide to put the kettle on to make tea. The strong occasionalist can say that I have a desire for tea, and that I believe that putting on the kettle will get me tea. The strong occasionalist can therefore agree with Davidson that I have a *reason* to put on the kettle.

But it is one thing to have a reason to do something, and another to do something *for* that reason. If my turning on the kettle were the result of a series of bodily spasms over which I have no control, then I could not be said to have turned it on *for the reason* of making tea, even though I *have* that reason for turning on the kettle. Isn't this similar to the strong occasionalist picture, where I have a reason for turning on the kettle but my turning it on is wholly caused by God?

No, because although the occasionalist does not believe that created things are causes, she does believe that they are *occasions*. Consider the case of the white billiard ball striking the black. According to occasionalism, the motion of the black ball is caused not by the white but by God. However, God does not move the black ball simply on a whim. God moves it because the white ball has just moved in a certain way, and God operates in a regular and orderly way. If God had not just moved the white ball in that way, God would not have moved the black ball. There is a sense, then, in which the occasionalist can say that the black ball moved *because of* the white, even though the white is not the *cause* of the black's moving.

A similar story can be told about reasons for human action according to strong occasionalism. God does not cause me to decide to turn on the kettle on a whim. God causes me to make that decision because I have certain beliefs and desires, and God operates in such a way that when anyone has beliefs and desires of a certain kind, God causes them to make decisions of a certain kind. So although my reason for acting did not *cause* my decision to act, it was the *occasion* for my acting, and we can say—loosely—that I decided to act in that way *because of* my reason for acting.

---

8. Jennifer Hornsby, "Agency and Actions," in *Agency and Action*, ed. John Hyman and Helen Steward (Cambridge: Cambridge University Press, 2004), 1.

We can go further. Davidson points out that primary reasons, as he describes them, are reflective of agents: "In the light of a primary reason, an action is revealed as coherent with certain traits, long-or short-termed, characteristic or not, of the agent, and the agent is shown in his role of Rational Animal."[9]

The strong occasionalist can say this too. What makes my action mine is—in part—the fact that it reflects my character: it is in virtue of beliefs and desires in *my* mind that God causes the action. And we can develop this further to explain not only why my actions are mine, but why I am morally responsible for them too. Building on Peter Strawson's account of "reactive attitudes" to other people's behavior such as gratitude or condemnation, John Fischer and Mark Ravizza suggest the following criterion for moral responsibility:

> Someone is morally responsible insofar as he is an appropriate candidate for the reactive attitudes. More specifically someone is a morally responsible *agent* insofar as he is an appropriate candidate for at least some of the reactive attitudes on the basis of at least some of his behavior (or perhaps his character). And someone is morally responsible *for a particular bit of behavior* (or perhaps a trait of character) to the extent that he is an appropriate candidate for at least some of the reactive attitudes on the basis of that behavior (or trait of character).[10]

But if my actions reflect *my* desires and beliefs, then I am an appropriate candidate for reactive attitudes even given strong occasionalism. The relation between my desires and beliefs on the one hand, and my actions on the other, is not accidental or coincidental—God causes my actions precisely on the *occasion* of my desires and beliefs. The former reflect the latter, then, even though they are not directly caused by them.

Fischer and Ravizza offer a reasons-responsive view of moral responsibility which meshes well with the strong occasionalist position I am suggesting here. A reasons-responsive theory is one under which a person has moral responsibility to the degree to which her behavior is guided by reasons, taking "reasons" in a broadly Davidsonian sense. Normally, this can be expressed modally: an action is guided by reasons if, in the absence of those reasons or the presence of different ones, the agent would have

---

9. Davidson, "Actions," 690.
10. John Fischer and Mark Ravizza, *Responsibility and Control: A Theory of Moral Responsibility* (Cambridge: Cambridge University Press, 1998), 6–8 (emphasis original).

acted otherwise. But Fischer and Ravizza note this criterion cannot apply to Frankfurt-type cases, that is, cases where we would ascribe moral responsibility to an agent even though she is unable to do otherwise. The example they give, building on Harry Frankfurt's original discussion of the idea,[11] is the assassin who—unknown to himself—has a chip in his brain, which will force him to carry out an assassination if he loses the nerve to do it. The assassin does, in the event, carry out the assassination through his own choice, and the chip is not activated. It looks like the assassin is morally responsible for the act, even though he could not have failed to do it.[12]

For Fischer and Ravizza, this indicates a distinction between "guidance control" and "regulative control." "Guidance control" is where an agent controls what actually happens; "regulative control" is where an agent has the ability to perform something different instead.[13] Frankfurt-type cases indicate that what matters for moral responsibility is guidance control, not regulative control. Fischer and Ravizza then go on to make the key point: "In a Frankfurt-type case the agent could not have done otherwise, and thus the *agent* is not reasons-responsive. But it is crucial to see that in these cases the kind of mechanism that *actually* operates *is* reasons-responsive, even though the kind of mechanism that *would* operate—that is, that does operate in the alternative scenario—is *not* reasons-responsive.[14]

The assassin himself is not reasons-responsive because he would kill the target no matter what reasons he had. But the *process* by which he actually does kill the target *is* reasons-responsive: it is a normal deliberative process in which he acts as he does because he has a reason to do it. The fact that, had he chosen otherwise, he would have killed the target as the result of a non-reasons-responsive process (the activation of the chip in his brain) does not change this fact.

To my mind, this analysis of Frankfurt-type cases is—so far as it goes—exactly right. It explains *why* we think that agents in these cases are morally responsible (something Frankfurt himself did not explain). Now apply this to the strong occasionalist picture. Suppose God causes me to turn the kettle on in order to make a cup of tea. Is this process reasons-responsive? Clearly it is: God causes me to perform this action rather than another because I have a Davidsonian reason to do it. If I had lacked that reason, or had some

11. Harry Frankfurt, "Alternate Possibilities and Moral Responsibility," *Journal of Philosophy* 66, no. 23 (December 1969): 829–39.

12. Fischer and Ravizza, *Responsibility*, 29–30.

13. Fischer and Ravizza, *Responsibility*, 31–34.

14. Fischer and Ravizza, *Responsibility*, 38 (emphasis original).

other, stronger reason not to do it, God would not have caused me to do it. It would seem, then, that on strong occasionalism, we are a little like characters in Frankfurt-type cases all the time. We lack "regulative control" over our actions because we are not able—in any given moment—to choose otherwise than how we do. God causes us to make the decisions we do, and we cannot overrule divine action. But we do have "guidance control," because the mechanism that causes our actions is responsive to reasons.

Fischer and Ravizza point out that one of the reasons we say an agent has guidance control over an action is that she "owns" the mechanism that produces it: it has to be peculiarly hers. Their account of "ownership" revolves around the agent's personal history and how she develops morally to come to take ownership of her actions.[15] But under strong occasionalism, it seems that the mechanism that produces my actions is not my own—it is God's. However, we can again point to the fact that this mechanism is driven by *my own reasons.*

Consider the following scenario. I am playing blackjack and have a twelve. I have to decide whether to hit or stand. I know that the chances of going bust on the next card are low (it would have to be a ten or higher). In my understanding, then, I have good reasons to hit. My understanding is in this state, of course, because God has put it in this state: God has caused me to have the belief that the next card will probably get me closer to twenty-one than the dealer. God has caused me to have this belief on the "occasion" of the identity of the cards in my hand, the card I can see that the dealer has, what I remember of the cards that have already been played from this deck, and so on.

But God, being omniscient, knows that in fact the next card *is* a ten, which will cause me to go bust. And God knows that if I knew that, I would have an excellent reason to fold. If I fold and the dealer gets that card, the dealer will go bust, and I will win. Nevertheless, God still causes me to decide to hit, and I go on to lose my chips. God does this because *my* understanding is such that it seems to *me* that this is the wisest course of action. And this is what makes the decision *mine,* even though it is God who directly causes it. If God had caused me to decide otherwise on the basis of special divine knowledge not available to me, then it would not really have been my decision; but as it is, God makes the decision that I would have made if, *per impossibile,* I could make decisions independent of divine action. Consequently it is my decision: the mechanism by which

15. Fischer and Ravizza, *Responsibility,* 170–239.

the decision has been produced is reasons-responsive, and the reasons it is responsive to are *my* reasons, not God's.

So on strong occasionalism, it can still be the case that I perform actions that come about through a reasons-responsive process that I can meaningfully be said to own. As a result, I can be held morally responsible for them. And we can say more: these actions can be meaningfully called *free* too. Many theists (including Plantinga) think that human actions are free only if we have incompatibilist freedom. They think that no account of compatibilist free will really offers free will at all. Suppose, for the sake of argument, that they are right, and that an act that is determined cannot be free. To count as free, an act must be caused by an *agent* who chooses to do it in the absence of determining factors, such that they might have chosen to do otherwise even given exactly the same situation. If that is so, then any account of human decision-making that locates our decisions within a creaturely causal network will struggle to make room for free will. But strong occasionalism does not face that problem. On strong occasionalism, our decisions are caused precisely by the freest agent conceivable: God. God may cause our decisions on the basis of our desires and knowledge, but those are only the *occasion* for God's actions. They are not the causes of our decisions. In other words, the freedom of *my* decisions is guaranteed because they are indeed caused by a perfectly free agent operating without any prior causes, namely God. My free will is not some faculty of mine distinct from God's free will. It *is* God's free will.

So Plantinga is wrong to rule strong occasionalism out of court on the grounds of being incompatible with creaturely responsibility. An account can be given of creaturely responsibility—even creaturely free will—that is compatible with strong occasionalism. Perhaps that account may be rejected, but if so, it needs to be shown where it is flawed—one cannot simply assume its inadequacy. To the extent that this account is plausible, Plantinga's primary reason for rejecting strong occasionalism as incompatible with Christianity fails.

STRONG VERSUS WEAK OCCASIONALISM

Weak occasionalism holds that God directly causes all physical events but not mental events. *I* am the cause of my own thoughts, intentions, and so on.[16] Plantinga himself is rather vague on precisely *which* mental events

---

16. Although Plantinga does not say so, such a view presumably requires some kind of substance

have creaturely causes according to weak occasionalism. At one point he seems to suggest that they all do. He states that rejecting strong occasionalism amounts to "taking it that human beings and perhaps other persons cause changes—decisions, for example, or undertakings—in themselves."[17] Here, "decisions" and "undertakings" are just *examples* of the changes that a person can undergo, and the implication is that *all* changes in a person—not just these—are done by that person if we reject strong occasionalism. Later, however, he defines weak occasionalism as "the thought that the only creaturely causation is of the sort involved in my causing my decisions, volitions, and undertakings (if indeed that relation is one of causation)."[18]

Let us call these *broad weak occasionalism* and *narrow weak occasionalism*, respectively. According to broad weak occasionalism, God's role as direct causative agent is restricted to the physical realm. All mental events have creaturely causes. According to narrow weak occasionalism, by contrast, some mental events have direct divine causes. The only mental events that have creaturely causes are those involving the will.

But both of these are problematic. Broad weak occasionalism stumbles over cases where it looks like mental events are caused by physical events. For example, I see a tree and form the concept of a tree in my mind. What causes the formation of that concept? It cannot be God, by hypothesis. So it must be the tree itself, or a combination of the tree and other creaturely causes. But in that case, physical objects do have causative power after all—not on each other but on minds. But if a physical object can cause an effect on a mind, why can't it do so on another physical object? It seems extraordinary to suggest that a mind can be acted upon by a physical object but another physical object cannot be.

Broad weak occasionalism, then, is extremely implausible. Does narrow weak occasionalism fare any better? On this view, God directly causes the formation in my mind of the concept of the tree; the tree itself is only the occasion for God's doing that. So God does act directly on my mind, leaving only my decisions untouched: I am the cause of those, but not of other mental events. Here we immediately face a problem: what if I decide to bring about mental events? What if, for example, I decide to think about trees, even in the absence of any external stimulus? According to narrow

---

dualism. If I am a physical thing or constituted solely by physical things, how could I acquire a new property without God's being the sole cause if God is the sole cause of all occurrences in the physical world?

17. Plantinga, "Law, Cause, and Occasionalism," 140.
18. Plantinga, "Law, Cause, and Occasionalism," 141.

weak occasionalism, that decision is caused by me. Does that decision then directly cause my thoughts of trees? Or does God cause me to think of trees in response to my decision to do so, just as (according to any form of weak occasionalism) God directly causes my arm to move in response to my decision to move it? If the former, then some of my thoughts will have a divine cause, and some will not: my thought of a tree upon seeing a tree will be caused by God, while my thought of a tree when not seeing one will be caused by myself. And yet it is qualitatively the same thought each time.

That seems odd, but it is perhaps possible for exactly similar effects to have very different kinds of causes.[19] A more serious problem is that narrow weak occasionalism depends upon the assumption that we can clearly distinguish between volitional mental events (which are not caused by God) and nonvolitional ones (which are). But is such a clear distinction possible? Medieval philosophy of action revolved around the assumption that it is, with philosophers agreeing that human beings have two distinct faculties—the intellect and the will—in addition to the desires that they share with nonrational creatures. For Aquinas, for example, the intellect establishes the agent's goal (by judging that it would be good to achieve it), and the will decides which course of action to take to achieve it.[20] But the history of scholastic philosophy—with its debates over how these two faculties relate to each other, and in particular over whether or not the will has the power to ignore what the intellect tells it—is testament to the fact that the distinction is not as straightforward as it might at first seem. In particular, if the domain of the will is supposed to be establishing the means to an end established by the intellect, why is it that deliberating about means often seems to consist solely of trying to work out which is the most effective course of action? For example, if I am trying to decide which route to take to a particular place, I will work out which is the quickest (or most scenic, or most fuel-efficient, depending on my priorities), and once I have established which one that is, I have chosen it—there is nothing more to choosing than that.[21] In other words, practical deliberation seems

---

19. Radically skeptical thought experiments, such as deceiving demons or brains in vats, presuppose that this is possible, as they rely on the assumption that an experience caused by a sophisticated computer or powerful demon would be indistinguishable from one caused by real perception.

20. Thomas Aquinas, *Summa Theologiae* II.6.1.

21. On this, see O. S. Franks, "Choice," *Proceedings of the Aristotelian Society* 34 (1933–1934): 275–76. As Franks puts it, "If a man fails to judge correctly about the means to an end, it is an intellectual mistake that he makes" (275). See also Robert Burton, "Choice," *Philosophy and Phenomenological Research* 42, no. 4 (June 1982): 584–85: "If I choose to do X rather than Y, there must be some reason for choosing to do X rather than Y . . . an act of choice is a deliberative act."

much like any other rational investigation—the result is discovered rather than selected. The same thing goes for deliberations that are more about desire than rationality. If I am trying to decide which dessert to choose, I will consider which one I desire the most; once I am aware of which one that is, that *is* the choice. If I choose another one instead (for reasons of expense, or health, or wanting not to seem greedy), then I have some reason for doing so, and again, my awareness of that reason and of my preference for it just *is* the choice.

Perhaps this is true of all choices. Certainly there seem to be some cases where there is no particular reason pushing me towards one option rather than another and where I "just decide" to go for one rather than the other, but perhaps in those cases I am making subconscious judgments—or following subconscious desires—of which my conscious mind is unaware. If that is so, then the "will" is not really a distinct faculty after all but is simply another word for the way the intellect and our desires determine our actions. I am aware, or feel that I am aware, of myself making decisions, but I am not aware of any content to those decisions distinct from judgments and desires. So there seems to me to be no explanatory need for any notion of a faculty of will distinct from both judgments and desires.

If that is the case, then narrow weak occasionalism cannot get off the ground at all, because there is no class of "volitional mental events," distinct from nonvolitional ones, that can be insulated from direct divine action. Narrow weak occasionalism would therefore collapse into strong occasionalism. Of course it may be that the theory I have just sketched is false, and in fact the will is quite distinct from the intellect and desires. But the onus is on the defender of narrow weak occasionalism to provide an account that shows this, and such an account has not, to my knowledge, been given.

One might say that if volitions or choices are really judgments or desires, or determined by them, then they are not free, and that is something a Christian could not accept. But plenty of Christians *do* accept that choices are not free, at least not in the sense of being undetermined; the Calvinist doctrine of predestination is the most obvious example. What is essential for Christianity is not the doctrine that the will is free (in that sense) but the intuition that people can be held genuinely responsible for their choices. But we have already seen a possible account of responsibility that is consistent even with those choices being directly caused by God. That account could easily accommodate a theory of choice that makes it a kind of judgment.

So weak occasionalism is a problematic position. Broad weak occasionalism is very implausible, while narrow weak occasionalism may be possible but requires an account of volitional mental events that shows how they are utterly distinct from nonvolitional mental events, despite the fact that such a distinction is very hard to demarcate. There is no positive reason to prefer weak occasionalism over strong occasionalism. So if someone is going to be an occasionalist, she should be a strong occasionalist. I turn, then, to the question whether she should be an occasionalist at all.

PLANTINGA'S ARGUMENT FROM CAUSATION

Arguments for occasionalism fall, broadly, into two main categories. Those in the first category are based on supposed problems with the notion of creaturely causation. The notion is claimed to be either obscure or impossible, and so divine causation is invoked instead. Arguments in the second category are based on the concept of God. These more theologically focused arguments hold that something about the traditional understanding of God entails that God is the sole cause and conclude from this that creaturely causation does not occur.

Plantinga offers an argument of the first kind. He begins by pointing out that the notion of creaturely causation is obscure:

> It pains me to agree with Hume, but is he not right here? We see the first billiard ball roll up to and strike the second, and we see the second roll away. We do not, of course, see or experience anything like a causal connection between the first ball and the second, or the motion of the first ball and the motion of the second, or the event consisting in the first ball's striking the second and the second's moving away. We just see the first ball roll up to the second and become juxtaposed with it, we hear a click, and then we see the second ball roll off. Furthermore, we do not seem to have a coherent idea of a necessity linking the two events. What is this idea of creaturely causation?[22]

But this problem does not affect the notion of *divine* causation. Plantinga writes,

> Divine causality, as we may suppose, just goes by way of divine fiat: God says, "Let there be light" and there is light. God wills that there be light, or that there be light at a particular time and place, and there is light then and there. And the connection between God's willing that there

---

22. Plantinga, "Law, Cause, and Occasionalism," 135.

be light and there being light is necessary in the broadly logical sense: it is necessary in that sense that if God wills that p, p occurs. Insofar as we have a grasp of necessity (and we do have a grasp of necessity), we also have a grasp of causality when it is divine causality that is at issue. I take it this is a point in favor of occasionalism, and in fact it constitutes a very powerful advantage of occasionalism.[23]

So Plantinga's argument can be summarized:

1. A theory that relies on obscure notions is, other things being equal, inferior to one that does not.
2. Secondary causalism relies on obscure notions, but occasionalism does not.
3. Therefore, secondary causalism is inferior to occasionalism.

Plantinga offers no defense of (1), though it is questionable.[24] But even if we grant (1), (2) is still more dubious. Plantinga thinks that divine causality is simply a species of necessity, which we understand. But there is a fatal elision here. It may be true that whatever God wills is necessarily so. But this tells us nothing about *how it comes about* that it *actually is* so. For example, we might say, "Necessarily, if God wills p, then p." But this does not tell us how God's will brings it about that p is true.

Consider: "Necessarily, if I know p, then p." That is also true, at least if we assume that knowledge entails true belief. But of course it does not follow that my knowledge of p explains the truth of p—quite the reverse. Similarly, from the mere fact that, necessarily, if God wills p, then p, it does not even follow that God's willing of p is the cause of p; it could equally well be that p causes God's willing of p. (Perhaps God just wills whatever is actually the case.) If we want to say, "Necessarily, if God wills p, then p *is a result of* God's willing p," then we have captured more accurately what the theist typically wants to say about the relationship between God's will and the state of affairs. But in so doing, we have added something to that relationship beyond mere logical necessity. We have added causation. So causation, in the case of God's will, is *not* a species of logical necessity. It is

---

23. Plantinga, "Law, Cause, and Occasionalism," 137.

24. Theism itself involves a notion that some theologians, at least, have considered obscure. Gregory Palamas, for example, claimed that any idea we think we have of God is really of his energies, not of his essence. (On Palamas and the sources for this doctrine, see Alexis Torrance, "Precedents for Palamas' Essence-Energies Theology in the Cappadocian Fathers," *Vigiliae Christianae* 63, no. 1 [2009]). By (1), atheism is superior to theism, at least Palamas-style theism.

an additional relation. And if it is obscure in the case of creaturely causation, there is no reason to think it any less obscure here.

So Plantinga's argument for the superiority of occasionalism over creaturely causalism fails. If the latter requires obscure concepts, so does the former. But the situation is worse than this. Hume and Plantinga may be right that when we perceive one billiard ball hitting another, we do not perceive any "causation" beyond the movement of the two balls. But we do at least perceive both balls. In the case of divine causation, we do not even have that. Suppose God causes a rainbow to appear in the sky. We perceive the rainbow, but we do not perceive any divine action distinct from the rainbow. From an empirical point of view, we can coherently deny that any divine action occurs at all—for all we can see, there is nothing but an ordinary rainbow. In other words, with ordinary creaturely causation, we perceive things that we take to be causes and we also perceive things that we take to be effects, and we are uncertain precisely how they relate to each other. But with supposed divine causation, we perceive only the things that we take to be effects, and we do not perceive either the supposed cause or the relation between cause and effect. I do not see, then, how one can reject creaturely causation on Humean, empiricist grounds while affirming divine causation. If we are entitled to say that the former is obscure because we do not perceive it, we must consistently say that the latter is even more obscure on the same grounds. A theist who believes in divine action, then, ought not to reject metaphysical claims on grounds of this kind.

THEOLOGICAL ARGUMENTS

The most common theological argument for occasionalism is the argument from continuous creation,[25] which goes back at least to Louis de La Forge and is developed at greater length by Nicholas Malebranche.[26] It can be summarized like this:

---

25. The claim that the doctrine of continuous creation entails occasionalism is sometimes used to support occasionalism (on the basis of the truth of continuous creation) and sometimes used to attack continuous creation (on the basis that occasionalism is absurd). For a modern example of the latter, see Craig, "Creation and Conservation," 183–86. Miller seeks to avoid the inference of occasionalism from continuous occasion but always presents occasionalism as something to be avoided, not to be seriously entertained. T. D. Miller, "Continuous Creation and Secondary Causation: the Threat of Occasionalism," *Religious Studies* 47, no. 1 (March 2011): 3–22.

26. For La Forge, see *Treatise* 16, in Louis de La Forge, *Treatise on the Human Mind*, trans. Desmond Clarke (Dordrecht: Kluwer, 1997), 146–47. For Malebranche, see Nicolas Malebranche, *Dialogues on Metaphysics and on Religion*, ed. Nicholas Jolley, trans. David Scott (Cambridge: Cambridge University Press, 1997), 115–16.

1. At every time that an object exists, God actively conserves its existence at that time.
2. If God creates some particular object, God must create it with all of its determinate properties such as size, location, motion, and the like.
3. If God creates the determinate properties of an object, God is the sole cause of its having those properties.
4. God's action of conservation is identical to God's action of creation.
5. Therefore, for any object at any time, God is the sole cause of its having whatever properties it has at that time.

As far as I can tell, this is a valid argument. If one accepts premises (1) to (4), one must accept the conclusion, (5), which is occasionalism. The question, then, is whether one should accept those premises.

Premise (1) is a basic theological doctrine. To deny (1) is to endorse deism or something like it. So I will take it that most Christians will want to accept (1).

In Malebranche's formulation of the argument, premise (2) is the most prominent. Malebranche devotes some time to showing that God cannot create an object—say a chair—without locating it in some particular place, time, and so on. Andrew Pessin has argued, though, that Malebranche intends this to apply only to material objects, not to minds, and that consequently Malebranche does not intend the argument from continuous creation to support strong occasionalism (although he does in fact hold strong occasionalism).[27] This is on the grounds that, for Malebranche, minds can exist without some of their determinate properties, and so God can create (or conserve) them without necessarily having to cause those determinate properties.[28]

Pessin points out that even if it is true that when God creates an object, it must be created with all of its determinate properties, it does not follow that God must will those particular properties.[29] God could, for example, will to create a chair without being bothered about where it appears, and its location could be random, uncaused by God. However, this does not seem to me to be very damaging to the argument. Even if we accept this possibility—and some, such as Craig, would probably regard it as inimical to the doctrine of providence[30]—the fact that God would not be the cause of the chair's determinate properties would not mean that anything else could

---

27. Andrew Pessin, "Does Continuous Creation Entail Occasionalism? Malebranche (and Descartes)," *Canadian Journal of Philosophy* 30, no. 3 (September 2000): 413–40.
28. Pessin, "Continuous Creation," 426–29.
29. Pessin, "Continuous Creation," 425.
30. William Lane Craig, "Creation and Conservation Once More," *Religious Studies* 34, no. 2 (May 1998): 185.

be. If the chair is being created from nothing then there is nothing for other objects to act upon until it actually exists—and once it exists, it already has its determinate properties. There is no moment when the chair exists indeterminately, giving other objects the opportunity to cause its determinate properties. So if God does not determine these properties, nothing else does: they must be wholly undetermined, uncaused, and genuinely random. In this case there are no causal agents other than God. Everything that is caused is caused solely by God; the fact that some things are uncaused does not undermine occasionalism, although it would yield a rather unusual form of occasionalism where some things are not caused by God or by anything else.

There is another possibility. Even if God's conserving action on an object from moment to moment is identical to God's creative action on that object from its first moment, it could still be the case that its determinate properties at one moment are inherited from those at a previous moment. Perhaps me-at-T1 can cause me-at-T2 to instantiate the same properties that me-at-T1 does. At the very least, one needs an argument to show why this cannot happen.[31]

Another possibility is to reject (3). Pessin suggests this too, pointing out that Malebranche frames the argument to rule out creaturely causes that compete with divine causes, but not to rule out creaturely causes that align with divine causes. That is, the fact that God causes an object to have certain properties does not, in itself, mean that other creatures might not also cause it to have those properties. That would require the possibility of overdetermination.[32] But to my mind at least, overdetermination in such scenarios is meaningless. If God's action is sufficient for an event to occur, then any putative creaturely contribution adds nothing, in which case it is hard to see in what sense it is a cause at all beyond the occasional sense.

Premise (4), then, is the crucial one—the doctrine of "continuous creation," which states that divine conservation is (from God's point of view, at least) the same thing as creation. This view has been widely held throughout Christian history. Oddly, though, arguments for it are very thin on the ground. Thomas Aquinas, for example, is often regarded as a key figure in its articulation. Yet his version of the doctrine appears simply as a brief assertion in the course of a reply to an objection without any argumentation at all.[33] Descartes's articulation of the doctrine is fuller but again lacks argument,

---

31. Jonathan Edwards does provide such an argument—see below.
32. Pessin, "Continuous Creation," 432–33.
33. *Summa Theologiae* I.104.1.4.

merely asserting that the natural light makes it plain.[34] Even Malebranche, who rests such importance on this argument, offers no reason to accept this premise but takes for granted that his interlocutor will agree with it. In modern authors, too, there is little overt attempt to argue for continuous creation.

The best reason I can think of to hold the doctrine of continuous creation is to appeal to a theory of diachronic identity. Suppose, for example, that one had a four-dimensionalist theory akin to stage theory, according to which anything that seems to persist through time is actually a succession of different "stages," distinct objects that do not last for any amount of time at all. If me-at-T1 and me-at-T2 are distinct objects, then it might seem that they must be separately created by God, in which case occasionalism would follow.

By itself, however, such a theory of diachronic identity does not necessarily entail continuous creation. It could be the case that me-at-T1 causes the existence of me-at-T2. To yield continuous creation, we also need an argument that causation of this kind is impossible. This is precisely what Jonathan Edwards provides; he argues that it would violate the principle that an object has no causal power in times when it does not exist. It is, he thinks, impossible for me-at-T1 to be the cause of me-at-T2; therefore God must be the sole cause of each of them, and occasionalism follows.[35]

Despite its similarities to the skeptical argument described above, this argument is based on quite different premises. Where Plantinga appeals to the obscurity of the notion of creaturely causation, Edwards appeals to its clarity. It is precisely because we know (he thinks) that causation requires (among other things) the temporal simultaneity of cause and effect that we can be certain that creatures have no causal power. And that is of course the weak point of the argument, because it is questionable whether we do know any such thing.

What about other accounts of diachronic identity? An alternative version of four-dimensionalism is perdurantism, or "worm theory," which differs from stage theory in viewing the different temporal stages as genuine parts of a greater, transtemporal whole rather than as distinct individuals. And the alternative to four-dimensionalism is three-dimensionalism, or endurantism. According to endurantism, an object is whole and entire at any given moment, and it persists through time by "moving" through it. Me-at-T1 and me-at-T2 are straightforwardly identical, just the same thing at different times.

---

34. René Descartes, *Meditation 3*.

35. Jonathan Edwards, *The Works of Jonathan Edwards*, vol. 3, ed. Clyde Holbrook (New Haven, CT: Yale University Press, 1970), 400–401. See also Oliver Crisp, *Revisioning Christology: Theology in the Reformed Tradition* (Aldershot: Ashgate, 2011), 49–56.

With endurantism, we can think of an object as coming into existence at the start of its timeline then moving, whole and entire, along its timeline until it ceases to exist. I see no reason why God could not create an object at the beginning of its timeline by one action and then move it along its timeline by another, just as a person may build a cart and then pull it along. Building and pulling are quite distinct actions. Indeed, not only does endurantism not require continuous creation, but they are arguably incompatible. For if God's conservation of an object from moment to moment is a recreation, then one and the same object does *not* endure from moment to moment—not unless we can conceive of God's recreating *one and the same* object over and over again. But that seems very peculiar—how would it differ from God's creating a series of qualitatively very similar objects?

What of perdurantism? If me-at-T1 and me-at-T2 are different temporal parts of a space-time "worm," and if that "worm" is a genuine unity, it does seem plausible to think that God might create the whole worm in a single creative act. One might take an Aristotelian view of mereology and say that if *x* is a proper part of *y*, then *x* cannot exist without the rest of *y*; a severed hand is not really a hand at all. In that case, if God is to create *x*, then God has to create the rest of *y* in the same creative act. And what goes for spatial parts goes for temporal ones. That would yield the result that if God creates me-at-T1, God must, in the same act, create me-at-T2 and every other temporal part of my space-time worm. And then it does indeed look like continuous creation results.

So a theist who holds perdurantism does seem to be committed to continuous creation, at least given other metaphysical commitments. Stage theory might also suggest continuous creation, but that requires what seems to me to be more questionable metaphysical commitments. Endurantism does not require continuous creation and is arguably inconsistent with it.

If Malebranche's argument that continuous creation entails occasionalism holds good—as I have suggested it does—then whether one should be an occasionalist or not comes down entirely to what theory of diachronic identity one accepts. A Christian who accepts perdurantism should be an occasionalist. And, as I have argued, she should be a strong occasionalist, not a weak one. An endurantist should probably not be an occasionalist, and a stage theorist is free to choose.[36]

---

36. I would like to thank the attendees at the 2019 Los Angeles Theology Conference for their helpful comments on an earlier version of this paper, particularly the organizers for putting on such a stimulating and enjoyable event.

CHAPTER 11

"SO THAT WHERE I AM, THERE YOU MAY BE ALSO"

Divine Action and Divine Providence in the Beatific Vision

DAVID EFIRD AND DAVID WORSLEY

THE BEATIFIC VISION CONCERNS our eternal union with God, which is our greatest good. If God loves us, and so wills our good, why does he not actualise that union now, in our earthly lives, instead of waiting until the life to come? Answering this question addresses some of the most fundamental issues of divine providence and of divine action, in particular, how divine providence is compatible with human freedom and how divine action is compatible with a law-governed creation. Building on previously published work,[1] in this chapter we develop an account of our knowledge of God that allows for divine providence to be compatible with human freedom and an account of God's grace that allows for divine action to be compatible with a law-governed creation. We then bring these two accounts together to create a unified theory of God's love for us and God's desire that we love him too. This allows us to account for the so-called problem of divine hiddenness as not so much a problem but rather a feature of God's providential care for us and for how he manifests that care in his action in the world.

---

1. In particular, David Efird and David Worsley, "What Can an Apophaticist Know? Divine Ineffability and the Beatific Vision," *Philosophy and Theology* 29 (2017): 215–29; and David Worsley and David Efird, "Divine Action and Operative Grace," *The Heythrop Journal* 58 (2017): 771–77.

INTRODUCTION

"You have made us for Yourself, and our hearts are restless until they rest in You," Augustine addresses God at the beginning of his *Confessions*.[2] According to Bishop Robert Barron, "Everything else in the psychological and spiritual life is essentially a footnote to [this] statement."[3] This chapter concerns the problem at the heart of Augustine's address and at the heart of the spiritual life: If God has made us for himself, why are our hearts not already at rest in him?

To state this problem more clearly, let us think about what it is for our hearts to rest in God. To begin, our hearts will be at rest when their desires are fulfilled, and when our desires are fulfilled, we are perfectly happy. So, for our hearts to be at rest is for us to be perfectly happy. But we are perfectly happy, as Augustine notes, only in God, which, as Aquinas writes, consists in that which we now call the beatific vision: for our "final and perfect beatitude," he concludes, "can consist in nothing else than the vision of the divine essence."[4] Why might he have thought this? Let us take a closer look at one argument he gives for this conclusion:

Two things must be considered. First, man is not perfectly happy so long as something remains for him to desire and seek. Secondly, the perfection of any power is determined by the nature of its object. The object of the intellect is "what a thing is," i.e. the essence of a thing . . . It follows that the intellect attains perfection, insofar as it knows the essence of a thing. If therefore an intellect knows the essence of some effect, whereby it is not possible to know the essence of the cause, i.e. to know of the cause "what it is"; that intellect cannot be said to reach that cause simply, although it may be able to gather from the effect the knowledge that the cause exists. Consequently, when man knows an effect, and knows that it has a cause, there naturally remains in the man the desire to know about the cause, "what it is." And this desire is one of wonder, and causes inquiry . . . For instance, if a man, knowing the eclipse of the sun, considers that it must be due to some cause, and yet not know what that cause is, he wonders about it, and from wondering proceeds to inquire. Nor does this inquiry cease until he arrives at knowledge of

---

2. Augustine, *Confessions* 1.1.

3. Christopher White, "Barron Tells Google Religion's the Ultimate Search Engine," *Crux*, March 21, 2018, https://cruxnow.com/church-in-the-usa/2018/03/21/barron-tells-google-religions -the-ultimate-search-engine/.

4. Thomas Aquinas, *Summa Theologiae* I-II.3.8.

the essence of the cause. If therefore the human intellect, knowing the essence of some created effect, knows no more of God than "that He is"; the perfection of his intellect has not yet directly attained the First Cause, and so the natural desire to seek the cause still remains for him. On account of which he is not yet perfectly happy. Consequently, for perfect happiness the intellect needs to attain to the very essence of the First Cause. And thus it will have its perfection through union with God as with that object, in which alone man's happiness consists.[5]

More simply put, if a person knows that something exists, but they do not know the essence of that thing, until they come to know its essence, there will remain in them a desire to know. If they remain desirous of something they do not have, that is, if they continue with an unfulfilled desire for knowledge, both their intellect and will cannot come to perfect rest. Furthermore, as each thing has a cause, and as every cause is itself caused by something else, this metastasising desire for knowledge will eventually bring that person back to the First Cause, that is, to God. And so, without some sort of knowledge of God's essence (something well beyond mere knowledge *that* God exists), a person's intellect and will can never come to perfect rest but rather will continue on in a state of perpetual intellectual frustration.

But there is more to this vision than mere intellectual itch-scratching. On the Thomist account of love recently popularised by, amongst others, Eleonore Stump, love is the function of two desires: the desire for the good of the beloved and the desire for union with the beloved. At the beatific vision, these two desires coalesce. If Aquinas is right, the beatific vision *is both* our greatest good[6] and also the vehicle by which we are finally and completely united to God.

On the Thomistic account of union that Stump develops, union with God requires a person's freely sharing both significant presence[7] and personal closeness with God, where personal closeness includes—as much as is possible for a finite creature—inhabiting God's mind, seeing the world as God sees it, and so forth.[8] The closer one is to God, that is to say, the more one knows God, the greater the union with God, the more intense

---

5. Thomas Aquinas, *Summa Theologiae* I–II.3.8; see also *Summa Contra Gentiles* 3.50 and *Summa Theologiae* suppl., 92.3.

6. On Aquinas's account at least, it is, after all, that in which our final and perfect happiness consists.

7. That is, presence that includes causal and cognitive contact, second-personal experience, and is marked by the sharing of either dyadic joint attention, or triadic joint attention.

8. See Eleonore Stump, *Wandering in Darkness: Narrative and the Problem of Suffering* (Oxford: Oxford University Press, 2010), 108–29.

the joy,[9] and the more perfect the happiness that person experiences. Whilst presently we may see God as though through frosted glass, at the beatific vision we will see God face to face, and we will know God even as we are known.[10] That is to say, at the beatific vision, we will be as close to God, and so as united with God, as it is possible for us to be. Our joy will be complete. Our happiness, perfect. Our restless hearts will be at rest.[11]

Now, this is all well and good. But such reflection raises an immediate concern. If God loves us, and so wills both our good and union with us, why does he not actualise that union now, in our earthly lives, instead of waiting until the life to come? Why, presently, do we only see God as through frosted glass (1 Cor 13:12)? Why is God hidden from us *now*?

Before going any further, let us set to the side one sort of answer to this question. It is certainly true that God told Moses he could not see God's face because "no one shall see God and live" (Exod 33:20). And it is true that it took the symbolic removal of Isaiah's guilt before he could behold even a *vision* of God.[12] So, plausibly, there may be some connection between God's present hiddenness and the guilt and shame that accompany our unatoned sin.[13] But whilst this connection might explain why, given our sin, we are *currently* unable to share a certain kind of significant personal presence with God, it cannot explain all historic instances of divine hiddenness.

Consider both primal and original sinners—at least as they have been understood in the Christian tradition. Aquinas, for instance, thought the object of the first evil desire was just that which is now called the beatific

---

9. Where, following Augustine, I take it joy properly emerges as a function of (1) a person's pure (or wholehearted) desire for God, where (2) this desire for God is for no further reason, and where (3) this desire is fully realized (i.e., a person is united with God). See David Worsley, "Augustine on Beatific Enjoyment," *The Heythrop Journal* (forthcoming) for a development of this claim.

10. "For now we see in a mirror, dimly, but then we will see face to face. Now I know only in part; then I will know fully, even as I have been fully known" (1 Cor 13:12). All Bible quotations come from the NRSV.

11. See Job 19:25–27; John 17:3; and Revelation 22:4.

12. Indeed, Isaiah initially considered himself undone because in his guilty state he had seen a vision of God with his eyes: "In the year that King Uzziah died, I saw the Lord sitting on a throne, high and lofty; and the hem of his robe filled the temple. . . . And I said: 'Woe is me! I am lost, for I am a man of unclean lips; and I live among a people of unclean lips; yet my eyes have seen the King, the Lord of hosts!' Then one of the seraphs flew to me, holding a live coal that had been taken from the altar with a pair of tongs. The seraph touched my mouth with it and said: 'Now that this has touched your lips, your guilt has departed and your sin is blotted out'" (Isa 6:1, 5–7).

13. As we shall explain, we shall take it that a certain sort of significant personal presence is required for the sort of "personal knowledge" of God necessary to "know God as God knows us." Guilt and shame inhibit our ability to be so significantly personally present, and so inhibit our ability to know God personally. Elsewhere, we argue that hell just is a place for those whose guilt and shame has not been dealt with, and so are unable to share significantly personal presence with God. See David Worsley, "(Affective) Union in Hell," *Religious Studies* (forthcoming) for more details. See also Genesis 3:7–10 and Daniel 12:2. "Many of those who sleep in the dust of the earth shall awake, some to everlasting life, and some to shame and everlasting contempt."

vision. That is to say, although created intellectually flawless, supremely happy (naturally speaking),[14] and morally good, the primal sinner was created without a certain kind of knowledge of God (a "supernatural" knowledge necessary for perfect union with God), and that inordinate desire for such knowledge caused them to stumble.[15] Aquinas writes,

> Therefore, the devil's first sin was that, to attain the supernatural happiness consisting of the complete vision of God, he did not elevate himself to God so as to desire with holy angels his ultimate perfection through God's grace. Rather, he wanted to attain his ultimate perfection by the power of his own nature without God bestowing grace, although not without God acting on his nature . . . the devil sinned not by desiring something evil, but rather by desiring something good, viz., ultimate beatitude, but not in a fitting manner, that is, not in such a way as to attain it by God's grace.[16]

And whilst scriptural support for this claim is, at best, tenuous,[17] we see a structurally similar story repeated in the Genesis account of Adam's sin where, once again, a certain lacked knowledge was desired over friendship with God. The Genesis account reads:

> The LORD God took the man and put him in the garden of Eden to till it and keep it. And the LORD God commanded the man, "You may freely eat of every tree of the garden; but of the tree of the knowledge of good and evil you shall not eat, for in the day that you eat of it you shall die." . . .

> Now the serpent was more crafty than any other wild animal that the LORD God had made. He said to the woman, "Did God say, 'You shall not eat from any tree in the garden'?" The woman said to the serpent, "We may eat of the fruit of the trees in the garden; but God said, 'You shall not eat of the fruit of the tree that is in the middle of the garden, nor shall you touch it, or you shall die.'" But the serpent said to the woman, "You will not die; for God knows that when you eat of it your eyes will be opened, and you will be like God, knowing good and evil." So when the woman saw that the tree was good for food, and that it was a delight to the eyes, and that the tree was to be desired to make one

---

14. Anselm, however, suggested Lucifer (along with all other angels) was not created supremely happy according to his natural order, and that such knowledge of God could have been attained without God's supernatural aid. But this is not Aquinas's view. See Anselm, *De casu diaboli*.

15. See Giorgio Pini, "What Lucifer Wanted: Anselm, Aquinas, and Scotus on the Object of the First Evil Choice," *Oxford Studies in Medieval Philosophy* 1 (2013): 61–82.

16. Thomas Aquinas, *De Malo* 16.3.

17. See Isaiah 14:12–15 and Ezekiel 28:12–19. See also Luke 10:18.

wise, she took of its fruit and ate; and she also gave some to her husband, who was with her, and he ate. Then the eyes of both were opened, and they knew that they were naked; and they sewed fig leaves together and made loincloths for themselves. They heard the sound of the LORD God walking in the garden at the time of the evening breeze, and the man and his wife hid themselves from the presence of the LORD God among the trees of the garden. (Gen 2:15–17; 3:1–8)

However, if in their state of innocence neither primal nor original sinners had anything inhibiting them from sharing significant personal presence with God,[18] what reason might God have had for withholding the beatific vision from them? Indeed, such a question is all the more pertinent as it seems it was this very divine withholding that rendered their sin a possibility.

One response, of course, is to follow Scotus and claim such knowledge was (and is) both naturally and supernaturally impossible, but one could nevertheless still wish it were possible.[19] But it seems going down this route downplays the possibility and extent of our own beatific enjoyment, something we are not willing to give up, at least just yet. Instead we suggest an adequate answer to this question will end up addressing some of the most fundamental issues of divine providence and of divine action, in particular for how divine providence is compatible with human freedom and for how divine action is compatible with a law-governed creation.

Divine Hiddenness and Human Freedom

To see how this might be so, consider the following question: What might prevent a primal or original sin like event from happening to the saints in heaven?[20]

---

18. That is, they had no guilt or shame, and they were both morally good.

19. Scotus writes, "With regard to the act of willing in the first way [i.e. as an efficacious volition], I say that the [evil] angel could not desire equality with God. In the second way [i.e. by a mere wish], he could, because he could love himself by as much love of friendship as that by which, according to right reason, he ought to have loved God. And nevertheless he could also have desired for himself as much good as he owed to God by love of desire, if one speaks of the act of the will that is called a 'wish' (velleitas)." Reportatio parisiensis 2.6.1n5.

20. For more on the impeccability of the saints in heaven, see J. F. Sennett, "Is There Freedom in Heaven?" *Faith and Philosophy* 16, no. 1 (1999): 69–82; Simon Gaine, *Will There Be Free Will in Heaven? Freedom, Impeccability, and Beatitude* (London: T&T Clark, 2013); Tim Pawl and Kevin Timpe, "Incompatibilism, Sin, and Free Will in Heaven," *Faith and Philosophy* 26, no. 4 (2009): 398–419; Steven Cowan, "Compatibilism and the Sinlessness of the Redeemed in Heaven," *Faith and Philosophy* 28, no. 4 (2011): 416–31; Tim Pawl and Kevin Timpe, "Heavenly Freedom: A Reply to Cowan," *Faith and Philosophy* 30, no. 2 (2013): 188–97; Richard Tamburro, "The Possibility and Scope of Significant Heavenly Freedom," *Paradise Understood: New Philosophical Essays about Heaven*, ed. Ryan Byerly and Eric Silverman (Oxford: Oxford University Press, 2017), 308–28; Benjamin Matheson, "Tracing and Heavenly Freedom," *International Journal for Philosophy of Religion* 84, no. 1

Or, for that matter, to Christ in his human nature?[21] As far as we can see, there is only one significant difference between the former sinners and the latter saints: unlike respective sinners, both Christ and the saints in heaven *have access to the beatific vision*.[22] Both already possess the knowledge desired by the primal and original sinners. Plausibly, their impeccability is connected to their beholding the essence of God.[23]

So, if beholding the beatific vision were to prove sufficient for a person's impeccability, were beatific knowledge immediately available to either primal or original sinner, the beholder would necessarily desire union with God. They could not do otherwise. But if the sort of union God desires requires both lover and beloved to freely and independently desire union with each other, it seems immediately granting beatific revelation would render free, independent desire, and so such God-desired-union, impossible.[24] If God does indeed desire such mutually freely willed union, and if God's immediate beatific revelation renders such union impossible, God might have a reason to hide, at least initially, from both primal and original sinners.[25] To see the implications this might have for our reflection on divine action and divine providence, let us consider one reason why mutually freely willed union with God might be impossible were God to immediately grant beatific knowledge.[26]

(2018): 57–69; and Simon Kittle, "The Problems of Heavenly Freedom," *TheoLogica* 2, no. 2 (2018): 97–115.

21. It seems plausible that the temptation Christ faced in the Garden of Gethsemane was the mirror of the temptation facing both primal and original sinners. Christ beheld the beatific vision. He had the knowledge of God both primal and original sinner's desired. However, on this view, he knew he must give this up on the cross—and during the cry of dereliction, in fact did, in order to render an efficacious atonement. His temptation was to keep this knowledge rather than let it go, through the severing of significant personal presence with the Father.

22. For a defense of the claim that Christ beheld the beatific vision in his earthly life, see, for instance, Simon Gaine, *Did the Saviour See the Father? Christ, Salvation, and the Vision of God* (London: Bloomsbury, 2015).

23. See also 1 John 3:2: "Beloved, we are God's children now; what we will be has not yet been revealed. What we do know is this: when he is revealed, we will be like him, for we will see him as he is."

24. Alternatively, God's hiddenness might grant some plausible deniability, and so the opportunity to repent in case of mistakes made. See Hebrews 6:4–6: "For it is impossible to restore again to repentance those who have once been enlightened, and have tasted the heavenly gift, and have shared in the Holy Spirit, and have tasted the goodness of the word of God and the powers of the age to come, and then have fallen away, since on their own they are crucifying again the Son of God and are holding him up to contempt."

25. Interestingly, such a reason need not (and likely cannot) be primarily for *our* benefit (either positive or negative), and so is best understood as being for God's own sake. Were we to receive the beatific vision immediately upon our creation, we would enter into as much union with God as we might desire, being as happy as it is possible for us to be in such a state. We thank Jonathan Hill for pushing this point.

26. We have suggested that were God to reveal himself fully and completely to a person free from guilt and shame, they could not but desire union with him. The only reason this would be the

To do this, let us return to Aquinas. On a Thomist moral psychology, a person's mind is composed of a will and an intellect. The will is an appetite or inclination for goodness in general; however, the will cannot apprehend what is good on its own. Apprehending something as being "good for a person" is the responsibility of the intellect, which is itself an appetite or inclination for truth.[27] Every act of will is, therefore, necessarily preceded by an act of intellect, such that the will (the "moved mover") is always an efficient cause, and the intellect is always the final cause. But because it is also possible for the will to move the intellect (so long as there is a preceding act of intellect), Eleonore Stump has suggested this Thomist account of the mind fits well with Harry Frankfurt's account of the hierarchy of the will, such that there are first-order intellect-will moves, second-order intellect-will-intellect-will moves, and (quite rarely) third-order intellect-will-intellect-will-intellect-will moves.[28]

If the will is an appetite for goodness, were God to fully reveal himself to a person's intellect, that person could not but desire union with God. Why? Well, if the doctrine of divine simplicity is correct, all transcendentals that can be predicated of God are coreferential.[29] So, if God is the greatest being—indeed, being itself—he is also the greatest good—indeed, goodness personified (and so on with truth and beauty). In their prelapsarian state,[30]

---

case is if God designed them that way. Were God to do this to a person not free from shame and guilt, God's presence (so Scripture tells us) would be unbearable for them. Plausibly, experiencing such beatific revelation would be worse than hell for that individual. See Worsley, "(Affective) Union in Hell," for more on this line of argument.

27. See *Summa Theologiae* I.16.1.

28. Stump suggests the possibility of infinite regress is avoided, as any possible fourth-order combination has in fact has exactly the same composition as a second-order combination, and any fifth-order combination will have exactly the same composition as a third-order combination (and so on). As a result, all higher-order combinations will collapse back into either second- or third-order combinations. See Eleonore Stump, "Aquinas's Account of Freedom: Intellect and Will," in *Thomas Aquinas: Contemporary Philosophical Perspectives*, ed. Brian Davies (Oxford: Oxford University Press, 2002), 275–94.

29. See, for instance, *Summa Theologiae* I.5.1, which reads, "Goodness and being are really the same, and differ only in idea; which is clear from the following argument. The essence of goodness consists in this, that it is in some way desirable. Hence the Philosopher says: 'Goodness is what all desire.' Now it is clear that a thing is desirable only in so far as it is perfect; for all desire their own perfection. But everything is perfect so far as it is actual. Therefore it is clear that a thing is perfect so far as it exists; for it is existence that makes all things actual, as is clear from the foregoing. Hence it is clear that goodness and being are the same really. But goodness presents the aspect of desirableness, which being does not present."

30. This is not necessarily true of the postlapsarian state, as both intellect and will can, through the removal of original justice, the warping of concupiscible desires, and through habit, become perverted, such that lesser goods are preferred over greater goods (as the doctrine of original sin teaches is in fact the case). We take it that in the prelapsarian state, moral agents—including primal and original sinners—are in fact morally good and do in fact prefer greater goods to lesser goods. (After all, if Aquinas is right, the object of the first evil desire, the desire for the beatific vision, is the greatest good a person could desire.)

nothing could overcome a person's desire for union with God, were God's essence to be immediately to them.[31] The essence of God *is* goodness, and that person's will is an appetite for goodness; again, the essence of God *is* truth, and the intellect an appetite for truth. God would therefore have created a person to respond in a certain way to a certain set of stimuli and then immediately provided said stimuli.[32] As far as we can make out, this is precious little different to our creating a robot that says, "I love you" on the press of a button and then pressing the button. Whatever else that might be said about this, the sort of union that might then ensue between yourself and said robot is unlikely to be worth much at all.

So, plausibly, God withholds beatific revelation from a person until such a time as they come to desire it *for God's sake*.[33] In this way, God's hiddenness is a manifestation of God's love for us. God is hidden so that we might freely love God and so that in time we may join in a significant sort of union with God. But even granting this, why dangle the possibility of such knowledge in front of either the primal or original sinner? Why not just wait a while before offering such revelation? Well, consider the following claim by Richard Swinburne concerning the seriousness of freely willed action:

> If reasons alone influence action, an agent inevitably does what he believes to be the best, so if desires alone influence action, an agent will inevitably follow his strongest desire. Free choice of action therefore arises only in two situations. One is where there is a choice between two actions which the agent regards as equal best which the agent desires to do equally; which . . . is the situation of very unserious free will. The other is where there is a choice between two actions, one of which the agent desires to do more and the other of which he believes it better to do . . . the more

---

31. This is, perhaps, a more formal version of Kierkegaard's parable "The King and the Maiden."

32. In answering the question whether God can be loved immediately in this life, Aquinas writes, "The act of a cognitive power is completed by the thing known being in the knower, whereas the act of an appetitive power consists in the appetite being inclined towards the thing in itself. Hence it follows that the movement of the appetitive power is towards things in respect of their own condition, whereas the act of a cognitive power follows the mode of the knower. Now in itself the very order of things is such, that God is knowable and lovable for Himself, since He is essentially truth and goodness itself, whereby other things are known and loved: but with regard to us, since our knowledge is derived through the senses, those things are knowable first which are nearer to our senses, and the last term of knowledge is that which is most remote from our senses. Accordingly, we must assert that to love which is an act of the appetitive power, even in this state of life, tends to God first, and flows on from Him to other things, and in this sense charity loves God immediately, and other things through God" (*Summa Theologiae* II-II.27.4).

33. For incorporeal—and so aeviternal—angels, this need only be an instant after their initial volition (the second instant after their creation). For corporeal—and so temporal—humans, this presumably takes some longer period of time.

serious the free will and the stronger the contrary temptation, the better it is when the good action is done.[34]

In his recent work on the primal sin, Kevin Timpe attributes to the primal sinner a first-order desire for happiness (or benefit) and a second-order desire for justice (or rectitude).[35] By presenting them with the possibility of such knowledge of God, both primal and original sinners are then left with a serious choice. Do they follow their desire for happiness and try to obtain knowledge of God—their greatest good—on their own terms as usurpers, or do they follow their desire for justice, and so wait for this knowledge to be granted to them by God, as friends? Plausibly, such a choice meets the criteria for the serious exercise of free will previously described by Swinburne; they desire the beatific vision because it will lead to their greater happiness, but they also desire to wait and trust in God's timing because that is the right thing to do.

In any case, if attending to beatific revelation necessarily moves a (prelapsarian) person to desire union with God, divine revelation (both "beatific" and ordinary) could be (and, we argue, is) a mechanism for God's acting in this world. And not just in this world but in the life to come too, for, plausibly, the impeccability of the saints in heaven (and of Christ on earth) might stem from the desire for (continued) union with God necessarily prompted by their beholding this beatific vision.[36] In a similar way, too, God's veiled self-revelation in creation, in the person of Christ, through holy Scripture, and so forth might all work to move (although not ineluctably) an attentive person to desire union with God and God's complete self-revelation (to the person able to behold it): God's providential way of ensuring the impeccability of the saints in their unending union of love with God where God is.

OBJECTION: KNOWING AN UNKNOWABLE GOD

Now such claims are, of course, not without serious objections. We will address two, both epistemic. First, if the doctrine of divine ineffability is

---

34. Richard Swinburne, *Providence and the Problem of Evil* (Oxford: Oxford University Press, 1988), 86–87.

35. See Kevin Timpe, "The Arbitrariness of Primal Sin," *Oxford Studies in Philosophy of Religion* 5 (2014): 234–57. "Justice" and "happiness" could just as easily be considered names for the two intelligible species by which the primal sinner understood all intelligible objects.

36. Note that in the reversal of the situation facing primal and original sinners in the garden of Gethsemane, Christ was (plausibly) tempted to hold onto the beatific vision rather than voluntarily give it up by subjecting himself to the cross.

correct, God is unknowable. If God is unknowable, how can we know God's essence? Consider Gregory of Nyssa's claim:

> The simplicity of the True Faith assumes God to be that which He is, namely, incapable of being grasped by any term, or any idea, or any other device of our apprehension, remaining beyond the reach not only of the human but of the angelic and all supramundane intelligence, unthinkable, unutterable, above all expression in words, having but one name that can represent His proper nature, the single name being "Above Every Name."[37]

So, can we uphold this belief in divine ineffability and also, at the same time, coherently hold to the doctrine of the beatific vision? We have elsewhere argued in the affirmative.[38] Whilst we may not know God's essence in a way that can be reduced to propositions, we can know God personally.

In *Wandering in Darkness*, Eleonore Stump introduces a distinction between two kinds of knowledge, namely, Dominican knowledge and Franciscan knowledge.[39] As she explains it, Dominican knowledge is propositional knowledge, that is, knowledge-*that*. Franciscan knowledge, on the other hand, is neither propositional knowledge nor reducible to propositional knowledge. Such knowledge might include knowledge gained from phenomenal experience, acquaintance, or experience of persons, or so she suggests.[40] This much is easy to say. However, in virtue of the irreducibility of Franciscan knowledge to Dominican knowledge, finding a way to *illustrate* the differences between each kind of knowledge is challenging; while

---

37. Gregory of Nyssa, *Against Eunomius* 1:42.

38. David Efird and David Worsley, "What Can an Apophatcist Know?"

39. Stump, *Wandering in Darkness*, 40–63.

40. Stump distinguishes "Franciscan knowledge" from the "knowledge-how" ability hypothesis that Laurence Nemirow ("Physicalism and the Cognitive Role of Acquaintance," in *Mind and Cognition: A Reader*, ed. W. Lycan [London: Blackwell, 1990], 490–99), David Lewis ("What Experience Teaches," in *There's Something about Mary: Essays on Phenomenal Consciousness and Frank Jackson's Knowledge Argument*, ed. P. Ludlow, Y. Nagasawa, and D. Stoljar [Cambridge, MA: MIT Press, 2004], 77–104) and Paul Churchill ("Knowing Qualia: A Reply to Jackson," in *A Neurocomputational Perspective: The Nature of Mind and the Structure of Science* [Cambridge, MA: MIT Press, 1989], 67–76) discuss. The knowledge-how ability hypothesis suggests that experience gives us an ability and nothing more—an ability to remember, imagine, or recognize what it is like to have that experience. There is no *new* knowledge gained at all in this process. The position that Stump takes up, then, is closer to Earl Conee's "acquaintance" hypothesis (Earl Conee, "Phenomenal Knowledge," *The Australasian Journal of Philosophy* 72, no. 2 [1994]: 136–50). For Conee, there is no new propositional knowledge gained by experience, but there is something gained beyond mere know-how, namely, acquaintance with the thing known. However, whilst Franciscan knowledge might include both knowledge of persons and acquaintance (or phenomenal) knowledge, knowledge of persons is not the same as acquaintance (or phenomenal) knowledge (see Stump, *Wandering in Darkness*, 52).

Dominican knowledge can be expressed propositionally—for example, Donald Trump knows that Barack Obama was his predecessor—Franciscan knowledge cannot be expressed propositionally. That is the very point of Franciscan knowledge. Stump explains this thought in the following way:

> I want to claim [she writes] that there is a kind of knowledge of persons, a Franciscan knowledge, which is non-propositional and which is not reducible to knowledge that. What could that possibly be?, a skeptical objector may ask. But, of course, if I give an answer to the skeptic's question, I will have an incoherent position: in answering the question, I will be presenting in terms of knowledge that what I am claiming could not be presented that way.[41]

If Franciscan knowledge of persons is indeed by its very nature beyond description, and if, roughly speaking, to be ineffable is to be beyond description—that is, to have the property of not being expressible—all Franciscan knowledge of persons must be in some sense ineffable. We can call this sort of ineffability "propositional ineffability"—the impossibility of capturing something through propositional description. Divine ineffability, where "ineffability" is understood as "propositional ineffability," seems fairly straightforward. If, as Stump suggests, knowledge of other persons can be propositionally ineffable, it is easy to see how God, too, could be, in some comparable sense, propositionally ineffable.

Now, there is one important difference between knowledge of God and knowledge of other persons. When it comes to knowledge of human persons, Franciscan knowledge *could* lie in you learning something old in a new way. But for the defender of ineffability so construed, that is simply not possible for our knowledge of God. It cannot be the case that what we learn of God at the beatific vision is something old presented in a new way, for if the doctrine of divine ineffability is correct, there is a sense in which we can know nothing old (i.e., nothing that is reducible to propositional form) about God.

If we can sensibly talk about God being propositionally ineffable, there is another sort of ineffability reserved for those who do not (or cannot) make themselves open to any sort of second-personal interaction. For want of a better expression, we can call this "personal ineffability." Could God be personally ineffable? Simply put, to qualify for personal ineffability, God would have to refrain from making himself open to any second-personal

---

41. Stump, *Wandering in Darkness*, 52.

experience (or more strongly, that God's creation would be necessarily incapable of second-personal experience of God). Furthermore, God would have to refrain from any self-revelation through narrative (or again, more strongly, that it is impossible for God to self-reveal through narrative) for, Stump argues, Franciscan knowledge can be conveyed through narrative just as it can through unmediated second-personal experience.

So, the claim that "God is unknowable" is ambiguous between "God is propositionally unknowable" and "God is personally unknowable." Given this, if we say that God is propositionally ineffable but personally effable, God remains both beyond description and beyond human concepts. Knowledge of God can never be fully comprehended by or captured in descriptions or concepts, and thus we can know God (personally) and yet at the same time uphold a doctrine of divine ineffability (propositionally).

DIVINE GRACE AND A LAW-GOVERNED CREATION

Having argued for the place of divine hiddenness in an account of human freedom, let us now turn to the place of divine grace in a law-governed creation. To begin, the account of divine action presented so far is perfectly compatible with a law-governed creation. Because we have wills that desire goodness and intellects that can apprehend goodness, God can act in a law-governed world through self-revelation. Although we may only come to share the sort of dyadically mediated divine significant personal presence ultimately hoped for at the beatific vision, we can, in this earthly life, come to enjoy a different kind of divine significant personal presence by sharing triadic attention with God mediated through God's (veiled) self-revelation in creation. Indeed, such (veiled) self-revelation need not require special divine action at all (although of course, as in the case of the incarnation, special divine action need not be ruled out entirely). According to the apostle Paul, God placed evidence of the divine nature, that is to say, God's goodness, into creation at the point of creation, and this revelation can still be seen by all. Paul writes, "For what can be known about God is plain to them, because God has shown it to them. Ever since the creation of the world his eternal power and divine nature, invisible though they are, have been understood and seen through the things he has made. So they are without excuse" (Rom 1:19–20).

Plausibly, then, reflecting on the beauty of a spectacular sunset on the ocean, the grandeur of a Himalayan mountain range, or even just the beauty of a tree, a mathematical proof, or one's spouse might be sufficient to perceive the goodness of their creator. If we can be moved to desire union with God through such revelations of God's goodness, and if this revelation is readily available to all in God's creation, it may be that which appears at first glance to be a divine intervention, for instance, God's giving of operative grace, does not in fact require an act of special divine action at all. If general divine action alone can explain creation as we perceive it, operative grace could always and everywhere be available to all and indeed may have been so since the divine first cause.

OBJECTION: KNOWING THAT GOD HAS ACTED

But if this is the case, how can we *know* that God has providentially acted? For whether God acts in a law-governed creation or not, it seems the outcome is going to look exactly the same, that is, it will seem as though God's action is compatible with, and could just as easily have been the function of, preexisting laws that govern creation. However, by drawing upon recent work done on the epistemology of friendship, we can provide an answer to this concern.

To begin, this is not a new concern. It is a version of a concern one might have with noninterventionist accounts of special divine action. Let us explain. The Christian God is a God who acts. He acts in two ways: either at a particular time and place in the world or at all times and all places in the world. The former is termed "special divine action" and the latter "general divine action." For example, God's creating and sustaining the world concerns general divine action, since God does this at all times and in all places, while God's becoming incarnate concerns special divine action, since God does this at a particular time and place.

Now, it might seem that God's sustaining the world conflicts with special divine action. For when God sustains the world, God does this through upholding natural laws, which require certain regularities to govern events in the world. But when God acts at a particular time and place, it seems that God violates these natural laws, since this event is an exception to the regularities which govern events in the world. This is the metaphysical problem of divine action.

In response to this problem, a great deal of work has been done to show that God's sustaining the world is, indeed, consistent with special divine action, in particular by reconceiving special divine action so that it does not require God's intervening in the natural laws. For example, according to

George F. R. Ellis[42] and Robert John Russell,[43] God acts by determining quantum events, outcomes of which, when taken together, have macroscopic outcomes, such as God's parting the Red Sea, becoming incarnate, raising Jesus from the dead, inspiring the Scriptures, healing people, and in encountering us today in worship, prayer, and the sacraments.

While the metaphysics of these theories have been subject to extensive critical evaluation, little work has been done on their epistemology. And this is a problem. For even if these noninterventionist theories of divine action are metaphysically adequate—that is, even if they show that God *could* act in the world—if they make it impossible for us to know that God has indeed acted, such theories must be inadequate. This is the epistemological problem of noninterventionist special divine action.

It is not hard to see that this epistemological problem of noninterventionist special divine action is the same as the problem we have raised for our account of divine action and divine providence in the beatific vision. Both seem to make it impossible for us to know that God has acted.

To counter this objection, we observe that it hinges on the claim that, given the metaphysics of divine action we have offered, we could not be justified in believing that God has acted. Here we argued that because of the response we gave above to the objection concerning divine ineffability, we could have such justification. The reason is this. On our account of divine ineffability, we appealed to an account of knowing God personally. This account can easily be extended to an account of friendship with God, something Jesus emphasises in his farewell discourse (John 14–15) and subsequently across spiritual literature. Now, as Simon Keller[44] and Sarah Stroud[45] have argued, being a good friend places demands not only on what you do but also on what you believe, in particular that you show your friends epistemic bias. That is, it should take less evidence for you to believe something good about your friend and more evidence to believe something bad about them, than it would a stranger. For example, we give our friends "the benefit of the doubt" when we would not do so for strangers.

While Stroud and Keller think that this means that being a good friend sometimes means being a bad believer, Mark Schroeder has recently offered

---

42. George F. R. Ellis, "Ordinary and Extraordinary Divine Action: The Nexus of Interaction," in *Scientific Perspectives on Divine Action: Chaos and Complexity*, ed. R. J. Russell, N. Murphy, and A. R. Peacocke (Berkeley: CTNS and Vatican Observatory Publications, 1995), 359–95.

43. John Russell, "Divine Action and Quantum Mechanics: A Fresh Assessment," in *Scientific Perspectives on Divine Action*, 293–328.

44. Simon Keller, "Friendship and Belief," *Philosophical Papers* 33 (2004): 329–51.

45. Sarah Stroud, "Epistemic Partiality in Friendship," *Ethics* 116 (2006): 498–52.

an alternative account, arguing that rather than conflicting with epistemic rationality, epistemic bias towards close, personal relations is *required* by epistemic rationality. The reason is that close, personal relationships are what Schroeder calls "stable high stakes cases," where it makes sense to hold out for more evidence than you would for a stranger to think something bad of your close, personal relation and to go with less evidence than you would for a stranger to think something good of your close, personal relation.[46] For the consequences of thinking bad of your close, personal relation and refraining from thinking good of your close, personal relation are significant. That is, it would hurt them if you thought bad of them or did not think good of them.

If Schroeder is right, and if it is possible for God to be our friend, then it follows that it is rational to believe good things about God with less evidence than it would if God were a stranger. Think now about divine action. From an impartial perspective, say from an atheistic or deistic perspective, it would seem that there is not enough evidence for us to believe that God is acting in the world, because what we might interpret as God's action could merely be due to natural laws. But for those who take themselves to be friends of God, that is, those who have close, personal relationships with God, this standard of evidence is not required; rather, they ought to believe that God is acting in the world, giving God "the benefit of the doubt." So we not only can but should—we who take ourselves to be friends of God—believe that God acts in the world, even though God might never violate a law of nature.

CONCLUSION

In concluding, we have suggested that if God's self-revelation serves as a mechanism for God's action in the world, divine providence might well be compatible with human freedom, so long as God (initially) hides from us. Hiddenness is therefore not so much a problem but rather a feature of God's providential care for us and for how God manifests that care in God's action in the world. God is thus hidden so that, in time, we can be with God and remain there forever in perfect happiness and in perfect rest.

---

46. Max Schroeder, "Rational Stability under Pragmatic Encroachment," *Episteme* 15, no. 3 (2018): 297–312.

Scripture Index

Scripture Index

SUBJECT INDEX

AUTHOR INDEX